AUTHORIAL ECHOES
TEXTUALITY AND SELF-PLAGIARISM IN THE
NARRATIVE OF LUIGI PIRANDELLO

LEGENDA

LEGENDA, founded in 1995 by the European Humanities Research Centre of the University of Oxford, is now a joint imprint of the Modern Humanities Research Association and Maney Publishing. Titles range from medieval texts to contemporary cinema and form a widely comparative view of the modern humanities, including works on Arabic, Catalan, English, French, German, Greek, Italian, Portuguese, Russian, Spanish, and Yiddish literature. An Editorial Board of distinguished academic specialists works in collaboration with leading scholarly bodies such as the Society for French Studies and the British Comparative Literature Association.

MHRA

The Modern Humanities Research Association (MHRA) encourages and promotes advanced study and research in the field of the modern humanities, especially modern European languages and literature, including English, and also cinema. It also aims to break down the barriers between scholars working in different disciplines and to maintain the unity of humanistic scholarship in the face of increasing specialization. The Association fulfils this purpose primarily through the publication of journals, bibliographies, monographs and other aids to research.

MANEY
publishing

Maney Publishing is one of the few remaining independent British academic publishers. Founded in 1900, the company has offices both in the UK, in Leeds and London, and in North America, in Boston. Since 1945 Maney Publishing has worked closely with learned societies, their editors, authors, and members, in publishing academic books and journals to the highest traditional standards of materials and production.

Authorial Echoes

Textuality and Self-Plagiarism in the Narrative of Luigi Pirandello

CATHERINE O'RAWE

Modern Humanities Research Association and Maney Publishing

2005

Published by the
Modern Humanities Research Association and Maney Publishing
1 Carlton House Terrace
London SW1Y 5DB
United Kingdom

LEGENDA is an imprint of the
Modern Humanities Research Association and Maney Publishing

Maney Publishing is the trading name of W. S. Maney & Son Ltd,
whose registered office is at Hudson Road, Leeds LS9 7DL, UK

ISBN 1 904713 03 3

First published 2005

LEGENDA series designed by Cox Design Partnership, Witney, Oxon

Printed in Great Britain

Copy-Editor: Dr Bonnie Blackburn

CONTENTS

ABBREVIATIONS

Unless otherwise stated, the following editions of Pirandello's work are referred to in this book, using the abbreviations shown:

Mn I, *Mn* II — *Maschere nude*, ed. A. d'Amico, 2 vols. published so far (Milan: Mondadori, 1986–)

Na I, *Na* II, *Na* III — *Novelle per un anno*, ed. M. Costanzo, 3 vols. in 6 (Milan: Mondadori, 1985–90)

Spsv — *Saggi, poesie, scritti varii*, ed. M. Lo Vecchio-Musti (Milan: Mondadori, 1977)

Tr I, *Tr* II — *Tutti i romanzi*, ed. G. Macchia and M. Costanzo, 2 vols. (Milan: Mondadori, 1973)

ACKNOWLEDGEMENTS

This book is the outcome of a Ph.D. project which was made possible by an AHRB postgraduate studentship, and I would like to express my thanks to the AHRB and to Robinson College, Cambridge for their financial support. My supervisor, Ann Caesar, guided the project with immense patience and tact and I am extremely grateful to her, as well as to my examiners, Robert Gordon and Anna Laura Lepschy, for constructive advice and comments. Recognition is also due to the Centro di Studi Pirandelliani in Agrigento, and especially Enzo Lauretta, and to the British Pirandello Society, in particular Shirley Vinall and Julie Dashwood, for help and support at various times. I am also indebted to the School of Modern Languages at Exeter, and the Italian Department, for providing such a supportive environment in which to prepare this book, and to Mark Davie for his always pertinent counsel. I would like to acknowledge the School of Modern Languages and Cultures at Leeds University, and the Modern Humanities Research Association, for financial support which has made possible the publication of this book. Thanks also to Peter Forte and Manuela Gieri.

On a personal level, I have many debts of gratitude and affection, too many to mention: I want to thank my siblings for their support, friends who read and advised on drafts of chapters, particularly Daragh O'Connell, Stephen Forcer, Tiarnan Ó Cléirigh and Olivia Santovetti, and those who provided other kinds of solidarity and inspiration, especially Marc, Julie, Debs and Stevie G.

Earlier versions of some of the chapters have appeared in journals: parts of Chapter 3 appeared as 'Pirandello's *I vecchi e i giovani*: History, Space, Metaphor' in *The Italianist*, 22 (2003), 102–22, and 'Authors, Texts and Pre-Texts: Pirandello's *Uno, nessuno e centomila* as *Romanzo testamentario*', in *Italian Studies*, 58 (2003), 133–49, contains material from Chapter 5.

Finally, this book is dedicated to my parents, with love and thanks for their support and belief.

INTRODUCTION

In Luigi Pirandello's underrated play of 1934, *Quando si è qualcuno*, the famous ageing author *** (Qualcuno) complains of the totalizing effect of the literary criticism which has locked him into a public literary persona, a persona which, as always in Pirandello's works, is inadequate and ill-fitting:

***. Perché io ormai non debbo più pensare altro, immaginare altro—sentire altro—Che!—Ho pensato quello che ho pensato (secondo loro) e basta!—Non s'ammettono di me più altre immagini.—[...] io non devo più muovermi dal concetto preciso, determinato in ogni minima parte, che si son fatte di me: là, quello, immobile, per sempre!

PIETRO. Morto!

***. Se fossi morto! La dannazione è questa, che sono vivo ancora, io! Questo si può fare solo coi morti—e neppure coi morti, neppure coi morti! perché ce n'è pur di quelli, già lontani nel tempo, che hanno, beati loro!—qualche raro appuntamento con la storia, e poi il resto della loro vita liberi, oscuri!—basta che rispondano all'appello e si presentino puntuali a quella data fissa per compiere il loro atto memorabile—12 aprile 1426—15 ottobre 1571—[...] E anche—morti—da quell'unico atto—ci può essere qualcuno che venga a rimuoverli, scoprendo qualche nuovo documento—a scomporli dall'idea che s'è fissata di loro nella storia—e li faccia rivivere sott'altro aspetto, faccia dir loro una parola nuova—li riapra alla vita rimettendoli a respirare in un'altra luce![1]

I have quoted this monologue in its entirety because of its relevance to several areas of the argument of this book. Firstly, ***'s attack on biographical and critical commonplaces (and their conflation in much literary criticism) offers a metacommentary on Pirandello's uneasy relationship with critics and with his own body of work. At the time of the play's publication (the year in which Pirandello received the ultimate official seal of literary approval with the award of the Nobel Prize for Literature) Pirandello's relationship with the critic Adriano Tilgher, which had dominated his literary career in the 1920s, had irrevocably broken down. Tilgher's description of Pirandello's work as

revolving around a central dualism of 'Vita' and 'Forma'—a critical
topos which still endures today—was embraced by Pirandello to the
extent that it formed the theoretical core of his 1926 play *Diana e la
Tuda*. Pirandello and Tilgher's complicity degenerated into hostility,
with both critics claiming intellectual ownership of this concept, and
with Tilgher being widely recognized as initiating a critical paradigm
of 'pirandellismo' whose echoes are still heard today.[2] Mirroring
Tilgher's 'invention' of *pirandellismo*, the outright hostility of Benedetto Croce had an equally creative effect on Pirandello: Croce's
disparaging review of 'L'umorismo' caused Pirandello to rewrite the
essay substantially.[3]

Similarly, the authorized biography of Pirandello by Federico
Nardelli, which appeared in 1932, conflated the author's life and work
to an unprecedented extent, appropriating passages from Pirandello's
fiction and using them as biographical or historical material.[4] This
procedure was actively encouraged by Pirandello, who called the
book his 'confession':[5] Pirandello more or less dictated Nardelli's biography, a work which succeeds in confusing biographer and subject,
art and life, and mystifying the authorial figure by emphasizing his
tortured personal life (as the subtitle suggests) and linking it to those
of his characters.[6] This technique of using passages from Pirandello's
short stories to explicate his life has been very influential: it has been
used by Gaspare Giudice and also by Andrea Camilleri in his recent
biography of Pirandello.[7] This process of exchange between text
and commentary on it will be one of the keys to my rereading of
Pirandello.

Secondly, the play comments on the self-presentation of the artist
and his relation to his work in the profusion of paratextual apparatuses
and devices it shows: interviews, press conferences, photo shoots and
public addresses, all show the artist as public figure and the writer and
artwork as commodity.[8] The closing, ironically D'Annunzian oration
by *** in which his words and then he himself become literally
petrified, signals the triumph of public persona over the work of art
itself. This satire on the practice of criticism is significant (and ironic),
given Pirandello's attempts to control and mystify his own persona and
also the tendency of Pirandello criticism, until relatively recently, to
accept Pirandello's own rhetorical and paratextual self-positioning and
to interpret his works in the light of this.[9]

Thirdly, the quotation from *Quando si è qualcuno* sums up the role
of the literary critic as detective. The hope of discovering a 'nuovo

documento', which propels the critical act, has a special relevance for Pirandello studies: in the late 1960s two critics, Claudio Vicentini and Gösta Andersson, following on from the work of Franz Rauhut in 1939 which had hitherto been little noticed, identified a series of heavily plagiarized or 'borrowed' passages, (particularly from the French spiritualist philosopher Gabriel Séailles and the Italian philosopher Giovanni Marchesini, as well as the experimental psychologist Alfred Binet) in Pirandello's theoretical works, in particular in the essay 'L'umorismo'.[10] This has recently been augmented by Paola Casella's scrupulously detailed excavation of 'L'umorismo', in which she traces borrowings and filiations between Pirandello and De Sanctis and Arcoleo, as well as reinterpreting the plagiarism of Séailles, Binet and Marchesini.[11] Their detective work (along with that of Pieter de Meijer on the borrowed sources of *I vecchi e i giovani*) provided a bibliographical and critical framework within which an equivalent examination of Pirandello's self-plagiarizing, his transposition of parts of his works directly into other works, could be studied.[12] (Plagiarism is also touched on in *Quando si è qualcuno*, when *** invents a fictional alter ego, the radical young poet Delàgo, whom ***'s eagle-eyed son recognizes to be a plagiarist of his father). It is one of the contentions of this book that the consequences of these practices of borrowing and self-plagiarism, and the concomitant fragmentation and recessive doublings they effect on Pirandello's texts, have yet to be fully examined.[13] Against the dangers and addictions of source-hunting must be balanced the need to recognize the provisional nature of Pirandello's work: the threat of the appearance of a 'nuovo documento' also highlights the problem of single-author literary criticism, its need for a reliable, complete and authenticated corpus on which to work. This problem is exacerbated in Pirandello criticism by the incomplete nature of the archives, the loss or disappearance of manuscripts and the constant revisions and rewritings to which Pirandello subjected his work, both pre- and post-publication.[14] In tackling this problem, it is essential that textual criticism come to terms with philological criticism—the material status of the text must be considered hand-in-hand with its narrative status.

The complicated gestation and genealogies of Pirandello's texts have traditionally been overlooked by most Pirandello criticism, with the exception of those scholars already mentioned and a few others.[15] It is my contention here that these processes of composition and movement of material between texts, these texts which give birth to myriad offshoots, are not extraneous to the analysis of Pirandello's narrative poetics: rather, they can be analysed in the context of an approach which sees them as intimately linked to Pirandello's poetics of *umorismo*, regarded as a poetics which permits and indeed privileges such repetitions and fragmentation, such textual interplay and intertextual play.

The focus of the first part of the book, Pirandello's 1908 essay 'L'umorismo', has been considered by recent critics as a narrative poetics, an act of autoexegesis:[16] this aspect has taken precedence over its status as a treatise on humour, as a cultural or philosophical or indeed psychological phenomenon in the manner of essays by contemporaries such as Freud, Baudelaire or Bergson.[17]

Gérard Genette broadens the definition of authorial paratext to include authors' journals, letters and commentaries.[18] Claire De Obaldia comments with regard to the literary essay on 'the paratextual status of a genre which functions like a paratext when it has not been published literally as a paratext'.[19] The essay has thus been considered in its status as an authorial paratext, and also as a 'hypotext', to use Genette's terminology.[20] It is seen as the point from which Pirandello's subsequent work radiates, and is placed as the centre or source of his creative writing by many critics, as theory is mapped onto practice.[21] The relation between essay and narrative needs further clarification, however: De Obaldia's considerations on the literary essay form are worth considering here. She describes how essays are commonly seen as a fragment or draft, 'which foreshadows completion and totalization'.[22] She argues that there is thus a linear relation between the theory elaborated in the essay which is felt to be 'completed' in the narrative. This idea has a powerful hold over considerations of the relation between Pirandello's essay as a theorization of narrative poetics and his narrative itself. In focusing on the 'paratext' represented by the essay 'L'umorismo', I will examine the dangers (as well as the rewards) of reading the essay as an explication of Pirandello's narrative practice, a reading which ignores the complexities and contradictions (both theoretical and chronological) involved in the movement between theory and fiction, and the mythologizing of Pirandello's creative processes which his theory presents.[23] Instead of a close study of the composition, rhetorical and narrative strategies and plagiarisms of 'L'umorismo', attention has been focused on its completion or enactment in Pirandello's narrative.

'L'umorismo' has a bipartite structure, divided into a first, 'objective' part which is a historical survey of European humorists, and a second, 'subjective' theory (thematizing the dichotomy which characterizes the essay as a form).[24] Ironically, the second part, Pirandello's personal expression of *umorismo* as a *Weltanschauung*, is by far the more heavily plagiarized. The first part of the text explicitly sets up an idiosyncratic personal canon of humorists into which Pirandello inserts himself. His humoristic canon is mainly composed of prose writers: Manzoni, Cervantes, Sterne, Dostoevsky and the little-known Mantuan writer Alberto Cantoni all figure prominently, but there is also room for Socrates, Leopardi and Copernicus. Yet, as well as these acknowledged influences, there is an underlying tension in the text, in an anxiety of influence which is, however, very un-Bloomian: the hidden authors who influence the text (and Pirandello's narrative) are not the great iconoclastic figures of Pirandello's 'humoristic' canon listed above, but writers whose unacknowledged presence in the text is equally agonistic and perhaps more radical. As I mentioned earlier, the works of Andersson and Vicentini have exhaustively charted Pirandello's borrowings from philosophical and psychological works, while Antonio Illiano has mapped the borrowings from theosophical writings.[25] It is not my intention to replicate their groundwork, but to examine the ultimate textual effect of such borrowings (and autoplagiarism) on conceptions of fictionality and the fictional world of the text, considerations which are at the heart of *umorismo*.

My approach is two-stranded, with the first strand being divided into two further parts: firstly, at the level of *sjuzet*, I examine the essay's dual compositional principles, the seemingly extraneous or ornamental elements which turn out to be narrative structuring devices, namely metaphor and epiphany. These two phenomena are very different: one is linguistic/semantic/rhetorical, the other psychological or existential, but I will discuss them both, as Pirandello does, as aesthetic phenomena. They are narrative techniques which exemplify Pirandello's *umorismo* as metafictional, as imbued with an awareness of its own fictionality, an awareness which is compounded by the incessant recurrence of metaphors and epiphanies as metatextual and intertextual moments across Pirandello's narrative oeuvre: this recurrence will be charted in the second strand of the book. The second strand examines, at the level of *fabula*, the relations and intertextual filiations between texts in Pirandello and attempts to map the trajectories of fragments of text between texts (between 'L'umorismo' and the novels, between novels and short stories, etc).

Umorismo is predicated upon Pirandello's theorization of the *sentimento del contrario*, a psychological and aesthetic process described as both a mode of composition in the writer and an effect elicited in the reader. Pirandello criticism has considered the semantic instability of humoristic writing and its problematizing of nineteenth-century narrative and linguistic models.[26] Yet between Pirandello's much-repeated definition of *umorismo* as 'perplessità' and the *umorista* as 'fuori di chiave', it is difficult to identify the specific innovations of *umorismo*.[27] The vagueness of its definition as 'ambiguità' or 'sfiducia' inscribes it within a vague modernism which has allowed Pirandello to be paralleled with every early twentieth-century writer.

In my view, an integration of the traditionally separate areas of compositional and stylistic studies is a potentially fruitful one. For example, Claudio Vicentini's recent reading of Pirandello's 'thefts' demonstrates how Pirandello's 'scrittura nera', to use his lovely phrase, counters the organic image of the artwork, derived from Romantic thought, theorized by Pirandello in his essay.[28] I will return to Vicentini's essay later in the book, and, while acknowledging a debt to him, would like to extend his reading to unite a consideration of the problems of textual fragmentation and chronology caused by self-plagiarism and 'theft' with an assertion that, rather than being extraneous to Pirandello's narrative poetics, such problems are essential to them. *Umorismo* as a mode of doubleness, which privileges the partial, the incomplete, the recessive, the self-questioning, is a 'fenomeno di sdoppiamento' that produces narratives which are literally 'double' and a narrative 'scomposizione' which is both literal and metaphorical.[29] Reusing and recycling texts and quotations produces a 'palimpsestous' reading, according to Genette, which sets the reader up as detective, as uncoverer of sources and maker of connections in the most radical way. As well as the paratextual devices and interpretations of Pirandello's oeuvre we have a palimpsestous one, in which one text lies underneath the other, as well as alongside.

Part I of the book examines metaphor and epiphany as techniques of *umorismo*: Chapter I is a study of the first of these heuristic devices, which Pirandello uses obsessively to create allusive intertextual relations between 'L'umorismo' and his narrative. Pirandello's innovative conception of metaphor is one which sees it as essential to discourse, a *modus componendi* rather than a poetic 'extra', and by reading through the metaphors of humoristic discourse (which, I will argue, is both inherently metaphorical and metafictional), it is possible to identify metaphor as containing and enacting the plots of fiction.

Chapter 2 looks at narrative epiphany as theorized in 'L'umorismo' and elsewhere, again as a specifically metatextual phenomenon, intimately linked to the creativity of the artist. Like metaphor, it is a compositional principle, a humoristic anagnorisis, linked to the doubleness of *umorismo* in its subversion of narrative norms. Again, like metaphor, epiphanies in Pirandello are intertextual: their imitative and repetitive quality means that they frequently constitute the point at which his self-plagiarism becomes most obvious.

Part II focuses on three Pirandello novels: I have excluded from my discussion *L'esclusa*, *Il turno*, *Il fu Mattia Pascal* and *Quaderni di Serafino Gubbio*, partly for obvious reasons of space, which preclude an exhaustive survey of Pirandello's novels. Rather than attempting to justify why I have excluded certain texts, it is perhaps more useful to focus on the reasons why I have chosen the particular three novels which I am examining: *I vecchi e i giovani* (1909), *Suo marito* (1911) and *Uno, nessuno e centomila* (1925). Firstly, *I vecchi* and *Suo marito* are relatively neglected texts, puzzled over by critics, as I discuss, because their 'realism' seems to place them outside the critical paradigm which represents Pirandello's 'progress' as a writer from nineteenth-century realism to modernist experiment, with a 'svolta' represented by *Il fu Mattia Pascal*.[30] *Uno, nessuno e centomila*, on the other hand, is much studied and heralded by Pirandello criticism as the *summa* of *pirandellismo*, and perhaps fits into a critical paradigm of *pirandellismo* rather too easily.

I vecchi and *Suo marito* are both texts with concealed sources: in *I vecchi* the work of Napoleone Colaianni, in *Suo marito* Pirandello's own earlier texts. Both texts thus contain or allow discussions about the nature of fictionality, as *I vecchi* subverts the relationship between writer and source in the historical novel genre, and challenges its ideas of referentiality; *Suo marito*'s sources being texts of Pirandello's, it thematizes the dissolution of the boundaries of fictional worlds which pervades Pirandello's work and makes the connection between plagiarism and concepts of the text as property, concepts which are demonstrated to be less antithetical to Pirandello's view of art than expected.

The study of these textual issues is allied to an uncovering of the metaphors which structure both texts and whose tensive function gives the texts an intertextual and interpretative doubleness. Similarly, an analysis of epiphany in both novels sees the continuities in its use between texts and also its differences: in *I vecchi e i giovani* the epiphanic moment contests history and its representation, whereas in *Suo marito* it is an index of the creativity of Silvia Roncella, Pirandello's alter ego, his 'Delàgo'. In both texts epiphany negotiates the threshold between the fictional and the real.

The final chapter interrogates *Uno, nessuno*'s status as touchstone (or tombstone) of Pirandello's narrative production. Again, an examination of its sources is rewarding: they are, as is known, earlier versions or 'pre-texts' of the novel. This has produced a problem of reading the text through its pre-texts, and the editorial and critical problems involved in isolating the text itself, as well as disentangling the text from the (auto)biographical myths surrounding it. A philological approach to this text is united with a consideration of metaphor and epiphany as humoristic tools which unlock the novel's intertextual and famously inconclusive conclusion.

Pirandello criticism is too vast to even attempt a typology of it here: although, as mentioned earlier, criticism on the novels only really began seriously in 1960, there is a huge body of critical work devoted to them. There are several good bibliographies of Pirandello criticism:[31] one of the best and most comprehensive of these is Corrado Donati's *Bibliografia della critica pirandelliana* (1986).[32] This has recently been updated in an essay by Gian-Paolo Biasin and Manuela Gieri, and they quote Donati's useful division of Pirandello criticism into three main threads: historicist or sociological, psychological or psychoanalytical, and stylistic, a division which they still hold to be valid.[33] Biasin and Gieri discuss feminist criticism of Pirandello as an important addition to the critical canon, and, interestingly, they conclude with a mention (albeit brief) of Franca Angelini's call for a new philological criticism in Pirandello studies.[34] Obviously it is too soon for this to have had any marked effect but it is an encouraging and pragmatic rallying call.

This book owes a debt to the work of Claudio Vicentini and Gösta Andersson first of all, and to Giovanni Macchia, Giacomo Debenedetti, Marziano Guglielminetti, Renato Barilli, Paola Casella and Annamaria Andreoli (among many others): it is significant that I show a bias towards Italian criticism, a bias which is repeated throughout the book, for the simple reason that Anglophone criticism is still relatively uninterested in Pirandello's novels, though the recent publication of the first English translation of *Suo marito* offers a promising hint that this situation may be about to change.[35] Other critics are cited in turn in each chapter as I attempt to negotiate a path for myself and for Pirandello through the mass of critical common-places that the vast amount of criticism on Pirandello has inevitably produced: while such topoi are not always without foundation, the tendency to repeat them uncritically is ultimately reductive.

My own critical approach is broadly narratological, and has been influenced particularly by Gérard Genette's work on paratexts and palimpsests: I will also, especially in Chapters 4 and 5, attempt to unite a narratological approach with a philological, historicizing one, and I hope that whatever the critical contradictions such a dual approach may lead me into, the reward will be a richer and more nuanced reading of key Pirandellian narrative texts.

It is ironic that although, as I point out in Chapter 1, Pirandello criticism has failed to deal with the topic of metaphor convincingly, his work constantly inspires (or forces?) critics to come up with metaphors for it. The second half of the book discusses some of those textual metaphors, as well as the one suggested by 'L'umorismo' and Pirandello's narrative, and I have already appropriated Genette's metaphor of the palimpsest to describe the material traces of writing which characterize Pirandello's output, but my starting point will be a metaphor from Annamaria Andreoli, who, in her scrupulously detailed account of Pirandello's compositional practices, calls his work a 'tela di Penelope', constantly weaving and unweaving itself.[36] Of course, this is an especially apt textual metaphor because of the etymological relation of 'tessere' and text, and my own text examines Pirandello's weaving of the theories of fiction into his fictions themselves, and the unweaving effect produced by the awareness of the fictionality of narrative which the theories themselves posit.

Notes to Introduction

1. *Maschere nude*, 2 vols. (Milan: Mondadori, 1958), ii. 984–5.
2. See Adriano Tilgher, *Studi sul teatro contemporaneo* (Rome: Libreria di scienze e lettere, 1923), 140. See Antonio Illiano, *Introduzione alla critica pirandelliana* (Verona: Fiorini, 1976), 47–53, on the Pirandello–Tilgher relation; I will return to Tilgher's 'invention' of Pirandello at the end of the book.
3. Croce's *stroncatura* of 'L'umorismo' will be discussed in Ch. 1; on their relationship generally see Claudio Vicentini, *L'estetica di Pirandello* (Milan: Mursia, 1985), 123–31.

4. Federico Nardelli, *L'uomo segreto: vita e croci di Luigi Pirandello* (Milan: Mondadori, 1932).

5. See Walter Starkie, *Luigi Pirandello 1867–1936* (Berkeley: University of California Press, 1965), p. ix.

6. Gaspare Giudice, who himself used the same kind of technique in his biography of Pirandello, and who repeats large passages from Nardelli, says that 'era come se scrivesse un'autobiografia', *Luigi Pirandello* (Turin: UTET, 1963), 52.

7. Andrea Camilleri, *Biografia del figlio cambiato* (Milan: Rizzoli, 2000).

8. The concept of paratext comes from Gérard Genette, who defines it as 'a certain number of verbal productions, such as an author's name, a title, a preface, illustrations [..]. These productions [...] surround [the text] and extend it, precisely in order to *present* it, in the usual sense of this verb but also in the strongest sense: to *make present*, to ensure the text's presence in the world, its "reception" and consumption in the form [...] of a book.'; *Paratexts*, trans. Jane E. Lewin (Cambridge: Cambridge University Press, 1997), 1. Genette's study considers primarily paratextual apparatus such as epigraphs, prefaces and titles, but he also discusses the 'epitext', which is 'any paratextual element not materially appended to the text within the same volume but circulating, as it were, freely, in a virtually limitless physical and social space' (p. 344). Epitexts can be both public, such as interviews, or private, such as letters or diaries. Both types will be discussed here.

9. Luigi Ferrante, writing in the proceedings of the first conference of the Congresso Internazionale di Studi Pirandelliani in 1961 (in which, incidentally, out of over sixty papers and contributions, a mere five are specifically devoted to narrative, indicating the direction in which critical attention was then focused) makes a brave, but ultimately unsuccessful, attempt to separate the paratextual elements ('interviste, noterelle pirandelliane, marginali, appunto, rispetto ai testi') which have led to a critical construction of 'pirandellismo' from the work itself; 'La poetica di Pirandello', in AA.VV., *Atti del Congresso Internazionale di Studi Pirandelliani* (Florence: Le Monnier, 1967), 371–8 at 371.

10. See Gösta Andersson, *Arte e teoria: studi sulla poetica del giovane Pirandello* (Uppsala: Almqvist & Wiksells, 1966), 142–229 on borrowings from Gabriel Séailles and *passim* on other borrowings; see Vicentini, *L'estetica di Pirandello*, 101–31 on borrowings from Séailles and pp. 116–17 and *passim* for lifts from Marchesini and other writers; also see the second, extended edition of Vicentini's study, published by Mursia in 1985, pp. 95–120 on Séailles, pp. 120–1 on Binet and pp. 109–11 on Marchesini.

11. Paola Casella, *L'umorismo di Pirandello: ragioni intra- e intertestuali* (Florence: Cadmo, 2002).

12. On Pirandello's autoplagiarism, see in particular Giovanni Macchia, 'Introduzione' to *Tutti i romanzi* (Tr I, pp. xiii–lii); parts of Macchia's essay are repeated verbatim (in a very Pirandellian fashion!) in his *Pirandello o la stanza della tortura* (Milan: Mondadori, 2000), 24–7 and in the section 'Scomposizione e unità', of his essay 'Luigi Pirandello' in *Storia della letteratura italiana*, ed. E. Cecchi and N. Sapegno, 9 vols. (Milan: Garzanti, 1969), ix. 441–92.

13. K. K. Ruthven points out that self-plagiarism goes unexamined both by literary criticism and by copyright law: 'the law takes no interest in self-plagiarism, which is the use of bits of one's earlier writings as unmarked components of a

"new" text'; Ruthven, *Faking Literature* (Cambridge: Cambridge University Press, 2001), 136.

14. The assertion by Manlio Lo Vecchio-Musti, Pirandello's first bibliographer, that 'Luigi Pirandello nulla conservava di suo: né volumi, né manoscritti, né appunti, né ritagli di giornale' ('Avvertenza' to *Bibliografia di Pirandello* (Milan: Mondadori, 1937), 3) is contested by Annamaria Andreoli, 'Nel laboratorio di Pirandello', in *Taccuino segreto di Luigi Pirandello* (Milan: Mondadori, 1997), 127–215 at 131 ff., indicating the state of doubt and confusion which still surrounds the existence of Pirandello's manuscripts.

15. Pieter de Meijer's work on unearthing Napoleone Colaianni as a source for *I vecchi e i giovani* is discussed in Ch. 3; Riccardo Scrivano has provided a valuable examination of the compositional and editorial history of *Suo marito*, which will be acknowledged in Ch. 4; Mario Costanza and Marziano Guglielminetti's work on *Uno, nessuno e centomila* will be discussed in this regard in Ch. 5; Annamaria Andreoli's essay discussing Pirandello's notebooks, which contain hundreds of set phrases which he will reuse over and over again, has been of great use to me; 'Nel laboratorio di Pirandello'. The recent publication of Pirandello's *Taccuino di Harvard* convincingly demonstrates his dependence on lists of set phrases and expressions borrowed from other writers; *Taccuino di Harvard*, ed. O. Frau and C. Grignani (Milan: Mondadori, 2002).

16. Antonio Illiano calls 'L'umorismo' 'una confessione, uno spontaneo atto di autoesegesi'; 'Momenti e problemi di critica pirandelliana: "L'umorismo", Pirandello e Croce, Pirandello e Tilgher', *PMLA* 83/1 (1968), 135–43 at 135; Gösta Andersson calls 'L'umorismo' 'un utile commento alle sue opere letterarie'; *Arte e teoria*, 11. See Franco Zangrilli on 'L'umorismo' as the defining moment of Pirandello's poetics; '"L'umorismo"—poetica morale', *Rivista di studi pirandelliani* 6 (1980), 26–41 at 35; Gavriel Moses discusses 'L'umorismo' as Pirandellian literary criticism; *The Nickel was for the Movies* (Berkeley: University of California Press, 1995), 24. Elio Gioanola sees the essay as a self-justificatory exercise; *Pirandello: la follia* (Genoa: Il Melangolo, 1983), 9–10. Marinella Cantelmo discusses it, as I do, as both 'teoria storico-critica' and 'poetica compositiva'; 'Di lemmi del riso', in ead. (ed.), *L'isola che ride: teoria, poetica e retoriche dell'umorismo di Pirandello* (Rome: Bulzoni, 1997). See also Paola Casella on the tensions evident in the essay between its theoretical and personal or impressionistic impulses; *L'umorismo di Pirandello*, 292–3.

17. On the relationship between 'L'umorismo' and other works on humour, see Renato Barilli, 'Il comico in Bergson, Freud e Pirandello', in A. Alessio (ed.), *L'enigma Pirandello* (Ottawa: Canadian Society for Italian Studies, 1988), 318–35; also Tullio Pagano, 'Modernisms: from Bergson's laughter to Pirandello's humour', *The Italianist* 17 (1997), 44–59.

18. Genette, *Paratexts*, 344–5.

19. Claire De Obaldia, *The Essayistic Spirit* (Oxford: Clarendon, 1995), 20.

20. Genette's typology of what he calls 'transtextuality', or 'all that sets the text in a relationship, whether obvious or concealed, with other texts', identifies 'hypertextuality' as 'any relationship uniting a text B (which I shall call the *hypertext*) to an earlier text A (I shall, of course, call it the *hypotext*)'; *Palimpsests: Literature in the Second Degree*, trans. Channa Newman and Claude Doubinsky (Lincoln: University of Nebraska Press, 1997), 5. This hypertextual relationship

is especially significant in the study of *Uno, nessuno e centomila* and will be instrumental in defining the 'palimpsestous' readings which Pirandello's layered narratives produce.

21. The first two major studies to be published on Pirandello both place 'L'umorismo' at the centre of his poetics: Carlo Salinari's 'La coscienza della crisi', in his *Miti e coscienza del decadentismo italiano: D'Annunzio, Pascoli, Fogazzaro e Pirandello* (Milan: Feltrinelli, 1960), says that 'L'umorismo' is 'collegato direttamente ai problemi del suo gusto e del suo modo particolare di concepire e realizzare l'opera poetica' (p. 249). However, Salinari's otherwise excellent contextualization of 'L'umorismo' within late 19th-c. decadentism and a crisis of bourgeois values tends to quote the text uncritically. Arcangelo Leone de Castris, the other major critic to publish on Pirandello at that time, implicitly critiques such an approach, noting the tendency of Pirandello criticism to 'spiegare la tematica pirandelliana [...] con la tematica pirandelliana', *Storia di Pirandello* (Bari: Laterza, 1962), 6. De Castris calls 'L'umorismo' a 'documento essenziale della poetica pirandelliana' (p. 20) and argues passionately for a historicizing criticism of Pirandello's work, seeing it as similarly rooted in the crisis of late 19th-c. society.

22. De Obaldia, *The Essayistic Spirit*, 18.

23. De Obaldia also sees in the literary essay a 'crossing over from criticism to literature, or of "critical" to "poetic" intertextuality' in its 'mediation between artistic and philosophical truths'; ibid. 56.

24. Ibid. 209.

25. Antonio Illiano, *Metapsichica e letteratura in Pirandello* (Florence: Vallecchi, 1982).

26. See especially Giacomo Debenedetti, *Il romanzo del Novecento* (Milan: Garzanti, 1971), 390–414; see also Carlo Salinari on Pirandello's 'singolare collocazione fra Ottocento e Novecento', leading to a narrative poetics which 'svuota dal di dentro [...] i miti e gli ideali ottocenteschi'; 'Luigi Pirandello fra Ottocento e Novecento', in *Boccaccio, Manzoni, Pirandello* (Rome: Riuniti, 1979), 171–2; Gioanola, *Pirandello: la follia*, 44.

27. These definitions have also provided titles for works of Pirandello criticism: hence Aldo Borlenghi's *Pirandello o dell'ambiguità* (Padua: R.A.D.A.R., 1968) and Enzo Lauretta's *Luigi Pirandello: storia di un personaggio 'fuori di chiave'* (Milan: Mursia, 1980).

28. Claudio Vicentini, 'I "furti" di Pirandello e l'illusione della forma artistica', in R. A. Syska-Lamparska (ed.), *Ars dramatica: studi sulla poetica di Luigi Pirandello* (New York: Lang, 1996), 43–54. Similarly, Fausto Curi talks of Pirandello's 'scrittura doppia'; 'L'umorismo di Pirandello nel sistema della modernità letteraria', in F. Nicolosi and V. Moretti (ed.), *L'ultimo Pirandello: Pirandello e l'Abruzzo* (Chieti: Vecchio Faggio, 1988), 19–61 at 37.

29. 'Scomposizione', a key term in the lexicon of 'L'umorismo', is touched upon by Salinari, *Miti e coscienza del decadentismo*, 253 and 273, and is highlighted by Marziano Guglielminetti as a syntactic phenomenon typical of *umorismo* in 'Il soliloquio di Pirandello', in *Il romanzo del Novecento italiano: strutture e sintassi* (Rome: Riuniti, 1986), 55–97 passim. In Giovanni Macchia's essay 'Il gusto della scomposizione', linguistic and textual breakdown and fragmentation are definitively linked. Pietro Milone provides a similar approach, interestingly asserting that Pirandello's self-plagiarism makes him a 'critico di se stesso', 'Prefazione' to *L'umorismo* (Milan: Garzanti, 1995), pp. lvi–cv at p. lvii.

30. It is possible that this paradigm emanates from the influence of Croce's essay on Pirandello in 1940, when he talks of Pirandello's 'modo veristico' which is followed by a 'seconda maniera', marked by the turning point of *Il fu Mattia Pascal* and famously characterized by what Croce calls 'un convulso inconcludente filosofare'; 'Luigi Pirandello', in *Letteratura della nuova Italia*, 6 vols. (Bari: Laterza, 1940), vi., 359–77 at 361–2. One of the first studies published on Pirandello, by Luigi Bàccolo in 1937, also talks of the 'svolgimento' of Pirandello's work 'dal punto di partenza a quello d'arrivo'. Bàccolo, *Luigi Pirandello* (Milan: Bocca, 1949), 9.

31. The first bibliography of Pirandello criticism, compiled by Manlio Lo Vecchio-Musti, appeared in 1937, and was republished in an updated form with an introductory essay by Stefano Pirandello, 'Le opere che Pirandello non scrisse', in 1952 by Mondadori. The next significant contribution to Pirandello bibliography was Pino Mensi's *La lezione di Pirandello* (Florence: Le Monnier, 1974), closely followed by Antonio Illiano's *Introduzione alla critica pirandelliana*, which divides Pirandello criticism into two phases: the biographical era lasting up until Pirandello's death in 1936 and the serious work which began after his death. Giulio Ferroni's thoughtful review of Pirandello criticism focuses on the lack of serious early criticism and points out, interestingly, that 'col saggio su "L'umorismo", egli è l'unico vero critico di se stesso'; 'Pirandello', in Walter Binni (ed.), *I classici italiani nella storia della critica*, 3 vols. (Florence: La Nuova Italia, 1977), iii. 57–129 at 60. Sergio Blazina's comprehensive overview of criticism on the novels highlights the 1961 conference as a turning point for Pirandello studies, in which criticism finally moved away from the Crocean and Tilgherian responses which had dominated the 20th c.; 'Rassegna di studi pirandelliani: i romanzi (1961–1983)', *Lettere italiane*, 36/1 (1984), 69–131. (Graziella Corsinovi made a similar point in her much more restricted survey of Pirandello criticism in the 1970s, 'Rassegna pirandelliana (1973–78), *Otto/Novecento*, 3 (1979), 357–67.)

32. *Bibliografia della critica pirandelliana 1962–1981* (Florence: La Ginestra, 1986). Donati's more recent bibliography of Pirandello criticism adopts both a thematic and a diachronic approach, although it restricts itself to criticism in Italian: *Luigi Pirandello: nella storia della critica* (Fossombrone: Metauro, 1998).

33. Biasin and Gieri, 'Pirandello at 360 degrees', in eid. (eds.), *Luigi Pirandello: Contemporary Perspectives* (Toronto: University of Toronto Press, 1999), 3–22.

34. 'It is time for the critic of both narrative and theatre to face the problems of variants in different editions; by now a philological study must (or should) accompany any edition of Pirandello's works'; Franca Angelini, 'Scenes and texts: perspectives in Pirandello criticism', in Biasin and Gieri (eds.), *Luigi Pirandello*, 23–34 at 30.

35. Luigi Pirandello, *Her Husband*, trans. and with an Afterword by Martha King and Mary Ann Frese Witt (Durham: Duke University Press, 2000): unfortunately, as I discuss in Ch. 4, the critical apparatus accompanying this translation fails to engage with the particular bibliographical and editorial problems which this text raises.

36. Andreoli, 'Nel laboratorio di Pirandello', 188. Andreoli is quoting Giovanni Macchia here.

PART I

CHAPTER 1

'Non parola ma la cosa stessa': Pirandello, Metaphor and 'L'umorismo'

Non sono filosofo [...] un contenuto filosofico nella mia produzione non c'è [...] il filosofo il mondo se lo pensa e se lo ragiona: io non riesco a vederlo e a sentirlo che in immagini.
LUIGI PIRANDELLO, interview in *La lettura*, 1927

Introduction

Benedetto Croce's famous 1909 review of 'L'umorismo' criticized what Croce saw as the essay's lack of philosophical precision, and in contesting the validity of Pirandello's designation of *umorismo* as a genre of literature, Croce's rebuke significantly attacks the essay's metaphorical and icastic qualities: 'Il P. si accorge, in qualche modo, che le distinzioni da lui adoperate sono assai imprecise; tanto che le ripete e modifica e tempera di continuo, e, quando altro non sa, ricorre alle immagini.'[1] The significance of Croce's statement is three-fold: firstly, it clearly expresses the idea that an essay or treatise is supposed to exhibit a kind of scientific linguistic precision.[2] Secondly, and this is derived from the first point, it expresses the idea that there should be a distinction between the aims and techniques of theory as opposed to those of fiction, so that theory has a clear explicatory or preparatory function. Thirdly, and most significantly, Croce's language reveals his view of metaphor as one which is derived from the comparison view of metaphor elaborated by Aristotle and classical rhetoric: this view, still prevalent in the nineteenth and early twentieth centuries, regarded metaphor as decorative or ornamental. In the *Poetics*, Aristotle makes clear that metaphor is a 'foreign' or 'alien' addition to poetic style, an inessential ingredient which adds distinction but militates against clarity.[3] The language of Pirandello's theories offers a radical challenge, as I will show, to the word-based, comparison theory of metaphor elaborated by Aristotle, in which the criteria for the comparison between the two terms in a metaphorical proposition are those of resemblance.[4] Pirandello anticipates later developments in metaphor theory by proposing a semantic theory of metaphor as a heuristic device, a theory which sees metaphor as essential to language. The radical nature of Pirandello's approach will become apparent: his novel approach to metaphor, which he regards as essentially a phenomenon of predication, becomes one of the central techniques of his *umorismo*, helping him to move from metaphorization of the noun to a broader notion of fictional discourse as itself metaphorical. A corollary of this approach will be the elision of generic boundaries between theory and fiction, as the 'tecnica e lo stile del grande narratore', adopted by Pirandello in 'L'umorismo', comes directly out of the metaphorizing process itself.[5] This metaphorizing process, as I will demonstrate, undermines the borders between fictionality and factuality and acts as a series of metonymic associations which disturb narrative linearity and chronology. The role and importance of metaphor and imagery in Pirandello's work has been, rather surprisingly, overlooked by most criticism.[6]

My intention in this chapter is to plot, through an examination of the metaphors and images which litter the essay, Pirandello's meta-linguistic poetics of *umorismo*, uncovering the fundamental fault lines which the essay traces and reveals in Pirandello's approach to language and fictionality.[7] By interpreting *umorismo* as, primarily, a theory of (figurative) reading and writing, and by placing the hermeneutic act at the centre of Pirandello's essay, I highlight the critical problems inherent in the idea of trying to read 'L'umorismo' as an act of auto-exegesis or as explication or genesis of his narrative. An examination of the metaphors and similes of 'L'umorismo' and their derivation from the philosophical and psychological treatises of Giovanni Marchesini and Gabriel Séailles, as well as a survey of some examples of such metaphorization in Pirandello's short stories and novels, will provide a clue to the patterning of metaphor in the novels I will look at in Part II. 'L'umorismo' presents the reader with interpretative problems and challenges from every angle: its bipartite structure, in which the first part of the essay is a historical, diachronic survey of Italian and European humorists, which aims to prove that there is such a genre as *umorismo*, using arguments borrowed from other sources,[8] is followed by the second part, 'Essenza, caratteri e materia dell'umorismo', which aims to provide a comprehensive definition of the process of *umorismo*, as well as presenting Pirandello's own narrative poetics.[9] As I will demonstrate, Pirandello is unable to explain the phenomenon of *umorismo* fully without placing his novel conception of metaphor at the formal and thematic core of the poetics of *umorismo*, and without rooting his relentlessly analogical text in the writings of others. The question of citation (or Pirandello's failure to cite his sources) as well as that of the audience for which the essay was written (as part of an application for an academic post) complicates the idea of reading the essay as prelude to or rehearsal of novelistic concerns and problematizes any attempt to see practice as unproblematically reflecting theory.[10] It is instructive to see how, in describing the processes of humoristic writing, Pirandello constantly reasserts questions about language and textuality, as the essay does not merely discursively render his fictional processes, but replicates them.

Finally, as is the case with all the texts I am discussing, the date and editorial status of the essay are significant: the edition normally used is the revised 1920 text which appears in the Lo Vecchio-Musti-edited *Saggi, poesie, scritti varii*, and which is generally used by critics without explaining that it is not the first edition. The essay was rewritten to include Pirandello's response to Croce's 1909 review of it, and I will be using the 1920 edition, but will discuss significant discrepancies between the two editions which affect my analysis.

Umorismo and Metaphor

'L'umorismo' begins with a discussion of the material origin of the word *umorismo*:

> La parola *umore* derivò a noi naturalmente dal latino e col senso materiale che essa aveva di corpo fluido, liquore, umidità o vapore, e col senso anche di fantasia, capriccio, o vigore [...] Sarà bene, infatti, trattando dell'umorismo, tener presente anche quest'altro significato di malattia della parola *umore*, e che *malinconia*, prima di significare quella delicata affezione o passion d'animo che intendiamo noi, abbia avuto in origine il senso di *bile* o *fiele* e sia stata per gli antichi un umore nel significato materiale della parola. (*Spsv* 17–18)

This discussion of the material basis of terms for spiritual states demonstrates how Pirandello's thinking will foreground the transfer between the abstract and the concrete and, also, how he will reawaken the 'dead' metaphors in language, delving down to the roots of language and focusing on its generative power.[11] Pirandello's awareness of language change is also tied up with his belief in the inherent fragility of language and meaning, and such semantic fragility is expressed throughout the essay in anguished metalinguistic outbursts: 'Ogni sentimento, ogni pensiero, ogni moto che sorga nell'umorista si sdoppia subito nel suo contrario: ogni sì in un no, che viene in fine ad assumere lo stesso valore del sì' (*Spsv* 139).[12] In the essay, Pirandello describes *umorismo* as a 'fenomeno di sdoppiamento' (*Spsv* 134), and this 'doubleness' is expressed in both of the quotations which could be said to be its dual mottoes—Pirandello's quotation of Giordano Bruno's chiastic epigraph to his *Candelaio*, 'In tristitia hilaris, in hilaritate tristis' (*Spsv* 110) and his rendering of the Socratic maxim 'Una è l'origine dell'allegria e della tristezza: nei contrapposti un'idea non si conosce che per la sua contraria' (*Spsv* 27). Chiasmus, doubling and ambiguity are the linguistic techniques of *umorismo*, mirrored by Pirandello's emphasis on the humoristic ambiguity of the visible. Thus, in Pirandello's work, a thing is only visible in and through its opposite, and what is there invariably stands for something else, leading to the problems of naming, designation and the dissolution of the visible in favour of its fantastic recreation, upon which I will focus.

Gösta Andersson has pointed out the nature and extent of Pirandello's borrowing from the French philosopher Gabriel Séailles's *Essai sur le génie dans l'art* (1883) throughout his theorization of the processes of humour, which are both psychological and aesthetic: in this theorization of the activity of the *coscienza* and *riflessione*, the only truly original point is the *sentimento del contrario*, represented as both a mode of composition in the writer and an effect elicited in the reader. Pirandello famously postulates the humoristic paradigm thus (in a passage which was added to the 1920 text): 'Vedo una vecchia signora, coi capelli ritinti, tutti unti con non si sa di quale orribile manteca [...] Mi metto a ridere. *Avverto* che quella signora è il contrario di ciò che una vecchia rispettabile signora dovrebbe essere. Posso così, a prima giunta e superficialmente, arrestarmi a questa impressione comica. Il comico è appunto un *avvertimento del contrario*' (*Spsv* 127, author's italics).

This idea of unproblematic acceptance of the visible is contested by Pirandello, who insists that the *umorista* should see beyond the potentially deceptive surface and read another interpretation into it: if we imagine, say, that the old lady is dressed thus in a vain attempt to hold on to a much younger husband, then, says Pirandello, the inappropriateness or anachronistic nature of the *vecchia* is recast and she is interpreted not according to the social codes of the time, but according to the codes of narrative fantasy: 'ecco che io non posso più riderne come prima, perché appunto la riflessione, lavorando in me, mi ha fatto andar oltre a quel primo avvertimento, o piuttosto, più addentro, da quel primo *avvertimento del contrario* mi ha fatto passare a questo *sentimento del contrario*. Ed è tutto qui la differenza tra il comico e l'umoristico' (ibid.).

The optic of the *umorista* sees beyond the object of perception, seeing it as both itself and other, creating a second reality other than the merely phenomenal and recasting the Pirandellian obsession with the ambiguous nature of perception as a model of reading and also of writing.[13] *Umorismo*, as an aesthetic which goes beyond the literal, surface meaning to a more profound revelation of a second meaning, emphasizes the centrality of Pirandello's conception of figurative meaning within it.

The problem of defining the *sentimento del contrario*, which, according to Casella, remains 'enigmatico', is not solved by Pirandello's addition in the 1920 text of the 'vecchia signora': this addition, in response to Croce's critique, is supposed to *clarify* the concept.[14] However, Casella argues that Pirandello has recourse to the image of the *vecchia* and the metaphor of the mirror of reflection precisely because the *sentimento del contrario* cannot logically be explained, an idea which again implies that metaphor can have no place in descriptive or analytical work.[15] I would argue that the use of these images in the definition of such a central and problematic idea in Pirandellian theory, rather than compensating for a lack of logic, exemplifies the importance of the figurative to Pirandello. The 'mirror' of reflection (which I will discuss in the next section), which permits the individual to reinterpret the 'vecchia', may be deliberately vague, but what it does is place the metaphorical capacity at the very heart of Pirandello's discursive prose. The *sentimento del contrario* may be underdetermined, but the attempts to articulate it through metaphor and indirection enact the conceptualizing process which is at the core of Pirandello's narrative.

Classical rhetoric had elaborated a word-based theory of metaphor, seeing it as the substitution of one name (or noun) for another, hence Aristotle's opinion that 'metaphor consists in giving the thing a name that belongs to something else'.[16] The Aristotelian theory of metaphor as comparison opposes literal meaning to figurative meaning, seeing metaphor as an impropriety or deviation, in which a stable term is substituted by a metaphorical one. One of the first challenges to this view came in the eighteenth century when Giambattista Vico outlined a theory of language which placed the capacity to make metaphors at the heart of human conceptualizing practice.[17] However, Vico's theory did little to displace the hegemony of the rhetorical approach to metaphor. In the twentieth century I. A. Richards challenged the still-dominant ornamental conception of metaphor by pointing out (in 1936) that metaphor is 'an omnipresent principle of language'.[18] Richards's theory, in which the vehicle or figure interacts with the tenor or thing being metaphorized to produce a new, metaphorical meaning, also moves away from the idea that metaphorical comparison must always be grounded in resemblance. Paul Ricoeur, one of Richards's most articulate followers, elaborates this idea to produce a semantic theory of metaphor, which views metaphor not as a trope, but as a 'phenomenon of predication'.[19] Ricoeur's emphasis on the limits of a purely tropological or rhetorical treatment of metaphor focuses on the semantic instability of such an approach: 'words have no proper meaning, because no meaning can be said to "belong" to them'.[20] This echoes Richards's view of what he terms the 'Proper Meaning Superstition', by which 'the word has a meaning of its own (ideally only one) independent of and controlling its use'.[21] Both Richards and Ricoeur emphasize that metaphors create resemblances as much as they seek them out.

The novelty and importance of considering metaphor as a heuristic device, something that stimulates the reader's imagination and regenerates language, producing a new way of seeing, can be seen in Pirandello as well as in Richards and Ricoeur: Pirandello's entire corpus can be interpreted in the light of 'L'umorismo''s performance of itself as a metaphorical mode of writing about language, which challenges the separation of literal from metaphorical, language from reality (and in *Uno, nessuno e centomila* transcends this separation seemingly definitively). Paul de Man also points out that 'to the extent that all language is conceptual, it always already speaks about language and not about things [...] all language is language about denomination, i.e. conceptual, figural, metaphorical metalanguage'.[22] This concept of metaphor as belonging to the very fabric of discourse itself is one which is crucial to any reading of Pirandello—the complex nature of metaphor is carried over into discussions of it which inevitably fall into the paradox by means of which, according to Ricoeur, 'there is no non-metaphorical standpoint from which to perceive the order and demarcation of a metaphorical field'.[23] This is vital to remember in examining the status of language in Pirandello's theoretical works, in which the fragility of language and meaning is highlighted and there is no assumption of an unproblematic meaning which 'belongs' to words. The 'transaction between contexts', of which Richards speaks in relation to metaphor, occurs in Pirandello's texts in the new insights which his metaphors produce, and comes from the semantic instability which pervades his work, in which both subject and predicate are implicated in the production of metaphorical meaning.[24]

The 'vecchia', as 'read' by Pirandello, thus becomes a figure of figure itself, of figurative writing and interpretation, in which a new meaning is produced by the interaction of subject and viewer. As an interpretative paradigm, linking the visual and linguistic (which are always connected in Pirandello), it demonstrates that in Pirandello metaphorical meaning retains the qualities not merely of similarity but also of difference inscribed within metaphor: the *avvertimento* or 'stable' first term is relativized by the interaction of the second term, the *sentimento del contrario*. The resulting meaning comes not from an opposition of the proper and the figurative, but from their interaction: the liberating coexistence of similarity and difference, rather than the quest for resemblance which was traditionally regarded as the function of metaphor, permits the acceptance and inclusion of differing interpretations and points of view, and, as we shall see in examining Pirandello's metaphorizing practice, focuses on the moments of insight in which two ostensibly dissimilar terms are yoked together. Rather than the comic 'avvertimento' (which in Henri Bergson's theory of comedy produces society's correction of the inappropriate or deviant),[25] the *sentimento del contrario* is a recognition of the interpretative and heuristic possibilites inherent in the seemingly absurd or anachronistic or inappropriate, as well as a recognition of the provisional status of meaning and its dependence upon context: meaning is always, in Pirandello, under threat of the change which comes from recontextualization. On a more macrocosmic level, such an extension of the possibilities of metaphor and language pervades Pirandello's attitudes to language and fictionality: the 'vecchia' therefore becomes both a rereading, a purportedly 'true' reading after a misreading and, in its focus on the duplicity of an unfaithful description which is open to revision by the viewer, an emblem of authorial desire for meaning despite a loss of faith in language's ability to signify definitively.

Sandro Briosi describes metaphor as a 'fenomeno di frontiera, caratterizzato da una tensione tra la logica e il sentimento, tra la verità e l'emozione',[26] and this tension is enacted in Pirandello's account of the *sentimento del contrario* as the interaction of conventional meaning ('è il contrario di ciò che una vecchia rispettabile signora dovrebbe essere') with the impressionistic and creative interpretation of the viewer/reader.[27] The idea of *umorismo* as operating on the threshold between the literal and metaphorical, in which the reader is poised between interpretations, is one to which I will return. The representation of the *sentimento del contrario* as a point of insight which is reached only after an initial stage of misreading or false knowledge also emphasizes the epistemological status of *umorismo* and its function as a metaphor for Pirandello's narrative practice: the uneasy relation between seeing and knowledge will be enacted in the cognitive and hermeneutic function of the Pirandellian gaze.[28]

The passage from *avvertimento* (knowledge based on the evidence of the senses) to *sentimento* (speculative, deductive and subjective interpretation, which to a certain extent undoes the previous interpretation) provides both a compositional and an interpretative paradigm for Pirandello's own work. *Umorismo* describes a poetics which undermines what is already present (hence the vocabulary of 'scomposizione'). This manifests itself at a diegetic level in the form of (and in the parody of) existing genres such as naturalism, and in digressions; the texts are also materially 'decomposed' by the endless textual displacement and echoing which Pirandello operates between texts, and thus the reader is also forced into constant interpretative readjustments as he or she traces the intertextual echoes of each text.[29] Pirandello's exegesis of the 'vecchia' adds something not found in the original description, it represents the 'something more' which metaphor promises, according to Max Black.[30] Metaphor's 'something more' than the literal, its creation of similarities and differences or its revelation of existing ones, its inability to be paraphrased, its often enigmatic and obscure correspondences, are delighted in and lingered over by Pirandello, both on a purely semantic level and as a structuring principle in his texts—this will become obvious when examining the various metaphors and figures which dominate the essay.

The Metaphors of *Umorismo*

In attempting to define the process of humour, Pirandello's language is profoundly metaphorical at its crucial moments (interestingly, most of the metaphoricity occurs in Part II of the essay, the part which attempts to pin down the essence of *umorismo*): Andersson and Vicentini have demonstrated the extent of Pirandello's debt to the treatises of Marchesini and Séailles, yet it is at precisely these moments of appropriation of the discourse of others that the Sicilian author's language interrupts and counters the scientific idiom of the treatises from which he is borrowing with a highly idiosyncratic and original use of personification and anthropomorphization. Also, in the figures he uses to describe the processes of *umorismo*, Pirandello switches almost interchangeably between metaphor and simile. Whilst metaphor theory postulates a radical difference between simile and metaphor, this difference is disregarded by Pirandello, who shifts between 'è' and 'è come', without regard for the fact that the nature of the relation between the two terms of the enunciation is completely changed by the omission or insertion of the word 'come'.[31] Pirandello's obsessive metaphorization will therefore question the status of both the terms contained within a metaphorical proposition.

Mirrors and Shadows

In Pirandello's description of the 'processo da cui risulta quella particolar rappresentazione che si suol chiamare umoristica' (*Spsv* 126), reflection occupies a prominent position. Andersson demonstrates convincingly how Pirandello's description of the interaction between the *coscienza* and the *riflessione* is borrowed wholesale from Séailles.[32] What is Pirandello's own, however, is the description of the intervention of reflection, the self-aware, self-critical function, in his play between the literal and metaphorical meanings of the term:

Abbiamo detto che, ordinariamente, nella concezione d'un'opera d'arte, la riflessione è quasi una forma del sentimento, quasi uno specchio in cui il sentimento si rimira. Volendo seguitar quest'immagine, si potrebbe dire che, nella concezione umoristica, la riflessione è, sí, come uno specchio, ma d'acqua diaccia, in cui la fiamma del sentimento non si rimira soltanto ma si tuffa e si smorza: il friggere dell'acqua è il riso che suscita l'umorista; il vapore che n'esala è la fantasia spesso un po' fumosa dell'opera umoristica. (*Spsv* 132)[33]

The technique which Pirandello has used here is one which will be very pervasive in his texts: it is that of *literalization*, a return to the etymological root of the word, which contrasts the meaning of literal reflection in a surface to the abstract concept of dispassionate observation which the word has acquired.[34] Thus *riflessione* in this context functions both literally and metaphorically, but each of the terms contains a trace or residue of the other and is defined (and read) with the knowledge of the other term. Pirandello's use of both literal and metaphorical meanings of a term simultaneously has, not incidentally, a punning quality, yoking two meanings together playfully in a manner proper to the pun.[35] It also interrogates the realist (in the philosophical sense) relation between word and thing, the idea of a necessary connection between the word and what it describes, and places it at the centre of Pirandello's narrative poetics. It is no surprise that Pirandello's last novel, *Uno, nessuno e centomila*, ends with the protagonist Moscarda desperately trying to set this realism against the metaphorizing which is transforming him into everything he sees: 'Se il nome è la cosa; se un nome è in noi il concetto d'ogni cosa posta fuori di noi; e senza nome non si ha il concetto' (*Tr* II, 901), as the connection between *res* and *verba* threatens to come apart completely.

It is significant that Pirandello thus places the mirror-image at the centre of his work: the 'specchio d'acqua diaccia', the externalization and spatialization of the action of reflection, embodies the relation between abstract and concrete terms which is so crucial to Pirandello's thought and foregrounds the act of perception, which in *umorismo* is paradoxically predicated upon the assumed unreliability of perception, as we saw with the 'vecchia'.[36] As well as the repercussions for the Pirandellian subject of the specular moment in his texts, which is always a recognition of the subject's own alterity, as discussed by Biasin and Donati amongst others, the mirror is also an important part of the symbolic economy of Pirandello's work:[37] it is a powerful metaphor, both for the self, suggesting as it does completion, an unproblematic monadic entity capable of being reflected in its totality—and also for the text, being the traditional metaphor of mimesis and therefore of naturalism and realism.[38] The mirror-image has an obvious analogue in the relation between signifier and signified and in *Uno, nessuno e centomila* the breakdown of the reflexivity of Moscarda's mirror signals the concomitant breakdown in the narrator's ability to name and denominate, which is also a breakdown in nineteenth-century realist modes of narrating.[39]

The mirror is thus one of the master metaphors of Pirandello's oeuvre, and the central image of *riflessione* as a 'specchio d'acqua diaccia' has the function in the essay of explaining the 'inexplicable'— the mental processes and abstract concepts which he then grounds in the physical or material, working to make the unknown known.[40] This epistemological function of metaphor has been widely discussed by theorists of metaphor, as has metaphor's tendency to represent the abstract in terms of the concrete, and we can apply to the technique of personification or anthropomorphization—which Pirandello uses in the specific instance of the mirror of *riflessione*—Hegel's view that 'personification is an important strategy for making the world seem less alien to us'.[41] I will discuss the exchange between the material and the abstract in Pirandello's language in more detail below.

The movement between the literal and the metaphorical and the physical and conceptual mimics the processes of metaphor itself, the transfer or *phora* which is at its heart.[42] The polyvalence of the mirror-image relation is paralleled in the metaphor of the *corpo/ombra*, the primary significance of which is also as a personified figure of the relation between *sentimento* and *riflessione*: 'La riflessione, dunque, di cui io parlo, non è un'opposizione del cosciente verso lo spontaneo; è una specie di proiezione della stessa attività fantastica: nasce dal fantasma, come l'ombra dal corpo; ha tutti i caratteri della "ingenuità" o natività spontanea; è nel germe stesso della creazione, e spira in fatti da essa ciò che ho chiamato il sentimento del contrario' (*Spsv* 134). Both the *corpo/ombra* and mirror/image relations can be deciphered as figures of metaphor itself, connoting its shadowy, reflective presence and standing for the relation of both interdependence and indivisibility, which defines the relation between literal and metaphorical meanings.[43] The *corpo/ombra* relation recurs at the end of the essay on humour as an emblem of the humorous enterprise itself, an enterprise which is represented as being double, deceptive and also de-hierarchizing, in the sense that the priority of the body is contested (in the same way as the challenge posed to the priority of the literal over the metaphorical). It also emphasizes how Pirandello is unable to escape from metaphorical language in his discussion—and, more to the point, does not attempt to, implying that metaphor is the natural condition of the *umorista*: 'L'artista ordinario bada al corpo solamente: l'umorista bada al corpo e all'ombra, e talvolta più all'ombra che al corpo; nota tutti gli scherzi di quest'ombra, com'essa ora s'allunghi ed ora s'intozzi, quasi a far le smorfie al corpo, che

intanto non la calcola e non se ne cura' (*Spsv* 160).[44] The reified
shadow, a negative, inverted image of the body, standing for the
betweenness and dualism of *umorismo*, also becomes, in the essay, a
heuristic metaphor for the fictional enterprise itself when Pirandello
uses the Romantic image of the 'favilla prometea favoleggiata', which
ostensibly stands for the perception humans have of life:

> Essa ci fa vedere sperduti su la terra; essa proietta tutt'intorno a noi un
> cerchio più o meno ampio di luce, di là dal quale è l'ombra nera, l'ombra
> paurosa che non esisterebbe, se la follia non fosse accesa in noi, ombra che
> noi però dobbiamo purtroppo creder vera [...] Tutta quell'ombra, l'enorme
> mistero [...] non sarà forse in fondo un inganno come un altro, un inganno
> della nostra mente, una fantasia che non si colora? [...] E non è anche qui
> illusorio il limite, e relativo al poco lume nostro, della nostra individualità?
> (*Spsv* 155)[45]

These ideas of the 'mistero', 'inganno' and 'fantasia' refer not merely
to the conditions of human existence, to the 'finzioni dell'anima' in
everyday life (which I will discuss below), but to the conditions of
narrative, the pretence and simulations of fiction, its shadow-casting
properties. Pirandello argues that the *umorista*:

> s'è finalmente accorto che Giove non è altro che un suo vano fantasma, un
> miserevole inganno, l'ombra del suo stesso corpo che si proietta gigantesca
> nel cielo [...] quell'ombra rimane, paurosa e tiranna, per tutti gli uomini che
> non riescono a rendersi conto del fatale inganno. Così il contrasto ci si
> dimostra inovviabile, inscindibile, come l'ombra dal corpo. Lo ha scoperto la
> riflessione, che vede in tutto una costruzione o illusoria o finta o fittizia del
> sentimento e con arguta, sottile e minuta analisi lo scompone. (*Spsv* 156)

Thus *umorismo* is represented as both the caster of shadows and also as
the source of the revelation of their fictitious, illusory character (in the
same way as writing 'humoristically' is both creation and simultaneous
undoing, decreation).[46] Narratively, this is paralleled by characters like
Mattia Pascal in *Il fu Mattia Pascal*; in the chapter entitled 'Io e l'ombra
mia', the shadow becomes a metaphor for Mattia's double personality
and also for his realization of this double nature (being both 'alive' and
'dead') and this realization anticipates the explicitly humorous self-
awareness of Moscarda in *Uno, nessuno e centomila*. Mattia's shadow is
a metaphor for his shadowy status, his existence between biographical
identity and the fiction he has created for himself:

> Mi guardai attorno; poi gli occhi mi s'affisarono su l'ombra del mio corpo, e
> rimasi un tratto a contemplarla [...] Chi era più ombra di noi due? io o lei?

Due ombre! Là, là per terra; e ciascuno poteva passarci sopra: schiacciarmi la
testa, schiaccarmi il cuore: e io, zitto; l'ombra, zitta. L'ombra d'un morto: ecco
la mia vita [...] 'E se mi metto a correre', pensai, 'mi seguirà!' [...] Ma sì!
Così era! il simbolo, lo spettro della mia vita era quell'ombra! (*Tr* I, 523–4)[47]

This typically Pirandellian process of metaphorization, through which
the idea of the body–shadow relationship becomes a metaphor for the
idea of 'character' within the novel, also points up the absurdity of the
idea of a fictional autobiography written by a 'dead' man: the illusion
of the character's existence is exploded by this humoristic self-
reflexive action. The 'moment' of the character's self-awareness is,
ultimately, a metafictional one, parallel to the 'momenti di silenzio
interiore', which I will discuss in the next chapter, and to the aporetic
gaze in the mirror. Thus Pirandello's trilogy of first-person novels (*Il
fu Mattia Pascal*, *Quaderni di Serafino Gubbio* and *Uno, nessuno e
centomila*) is bookended by novels whose master metaphors are,
respectively, the shadow and the mirror, both also figures of the
complex relation between reality and fiction.

Trees and Plants

If it is possible to speak of a figurative economy of *umorismo*, it is one
which is pervaded by organic metaphors, and these metaphors of trees
and plants, or natural growth and fructification, as figures of both the
work of art and the self, form a subtext in which Pirandello's narrative
is grounded. These images will be crucial for him in attempting to
create a myth of artistic originality. Pirandello borrows from the work
of Gabriel Séailles the Romantic metaphor of the work of art as an
organic form.[48] This first appears, translated almost directly from
Séailles, in Pirandello's 1899 essay 'L'azione parlata' to describe the
spontaneity and naturalness which must produce the work of art:
'Non il dramma fa le persone; ma queste, il dramma. E prima d'ogni
altro dunque bisogna aver le persone: vive, libere, operanti. Con esse
e in esse nascerà l'idea del dramma, il primo germe dove staran
racchiusi il destino e la forma; ché in ogni germe già freme l'essere
vivente, e nella ghianda c'è la quercia con tutti i suoi rami.'[49] Here
Pirandello does not limit himself to a mere appropriation of this
conventional metaphor for the work of art.[50] Rather, in typical
fashion, he takes the conventional metaphor and extends it, inserting
it into his own metaphorical network to produce a punning, playful
narrativization of this image, as in this attack on rhetoric:

La coltura, per la Retorica, non era la preparazione del terreno, la vanga, l'aratro, il sarchio, il concime, perché il germe fecondo, il polline vitale, che un'aura propizia, in un momento felice, doveva far cadere in quel terreno vi mettesse salde radici e vi trovasse abbondante nutrimento e si sviluppasse vigoroso e solido e sorgesse senza stento, alto e possente nel desiderio del sole. (*Spsv* 48)

This descriptive excursus, in which the landscape of the history of literature is rewritten as a literal landscape, is generated by Pirandello's punning on the double meaning of 'coltura': again, the literal and metaphorical significance of the terms are held in balance as the extended and complex nature of the metaphor ensures that the literal meaning is not overwhelmed by the metaphorical. It is of course typically ironic that Pirandello's anti-rhetorical polemic is couched in such icastic and rhetorical terms, his rhetoric of anti-rhetoric dramatizing the failure of the truly 'humoristic' author to reach any kind of linguistic revelation outside of metalinguistic discourse. It is a rhetoric of authenticity, of origins, contrasting the natural, spontaneous and 'rooted' language of the *umorista* with the artificiality and 'inauthenticity' of rhetoric: 'No: la coltura, per la Retorica, consisteva nel piantar pali e nel vestirli di frasche. Gli alberi antichi, custoditi nella sua serra, perdevano il loro verde, appassivano; e con le fronde morte, con le foglie ingiallite, coi fiori secchi essa insegnava a parar certi tronchi di idee senza radici nella vita' (*Spsv* 48). This metaphor will be used as an important narrative strategy in Pirandello's novels, especially in *I vecchi e i giovani* and *Suo marito*: what is significant is that in the novelistic context, such figures take on the same kind of explicatory or communicative force that Pirandello claims for them here in the riposte to Croce, when he argued that they add greater precision to the argument. In the novels, these figures are not isolated 'poetic' images, as I will show, but communicative devices which create metaphoric networks whose patterning acts as a structuring principle (and as an interpretative key) to the texts.[51] It is interesting to note, in discussing the challenge to chronology presented by chains of metaphors, that the very nature of metaphor itself is a denial of sequentiality, being rather an assertion of simultaneity, a placing of two bodies in the same space at the same time, which produces a dissolution of historical time. In Pirandello's novels, such metaphors take on a function of commentary or exegesis, both interrupting and explicating the plot: for example, my discussion of *I vecchi e i giovani* will show the importance of the tree as a symbol of the exchange between inside and outside which paralyses the Pirandellian subject in the (literal) landscapes of his novels.

In this sense, the creation of analogical relations within texts and between different texts constitutes another aspect of the inter-textuality provided by Pirandello's borrowings and plagiarizing. The creation of syntagmatic chains of metaphors (as will be shown in *I vecchi e i giovani*, for instance) provides a metonymic counterpart to the poetic function of metaphor attributed to it in the work of Roman Jakobson. Jakobson's immensely influential view, derived from Saussurean linguistics, sees verbal discourse as being divided into the twin axes of the metaphorical (represented in literature by Romanticism and Symbolism) and the metonymic (seen in realism), with the former relying upon relations of similarity and the latter on relations of contiguity. Jakobson asserts: 'Since poetry is focused upon the sign, and pragmatical prose primarily upon the referent, tropes and figures were studied mainly as poetic devices. The principle of similarity underlies poetry [...] Prose, on the contrary, is forwarded essentially by contiguity. Thus for poetry, metaphor—and for prose, metonymy—is the line of least resistance.'[52]

Drawing upon Teresa Bridgeman's essay on metaphor in Jarry, in which she identifies the presence of a series of recurring metaphors and similes as forming an 'intratextual collage', I want to postulate the existence of a series of metonymic associations between images in Pirandello's work, which, rather than referring to any extra-textual reality, similarly form 'part of a semantic seriality based purely on the metonymic relationships between elements of the text which are therefore only linked in language [..] and not through external reference'.[53] Pirandello's repetition and patterning of metaphor will be most notable in *I vecchi e i giovani*, in which the recurring metaphors of trees and fire for psychological states and historical events construct a matrix of natural images which parallel the narration's 'telling' with its own 'showing', not building up a fictional world which resembles the real but forming a constellation of moments of auto-referential and inter- and intratextual connotation.

Metaphor is both an interruption to the diegesis, a 'language of hesitation',[54] and a narrative tool: Patricia Parker writes persuasively of the 'plots' of metaphor, and of its emphasis on the notion of 'place', 'of the tropological as inseparable from the topological', and I would suggest that in Pirandello's essay, through such metaphorical 'plots', he has conceptualized language as a terrain, and ideas as a landscape, mapping the psychological onto the topological and creating master metaphors which are then layered through all of his other texts.[55] I will be examining the intertextual ramifications of Pirandello's repetitions and reuse of images and passages throughout his works in later chapters, but it is interesting to note that this idea of the artist as Romantic genius simultaneously places the author at the centre of the artistic process and also paradoxically emphasizes the autonomy of the art work.[56] In a suggestive passage of 'L'umorismo', the *umorista* is likened to a gardener, preparing the terrain for the growth of the work of art, and Pirandello quotes the idea that:

nei capolavori del genio umano viva nascosta una *plusvalenza* futura, la quale si svolge di per sé sola, indipendentemente dagli autori medesimi, come dal germe si svolgono il fiore ed il frutto senza che il giardiniere abbia fatto altro se non avere zappato bene, rastrellato, innaffiato il terreno, e dato ad esso tutte quelle cure e conferito quegli elementi che meglio valessero a fecondarlo. (*Spsv* 101)

Pirandello's metaphors of authenticity and fructification assert the originality of his work: this rhetoric of originality will be examined more closely in the chapter on *Suo marito*, where the figure of the gardener recurs with a more ambiguous role in the creative process, promoting not the organic growth of the 'natural' work of art, but the hybrid, grafted (humoristic) text. Pirandello's tendency to create metaphors for his own works will be discussed in examining each novel, but a key image in this lexicon of artistic creation is that of *umorismo* as a grafted or hybrid plant:

Quando un sentimento scuote violentemente lo spirito, d'ordinario, si svegliano tutte le idee, tutte le immagini che son con esso in accordo: qui, invece, per la riflessione inserta nel germe del sentimento, come un vischio maligno, si sveglian le idee e le immagini in contrasto. È la condizione, è la qualità che prende il germe, cadendo nel terreno [...] gli s'inserisce il vischio della riflessione; e la pianta sorge e si veste d'un verde estraneo e pur con essa connaturata. (*Spsv* 134)

Metaphors in/and/of Narrative

I have already discussed the tendency of Pirandello's discourse of *umorismo* to render material the abstract; this technique is elaborated throughout his narrative, as his metaphors work both to extend the possibilities of language and constantly to cross over between the real and the ideal. In the process, it forges new relationships, linking previously unrelated or heterogeneous terms by asserting their similarity. The task imposed upon the reader is thus a hermeneutic one, of undoing or taking apart the associations which the text has created through its metaphors.

There are too many examples of this Pirandellian metaphorization to enumerate, but one of the most celebrated examples is that of the episode in *Il fu Mattia Pascal* where Mattia encounters Tito Lenzi, who counters the Ciceronian rhetorical aphorism *Mea mihi conscientia pluris est quam hominum sermo* with a typically Pirandellian rhetoric of anti-rhetoric: 'La coscienza? Ma la coscienza non serve, caro signore! La coscienza, come guida, non può bastare. Basterebbe forse, ma se essa fosse castello e non piazza, per così dire; se noi cioè potessimo riuscire a concepirci isolatamente, ed essa non fosse per sua natura aperta agli altri' (*Tr* I, 424). This literalization of the image of the mind as a fortress, like metaphor itself, takes the form of a mediation between inside and outside: the idea of subjectivity is turned into an image of externality.[57] The metaphor is also immediately explicated by the speaker, its meaning is revealed and the enigma of metaphor is 'solved'. It is useful to compare this episode with its analogue in Pirandello's novel *L'esclusa*, written in 1893 and published in 1901. In *L'esclusa*, Gregorio Alvignani adopts the same (anti)rhetorical mode as Tito Lenzi and declares that:

La retorica ha foggiato questa frase: 'Ho la mia coscienza e mi basta!' Sì, quando però della coscienza non si abbia un concetto preciso [...] Mi basterebbe forse, se potessi riuscire a concepirmi isolatamente, se essa cioè non fosse per sua natura aperta agli altri e non esistesse in lei una relazione, continua, tra me che penso e gli altri esseri che io penso. (*Tr* I, 908)

This passage is almost identical to the later one, except for the absence of the castle metaphor—in this occasion, however, the passage is purely explicatory, as the entire speech works towards clarification as clauses and subclauses seek to define and chart a precise relation between what is said and what is meant or what is accepted to be meaningful. It constitutes a paraphrase of the castello–piazza metaphor in *Il fu Mattia Pascal* and raises the question of what is, in fact, added by the metaphor: what is added, the 'something more', as well as the visibility of the metaphor, in the Aristotelian sense, is the positioning effected by the metaphor of the Pirandellian subject within a matrix of metaphors of the self, all of which serve to emphasize the self's fragility.[58] The metaphor of the self as (literal) construction is central to *Uno, nessuno e centomila* and will be discussed in more detail in that chapter: here, however, I will merely point to that novel's logical extrapolation of the image of the self as construction: 'L'uomo piglia a materia anche se stesso, e si costruisce, sissignori, come una casa [...] E la costruzione dura finché non si sgretoli il materiale dei nostri sentimenti e finché duri il cemento della volontà' (*Tr* II, 786). Pirandello puns on the meaning of 'costruzione', 'materia' and 'materiale' here to produce the humorous doubling which characterizes his metaphors. The prepositional complement, 'il cemento della volontà', is a familiar construction in Pirandello's work: it enacts the union of the twin realms of the physical and the conceptual, writing one exactly in terms of the other, offering a syntactic equivalence which yet retains a semantic equivocation.[59] Some other uses of the prepositional complement can be seen in expressions such as the following passage from 'L'umorismo': 'Il comico e il satirico sanno della riflessione quanta bava tragga dalla vita sociale il ragno dell'esperienza per comporre la ragna della mentalità in questo e in quell'individuo, e come in questa ragna resti spesso avviluppato ciò che si chiama il senso morale' (*Spsv* 146–7).

Pirandello's technique is one of accretion, in which a complex of images radiates out from the same source, constructing a denser 'web' of meaning: the 'ragna della mentalità' becomes part of a signifying web, which is an apt metaphor to describe the laborious and dense metaphorical constructions in Pirandello. Another recurring expression comes from 'L'umorismo''s anti-rhetorical diatribe and is reused by Pirandello on several occasions:

La Retorica, in somma, era come un guardaroba: il guardaroba dell'eloquenza dove i pensieri nudi andavano a vestirsi. E gli abiti, in quel guardaroba, eran già belli e pronti, tagliati tutti su i modelli antichi, o meno adorni, di stoffa umile o mezzana o magnifica, divisi in tante scansie, appesi alle grucce e custoditi dalla guardarobiera che si chiamava Convenienza (*Spsv* 48).[60]

This playful extension of the possibilities of language in the direction of creating new connections between concepts and words can be read as a whimsical stylistic tic which at times verges on self-parody, as in this example from the essay 'Un critico fantastico' (1905), Pirandello's homage to the Mantuan writer Alberto Cantoni. Pirandello describes Cantoni's style thus: 'mordeva in sé e negli altri col veleno dello stile lo scaltro capriccioso che si metteva a far le smorfie all'ingenuo e a beffarlo, il monello della riflessione che acchiappava per la coda la lodoletta del sentimento nell'atto ch'essa spiccava il volo'.[61] This parodic excess of metaphor is an assertion of the importance of difference in the relation of comparison between word and thing as much as similarity: it is also a violation of the decorum advised by Aristotle with regard to its use: 'we must make use of metaphors and epithets that are appropriate. This will be secured by observing due proportion; otherwise there will be a lack of propriety, because it is when placed in juxtaposition that contraries are most evident'.[62]

There are many other examples of this kind of formulation and this series of exchanges between the abstract and the concrete has intriguing consequences for language itself:[63] I have already argued that, in the poetics of *umorismo*, meaning is always deferred and transfigured and that each thing always stands for another thing—thus language itself is foregrounded in its materiality, unsure of its status as transparent medium or material entity. In this context, Pirandello writes admiringly of Verga in his 'Discorso alla Reale Accademia d'Italia' in 1933, defining him as a 'scrittore di cose' as opposed to the 'stile di parole' epitomized by D'Annunzio: Pirandello sees in Verga's work 'la parola che pone la cosa, e per parola non vuol valere se non in quanto serve a esprimere la cosa, per modo che tra la cosa e chi deve vederla, essa, come parola, sparisca, e stia lì, non parola ma la cosa stessa' (*Spsv* 392). The implication that Pirandello is attempting to situate himself as a 'scrittore di cose' is inescapable, and yet it is his attempts to articulate the relationship between 'cose' and 'parole' which constitute the fault line running through his fiction. Pirandello's relentless metaphorization undermines any attempt at unproblematic description and counters the illusion of transparency by focusing attention on the signifying process itself; as Paul Ricoeur asks, 'is not the property of figure as such to convey visibility, to make discourse appear?'[64] The humoristic model is one which, as I have emphasized, vainly attempts to transcend the visible, to 'smascherare', to strip away the false exterior and reach the core of things, yet Pirandello's narratives continually return to the word itself, a word which points both outwards and inwards, in a contest of reference and self-reference. An extreme example of this comes from the 1920 *novella* 'Pena di vivere così', in which words themselves are literally reified: 'Le posa come se fossero cose, le parole, il signor parocco: cose pulite e levigate—là—là—là—là—bei vasetti di porcellana sul tavolino che gli sta davanti' (*Na* I, 208). In the essay 'Soggettivismo e oggettivismo nell'arte narrativa', Pirandello's metalinguistic play reaches new levels when he discusses abstract language:

Natura, reale, vero, ideale, ecc. sono termini astratti, quasi vaselli elastici, che ciascuno può riempire del proprio sentimento [...] Il fornaciaio che fabbrica questi vaselli è il tempo, il quale di tanto in tanto ne varia più o meno la foggia [...] Sopravvengono però al vecchio fornaciaio certi momenti di delirio febbrile, in cui, scontento dei vaselli vecchi, si mette a tentare smaniosamente le più strane fogge [...] I vaselli restano vuoti: i pensieri e i sentimenti, che dovrebbero andar dentro, stanno tutt'intorno ad essi come un liquor versato. Tale effetto mi fanno appunto tutti quegli aggettivi e avverbii e giri di frase attorno ai termini astratti nelle prose e nelle poesie moderne. (*Spsv* 184–5)[65]

In their endless movement between the literal and the metaphorical, Pirandello's texts probe the limits of language and description. This obsessively metalinguistic practice is not, however, restricted to word-based metaphorization: rather, the entirety of Pirandello's fictional discourse (and his ideas of the fictional itself) becomes a focus of figurative play.

'La metafora odiosa': Character and Metafiction

In his many metaphors for the strategies of fiction, Pirandello is also implicitly paralleling the 'inganno', the 'finzioni' which humans create for themselves to themselves, with the conditions of fiction itself, its pretence and simulation, its shadow-casting properties: the idea of metaphor as symbolizing the relation between reality and fiction is highlighted by Pirandello's eager adherence to the ideas expressed by the positivist philosopher Giovanni Marchesini in his 1905 book, *Le finzioni dell'anima*. Once again the dominant concept is that of fictionality (in this case the philosophical concept of 'fiction' as both psychological and sociological illusion).[66] Pirandello adapts Marchesini's philosophical idea of 'finzione' to a more general idea of an awareness of the illusory nature of social and personal constructions of reality and to the conception of the work of art itself. As Marchesini writes, in a language which Pirandello will imitate wholeheartedly:[67]

E se intanto l'individuo crede di avere di sé una precisa conoscenza e assume come assolutamente valida e sincera quell'interpretazione ch'egli dà del suo essere interiore [...] non sarà improprio affermare che questo stato della sua coscienza [...] è uno stato in cui domina la finzione, e che, in ultima analisi, l'individuo in questa guisa *vive* non tanto la *realtà* quanto la *metafora* di se stesso.[68]

Marchesini's ideas profoundly shaped Pirandello's conceptions of the parallels between 'real' and 'fictional' worlds and characters.[69] The illusions of everyday reality become obvious analogues of the illusions created by fiction itself. Pirandello adapts and appropriates Marchesini's positivist psychological discourse to his own conception of 'l'interpretazione fittizia e pur sincera di noi stessi' (*Spsv* 146) and discusses how the comic author must 'sgonfiar questa metafora di noi stessi messa su dall'illusione spontanea' (ibid.). The idea of the self as metaphor becomes itself a metaphor for the narrative process in Pirandello, as is evident from the terms in which he frames the discussion of the 'finzioni dell'anima', arguing that the 'comune menzogna' which unites mankind—the deceptive idea that our social identity is coherent and coextensive with the idea that we have of ourselves—is played out in the way we both create and interpret ourselves. Pirandello expresses this, inevitably, by plagiarizing Marchesini (or rather by recontextualizing him), appropriating words which orginally refer to psychological and sociological processes and placing them in the context of narrative processes.[70] Marchesini's references to the social and psychological 'infingimenti' and 'arti trasfigurative' are transposed into a discussion of the act of narrating, as imitation and appropriation, as always in Pirandello, become discursive strategies and the boundaries between his own text and its model are fluid.

Antonio Illiano has discussed the way in which Pirandello's concept of the creation of fictional characters is derived from the turn-of-the-century theosophical ideas of C. W. Leadbeater and Annie Besant:[71] Pirandello, again borrowing his language from scientific or philosophical texts, seized upon the images of 'thought-forms' existing on another psychical plane in its utmost literality. The idea of characters coming from another realm thus becomes a staple of his metafiction, particularly in *Sei personaggi* and 'La tragedia d'un personaggio', and this literalizing process is on display in the appropriation of Marchesini in the following crucial scene from Pirandello's 1909 *novella*, 'Stefano Giogli, uno e due', in which the protagonist's wife 'reads' him incorrectly, creating an interpretation of him which does not match his real self: 'Quando Lucietta lo abbracciava, non abbracciava lui, ma quell'odiosa metafora di lui ch'ella s'era creata' (*Na* III, 1121). 'Stefano Giogli, uno e due' anticipates Pirandello's novel *Uno, nessuno e centomila* and I will discuss it further in that chapter, but this example of Pirandello's subordination of Marchesini's discourse to his narrative purposes is highly significant: the moment of insight into the fictional or meta-phorical status of characters which will be staged through epiphany in *I vecchi e i giovani* and *Suo marito*, and through metafictional techniques in *Uno, nessuno e centomila* and 'La tragedia d'un personaggio', is here pronounced in terms of the utmost literalism.

In the next chapter I will discuss the 'momenti di silenzio interiore' which punctuate Pirandello's essays and fictions, the 'epiphanic' moment in which, according to Pirandello, 'l'anima nostra si spoglia di tutte le finzioni abituali, e [...] noi vediamo noi stessi nella vita' (*Spsv* 152). This moment of revelation of the fictional nature of the self is a direct mirror of the humorist's revelation of the fictional nature of his own narrative: 'l'umorista coglie subito queste varie simulazioni per la lotta della vita: si diverte a smascherarle' (*Spsv* 148). The metaphor of the mask, so central to Pirandello's oeuvre in the massive presence of the *Maschere nude*, is itself a figure of revelation and concealment, and is also a metaphor for fiction, the *prosopon* of the mask becoming the prosopopeia of personification:

Ciascuno si racconcia la maschera come può—la maschera esteriore. Perché dentro c'è poi l'altra, che spesso non s'accorda con quella di fuori. E niente è vero! Vero il mare, sì, vera la montagna; vero il sasso; vero un filo d'erba; ma l'uomo? Sempre, mascherato, senza volerlo, senza saperlo, di quella tal cosa ch'egli in buona fede si figura di essere (*Spsv* 153).[72]

I think that we are here at the theoretical core of Pirandello's thought: the self is viewed as non-literal, as a site of interpretation, a locus of coexistence of identity and non-identity, similarity and difference. The self is also viewed as a meaning-producing process which requires different interpretative stances. Pirandello's concept of metaphor thus moves out from word to text to fictional discourse and fictional world as a phenomenon embracing predication itself. Similarly, the ways in which characters in Pirandello's narrative become aware of their own fictional status (which is what I will argue takes place in the 'epiphanic' moments) can be said to replicate or parody the way in which readers 'see' or believe in the fictional worlds which are inhabited by fictional characters. The 'momenti di silenzio interiore', as I will show, represent, in their interruptions to the diegesis, a laying bare of fictional illusion: this strategy of laying bare is of course explicit in the very idea of metafiction, represented in Pirandello's oeuvre in works such as the 'teatro nel teatro' trilogy and *novelle* such as 'La tragedia d'un personaggio'.

Metaphor and metafiction are intimately linked in Pirandello's narrative: metafiction, in which the concept of character and 'world' are exposed as absurd but necessary fictions, can also be read as a self-consciously metaphorical mode, and I will discuss this in greater detail in Chapter 5. Thomas Pavel remarks of metafiction that it is a 'juggling with ontological structures';[73] in *Suo marito* Pirandello dexterously violates the conventions surrounding fictional worlds by moving in and out of them, both by transposing textual material and characters from one text to another, and by deliberately confusing the writing of the protagonist of that novel, Silvia Roncella, with his own. The continued insertion and transposition by Pirandello of portions of his own texts into his other texts—distinct from the plagiarism evidenced in 'L'umorismo'; these are Macchia's '"plagi" da se stesso'—seems a provocative and parodic gesture, on a par with metafictional devices like the anthropomorphized 'Fantasia' of *Sei personaggi*, designed to highlight the illusory nature of the fictional enterprise.

Patricia Parker has identified the 'plots of metaphor' contained within the trope itself as, variously, 'transference, transport, transgression, alienation, impropriety, identity'.[74] In contrast to readings of Pirandello which assume his theoretical writings to be self-stating and self-summarizing, it can be seen that his language and his rhetoric of language, his 'tecnica e stile del grande narratore', is a symptom of the need shown by his theory for the techniques and procedures of fiction. More profoundly, the tensions contained in his metaphors of theory point towards the tensions inherent in his narrative: the organic metaphors which insist on the originality of Pirandello's artistic creation also constitute a proleptic defence of his later work against any charges of impropriety and point to the tensions in his work between originality and appropriation. Similarly, the metaphors of the mirror and shadow, in their emphasis on doubleness and schisms of identity, hint not only thematically at the problems of identity and alienation which run throughout Pirandello, but at the divided nature of his texts themselves, countering the fiction of origins created by the organic metaphors.

Notes to Chapter 1

1. Benedetto Croce, review of 'L'umorismo', *La critica* 7 (1909), 219–23 at 222. In the revised edition of the essay, Pirandello defended himself against this charge, arguing intriguingly that his use of images works to explicate and clarify his discourse: 'negli esempi ch'egli [Croce] cita di queste mie pretese ripetizioni modificazioni e soccorrevoli immagini, sfido chiunque a scoprire il minimo disaccordo, la minima modificazione, il minimo temperamento della prima asserzione, e non piuttosto una più chiara spiegazione, una più precisa immagine' (*Spsv* 136).

2. Paola Casella highlights this tension in the essay between its philosophical and speculative ends, noting that Pirandello 'nel sottotitolo chiama il proprio libro "saggio" e non trattato filosofico o estetico'. *L'umorismo di Pirandello*, 243.

3. 'The clearest diction is that made up of ordinary words, but it is commonplace [...] That which employs unfamiliar words is dignified and outside the common usage. By "unfamiliar" I mean a rare word, a metaphor, a lengthening, and anything beyond the ordinary use [...] We need then a sort of mixture [of ordinary and unfamiliar words]. For the one kind will save the diction from being prosaic and commonplace, the rare word, for example, and the metaphor and the "ornament", whereas the ordinary words give clarity'; *Poetics*, 1458^{a}1–7, trans. S. Halliwell, Loeb Classical Library 23 (London: Heineman, 1999).

4. 'By far the greatest thing is the use of metaphor. That alone cannot be learnt: it is the token of genius. For the right use of metaphor means an eye for resemblances'; *Poetics*, 1459^{a}17.

5. This description comes from Antonio Illiano's 'Momenti e problemi di critica pirandelliana': 'Pirandello usa la tecnica e lo stile del grande narratore anche quando scrive di critica e di filologia'; p. 138.

6. Exceptions to this are the essay by Antonio Alessio, 'Colori e metafore nell'immagine pirandelliana', in Enzo Lauretta (ed.), *Pirandello e la lingua* (Milan: Mursia, 1994), 177–83; also Luciana Salibra's study on a restricted corpus, 'Appunti sulle metafore delle *Novelle per un anno*', in *Lessicologia d'autore: studi su Pirandello e Svevo* (Rome: Edizioni dell'Ateneo, 1990), 77–105. There are, of course, critical studies of individual recurring images in Pirandello's narrative lexicon, chief among which is the mirror: on this topic see, *inter alia*, Corrado Donati, *La solitudine allo specchio* (Rome: Lucarini, 1980), Renato Barilli, 'La poetica dello specchio', in *La linea Svevo-Pirandello* (Milan: Mursia, 1981), 211–15 and Gian Paolo Biasin, 'Lo specchio di Moscarda', in *Malattie letterarie* (Milan: Bompiani, 1976), 125–55.

7. There are interesting parallels to be drawn with the metaphors and figures of Freud and Lacan in their theoretical works: see Malcolm Bowie, *Freud, Proust and Lacan: Theory as Fiction* (Cambridge: Cambridge University Press, 1987), especially 100–33.

8. The borrowings, quotations and plagiarism in Pirandello's essays were first identified by Franz Rauhut in *Der junge Pirandello* (1939; Munich: Beck, 1964) and have been discussed at length by Vicentini, Andersson and Casella.

9. The complex and often contradictory nature of *umorismo* militates against any attempt to define it, as Pirandello admitted in the 1896 article, 'Un preteso poeta umorista del secolo XIII': 'La verità è che il dare una definizione dell'umorismo,

la quale sia a un tempo comprensiva e comprensibile, è in sommo grado difficile, e ciò per l'essenza stessa dell'umorismo, diversa nell'intimo senso della parola' (*Spsv* 248).

10. On the conditions of the essay's composition, see Giorgio Patrizi, *Pirandello e l'umorismo* (Rome: Lithos, 1997), 29; Giudice, *Luigi Pirandello*, 110; Pietro Milone, 'Prefazione' to 'L'umorismo' (Milan: Garzanti, 1995), pp. lvi–cv at lvi–lvii; Casella, *L'umorismo di Pirandello*, 13–15 and 182–3.

11. See Kenneth Burke's view that 'all our terms for "spiritual" states were metonymic in origin [...] Language develops by metaphorical extension, in borrowing words from the realm of the corporeal, visible, tangible and applying them by analogy to the realm of the incorporeal, invisible, intangible, and then in the course of time, the corporeal reference is forgotten'; *A Grammar of Motives* (New York: Prentice-Hall, 1945), 506.

12. Pirandello's belief that language, far from being a tool for discovering and recording reality, is actually an agent of mystification and doubt (a belief expressed paradoxically with persuasive power) informs such outbursts. Similarly, Moscarda in *Uno, nessuno e centomila* articulates these problems of articulation and communication: 'Abbiamo usato, io e voi, la stessa lingua, le stesse parole. Ma che colpa abbiamo, io e voi, se le parole, per sé, sono vuote. Vuote, caro mio. E voi le riempite del senso vostro, nel dirmele; e io nell'accoglierle, inevitabilmente, le riempio del senso mio. Abbiamo creduto d'intenderci; non ci siamo intesi affatto' (*Tr* II, 769). This conceptualization of the spatial, material quality of language is one which is central to Pirandello's thought, and is one to which I will return.

13. Salvatore Guglielmino's reading of the 'vecchia' as Pirandello's 'superamento della poetica veristica o meglio la teorizzazione di questo superamento' is apposite here: 'Retroterra e implicazioni del saggio sull'*umorismo*', in Stefano Milioto (ed.), *Pirandello e la cultura del suo tempo* (Milan: Mursia, 1984), 143–55 at 148.

14. 'Il concetto centrale del sentimento del contrario resta determinato in modo enigmatico sia in termini propri [...] che in termini metaforici'; Casella, *L'umorismo di Pirandello*, 292.

15. 'Questi chiarimenti supplementari non eliminano però quel che di enigmatico ha la definizione pirandelliana, anzi le riformulazioni e il frequente ricorso a metafore filate sono sintomatici [...] per la difficoltà dello scrittore a esprimerla in termini logici'; ibid. 272.

16. *Poetics* 1457[b]6–9.

17. On Vico's ideas of the fundamental role played by metaphor in human psychology and the origin of language, see Marcel Danesi, *Vico, Metaphor and the Origin of Language* (Bloomington: Indiana University Press, 1993), esp. 121–42.

18. I. A. Richards, *Philosophy of Rhetoric* (Oxford: Oxford University Press, 1965), 92; Richards argued that 'throughout the history of rhetoric, metaphor has been treated as a sort of happy extra trick with words [...] in brief, a grace or ornament or added power of language, not its constitutive power' (p. 90). He counters this rhetorical view of metaphor with the argument that '*thought* is metaphoric, and proceeds by comparison, and the metaphors of language derive therefrom' (p. 94, author's italics). The semantic view of metaphor is continued by Max Black in his seminal 1962 article 'Metaphor', in *Models and Metaphors* (Ithaca: Cornell University Press, 1962), 25–47.

19. Paul Ricoeur, *The Rule of Metaphor* (Toronto: University of Toronto Press, 1975), 44. See also the chapter on 'Metaphor and Symbol' in Ricoeur, *Interpretation Theory: Discourse and the Surplus of Meaning* (Fort Worth: Texas Christian University Press, 1976), 45–69 for a synthesis of some of Ricoeur's ideas on metaphor expressed in the earlier text.

20. Ricoeur, *Rule*, 77.

21. Richards, *Philosophy*, 11.

22. Paul de Man, 'Metaphor in Rousseau', in *Allegories of Reading* (Yale: Yale University Press, 1979), 135–62 at 152.

23. Ricoeur, *Rule*, 287.

24. Richards, *Philosophy*, 94.

25. 'The comic is that side of a person which reveals his likeness to a thing, that aspect of human events which, through its peculiar inelasticity, conveys the impression of pure mechanism, of automatism, of movement without life. Consequently it expresses an individual or collective imperfection which calls for an immediate corrective. This corrective is laughter, a social gesture that singles out and represses a special kind of absentmindedness in men and in events'; Bergson, *Laughter*, in *Comedy*, ed. Wylie Sypher (Baltimore: Johns Hopkins University Press, 1980), 117. See also Umberto Eco, 'The frames of comic freedom', in Thomas A. Sebeok (ed.), *Carnival!* (New York and Berlin: Mouton, 1984), 1–9 on the transgressive possibilities inherent in the reframing act performed by the *sentimento del contrario*.

26. Sandro Briosi, *Il senso della metafora* (Napoli: Liguori, 1985), 15.

27. Pirandello's comment that, in the moment of humorous creation (which is, significantly, postulated as a moment of interpretation, 'la riflessione, lavorando in me, mi ha fatto andar oltre a quel primo avvertimento, o piuttosto, più addentro' (p. 127) points to the presence of 'avvertimento' within 'sentimento' and also to the notion, described by David Cooper, that 'metaphorical meaning is "submerged" beneath literal meaning', a conventional notion that is itself, of course, figurative. David Cooper, *Metaphor* (Oxford: Blackwell, 1986), 61.

28. See Marinella Cantelmo, 'Vedere, far vedere, essere visti: dalla *Weltanschauung* dell'autore alla visione narrativa', in *Strumenti critici* 11 (1996), 111–35 on ambiguous vision in Pirandello.

29. Thus Pirandello defines the narrative characteristics of umorismo as 'questa scompostezza, queste digressioni, queste variazioni', which are 'necessaria e inovviabile conseguenza del turbamento e delle interruzioni del movimento organatore delle immagini per opera della riflessione attiva' (*Spsv* 133).

30. Max Black, *Perplexities: Rational Choice, the Prisoner's Dilemma, Metaphor, Poetic Ambiguity and Other Puzzles* (Ithaca: Cornell University Press, 1990), 91. On the indefinable quality which metaphor imparts, its mystifying properties, see also Patricia Parker, 'The metaphorical plot', in David S. Miall (ed.) *Metaphor: Problems and Perspectives* (Brighton: Harvester, 1982), 133–57 at 149.

31. Paul Ricoeur concludes that 'simile explicitly displays the moment of resemblance which operates implicitly in metaphor' (Ricoeur, *Rule*, 27) and that 'bringing two concepts together in simile does not destroy their duality whereas it is destroyed in metaphor': what unites them is their 'perception of otherness' (p. 109). Thus the separateness of the two terms of an analogy is retained in simile but destroyed in metaphor. Teresa Bridgeman, discussing simile as a literal

and unpoetic trope as opposed to the poetic nature of metaphor, argues, however, that simile is as ambiguous as metaphor, despite its 'explanatory syntactic form': 'the tension between "is like" and the reader's referential awareness that the two terms are not like, is similar to that which exists in metaphor'; 'On the *like*ness of similes and metaphors', *Modern Language Review* 91/1 (1996), 65–77 at 69. Paul de Man sees simile as performing a balancing act between equivalence and self-loss: '"comme" maintains a balance between difference and identity'; 'Anthropomorphism and trope in lyric', in *The Rhetoric of Romanticism* (New York: Columbia University Press, 1984), 239–62 at 248. See also Patricia Parker's essay on 'The metaphorical plot' for the 'violation' which metaphor performs 'in its radically copular form', as in the example 'I am Heathcliff', which violates 'the law that two bodies cannot occupy the same space at the same time' (p. 138). This view of metaphor as violation, whilst Aristotelian in origin, can be assimilated to a view of metaphor which, like Ricoeur's, sees the trope in terms of suspension, identity and non-identity. The copular form will be radically reasserted at the end of *Uno, nessuno e centomila* in Moscarda's 'Sono quest'albero' and will be discussed in Ch. 5.

32. See *Arte e teoria*, 192–8 (esp. 195) and especially Andersson's demonstration of how 'Pirandello ha qui innalzato la riflessione a "potenza creatrice" mentre essa nel pensiero di Séailles si limita al compito di accompagnare il processo artistico controllandolo ed integrandolo in modo armonico' (p. 195).

33. Earlier in the essay Pirandello had written, however, that 'la coscienza, in somma, non è una potenza creatrice, ma lo specchio interiore in cui il pensiero si rimira' (*Spsv* 126), i.e. not as a simile but as a metaphor.

34. Maurice J. Quinlan, in an article on literalization in Swift, says that literalization is 'closely related to an interest in language and a knowledge of etymology' and that 'contrasting the literal and metaphorical significance of a term reveals the ironic disparity between the two terms'; 'Swift's use of literalisation as a rhetorical device', *PMLA* 82 (1967), 516–21 at 516.

35. Jonathan Culler writes of the link between etymology and punning: 'the tradition of ancient etymologizing, in Plato's *Cratylus*, in Varro, in Isidore of Seville, was one of motivating the meaning of words through punning derivations' and quotes Derek Attridge's view that 'in both etymologies and puns "two similar sounding but distinct signifiers are brought together, and the surface relation between them invested with meaning through the inventiveness and rhetorical skill of the writer"'; 'The call of the phoneme', in Culler (ed.), *On Puns: the Foundation of Letters* (Oxford: Blackwell, 1986), 1–16 at 2. Pirandello's punning and metaphorizing can be read in this context of extending the possibilities of language, of regenerating meaning through a return to a buried or forgotten origin.

36. For a more detailed discussion of optical metaphors in Pirandello's work, especially that of the lens of the humorist as a *cannocchiale rivoltato*, see my 'Pirandello's "macchinetta infernale" and "lente diabolica": *umorismo*'s devilish double visions', *Pirandello Studies* 20 (2000), 102–16, in which I discuss the complexities of vision as a metaphor for narrative practice in Pirandello.

37. From Pirandello's own categorization of his *novelle* as 'tanti piccoli specchi' ('Prefazione' to *Novelle per un anno* (1923), repr. in *Na* I, 1071) to Adriano Tilgher's invention of the term 'teatro dello specchio' to describe Pirandello's

dramaturgy, the mirror has functioned as a classifying principle in Pirandello's work. See Tilgher, 'Il teatro di Luigi Pirandello', in *Studi sul teatro contemporaneo* (1923), 135–93 *passim*.

38. Cristopher Nash comments that 'The Realist novel takes as its overriding metaphors the window, the mirror, the lens (of a telescope, microscope, spectacles)', *World-Games: the Tradition of Anti-Realist Revolt* (London: Methuen, 1987), 81. For further critical work on ideas of narrative transparency or opacity based on the mirror metaphor, see J. Wimsatt, 'The mirror as a metaphor for literature', in P. Hernadi (ed.), *What is Literature?* (Bloomington: Indiana University Press, 1978), 127–40; Richard Rorty, *Philosophy and the Mirror of Nature* (Oxford: Blackwell, 1998), esp. 12–13; Dorrit Cohn, 'Optics and power in the novel', *New Literary History*, 26 (1995), 3–20; Umberto Eco, 'Sugli specchi', in *Sugli specchi e altri saggi* (Milan: Bompiani, 1985), 9–37. The image of the mirror as metaphor of realism is also prominent in Séailles's essay: 'l'art, c'est l'imitation de la nature, dit le réaliste. Conséquent il élèverait au-dessus de tous les chefs d'oeuvre l'image que donne le miroir'; *Essai sur le génie dans l'art* (Paris: Alcan, 1911), 161.

39. I have drawn the analogy between mirror/image and signifier/signified from Umberto Eco's *Sugli specchi*, 261–70. See also Paola D. Giovanelli, *dicendo che hanno un corpo [sic]* (Modena: Mucchi, 1994), for her comments on the Pirandellian mirror as a 'strumento allo stesso tempo materiale e simbolico' (p. 33).

40. 'Metaphor is a way of knowing [...] a way to grasp the unknown through the known or to let the known stand for the unknown'; James Olney, *Metaphors of the Self* (Princeton: Princeton University Press, 1972), 31.

41. Quoted in Cooper, *Metaphor*, 166. Pirandello, in making the unknown known, exerts control over the realm of language, and grounds his images in the knowable and very bourgeois world—thus *Fantasia*, for example, becomes the author's servant-girl and logic is metaphorized into a 'pompa a filtro', whose workings, described in great detail by Pirandello, bear a striking similarity to those of the steam engine, so familiar as a symbol of the industrial revolution: 'il cervello pompa con essa i sentimenti dal cuore, e ne cava idee. Attraverso il filtro, il sentimento lascia quanto ha in sé di caldo, di torbido: si refrigera, si purifica, si i-de-a-liz-za' (*Spsv* 154). I will discuss this further in the next chapter. On the representation of the abstract in terms of the concrete in metaphor, see the following: on the non-physical in terms of the physical as part of a series of metaphors which make up the human conceptual system, G. Lakoff and M. Johnson, *Metaphors We Live By* (Chicago: University of Chicago Press, 1980), 59, 115–18; also E. E. Sweetser, *From Etymology to Pragmatics* (Cambridge: Cambridge University Press, 1990), 18–19; Cooper, *Metaphor*, 24–6. See the *novella* 'Il treno ha fischiato' (1914) for anthropomorphism run wild (and anthropomorphizing as a sign of madness), where the delirious protagonist begins to say 'cose inaudite; espressioni poetiche, immaginose, bislacche [...] ora parlava di *azzurre fronti* di montagne nevose' (*Na* I, 665), author's italics.

42. The idea of transfer implicit in metaphor (from the Greek *metaphora*, 'carrying over') is made explicit in Aristotle's definition in the *Poetics*: 'Metaphor consists in giving the thing a name that belongs to something else; the transference being either from genus to species, or from species to genus, or from species to species, or on grounds of analogy'; *Poetics* 1457[b]6–9.

43. On this copresence of the literal and the metaphorical, and the difficulty of
assigning a priority to one over the other, Jonathan Culler states that 'the terms
in which the figurative is defined so as to be distinguished from the literal lead
me, paradoxically, to recognize the primacy of the figurative, either by
identifying it with general cognitive processes and seeing the literal as figures
whose figurality has been forgotten, or else by focusing on cases of catachresis
where the figurative seems to work without being contrasted with the literal';
The Pursuit of Signs (London: Routledge, 1981), 207.

44. Elio Gioanola reads the shadow as a symbol of both 'divisione' and 'identificazione',
in which the shadow is both the 'vero se stesso' and 'altro da sé', thus inserting it
into a humoristic dualism of identity and alterity; *Pirandello: la follia*, 47; Vittorio
Stella sees the body/shadow relationship as a 'dialettica reciprocità della coscienza
inautentica e della coscienza autentica'; 'Pirandello e la filosofia italiana', in Milioto
(ed.), *Pirandello e la cultura del suo tempo*, 5–30 at 11.

45. Prometheus is, of course, as Nick Groom points out, the maker and creator, and
also the imitator, copier and forger: Pirandello's use of the image of Promethean
fire thus suggestively yokes artistic creation and artistic deception together, and
already hints at the problems inherent in attempting to talk of artistic originality;
The Forger's Shadow (London: Picador, 2002), 1–3.

46. As seen in this aphorism from the first edition of 'L'umorismo' (subsequently
removed): 'L'arte, in genere compone; l'umorismo decompone', *L'umorismo*
(Lanciano: Carabba, 1908), 183.

47. Pirandello's debt to Chamisso's *Peter Schlemihl* in this novel is apparent: he
rewrites Chamisso's tale, in which the loss of the shadow through an economic
transaction has profound consequences for *homo oeconomicus*, for a society
exploring the new science of psychology, and provides a suitable metaphor for
the divided psyche. Pirandello concludes 'L'umorismo' with the admonitory:
'Quanto valga un'ombra l'umorista sa bene: il *Peter Schlemihl* di Chamisso
informi' (*Spsv* 160).

48. See Andersson, *Arte e teoria*, 150 ff. for the influence of Séailles on Pirandello's
organic images—he identifies its first appearance in Pirandello's 1899 essay
'L'azione parlata'; see also Vicentini, *L'estetica di Pirandello*, 111–12 and Casella,
L'umorismo di Pirandello, 209–11. Vicentini also discusses the influence of
Capuana and Goethe on the prominence of this metaphor in Pirandello's
thought, cf. 64–6.

49. 'L'azione parlata' (*Spsv* 1016); the 'germe' reappears in 1905 in 'Un critico
fantastico' (*Spsv* 369); see Andersson, *Arte e teoria*, 150, for a comparison of this
passage with Séailles. See also Illiano, *Metapsichica e letteratura in Pirandello*, 60 on
the 'germe' as textual metaphor.

50. For the importance of the vegetal metaphor in Romantic thought, see M. H.
Abrams, *The Mirror and the Lamp* (New York: Norton, 1958), 184–208.

51. This ties in with Ricoeur's view that, in the heuristic model of metaphor with
which he proposes to counter the ornamental model, 'metaphor bears
information because it "redescribes" reality'; *The Rule of Metaphor*, 22.

52. Roman Jakobson, 'Two aspects of language and two types of aphasic
disturbance', in Krystyna Pomorska and Stephen Rudy (eds.), *Language in
Literature* (Cambridge: Harvard University Press, 1987), 95–114 at 114. For a
critique of the metaphor/metonymy division see Hugh Bredin, 'Roman

Jakobson on metaphor and metonymy', *Philosophy and Literature* 8/1 (1984), 89–103.

53. Bridgeman, 'On the *like*ness of simile and metaphor', 74.

54. Parker, 'The metaphorical plot', 148.

55. Ibid. 133. Parker's reading of classical rhetoric's emphasis on *locus*, transfer and property has proved very useful to my interpretation of Pirandello's essay.

56. The recurrence, throughout Pirandello's texts, of the tree as a double image, standing for both man's desire to be self-forgetting, to lose himself in the other, and for the text as natural, unself-conscious construction, concurs with M. H. Abrams's analysis of the Kantian tree motif from the *Critique of Judgement* as 'the natural image as immanently but unconsciously teleological, a "self-organising" being' (*The Mirror and the Lamp*, 208). Pirandello's 'l'albero vive e non si sente: per lui la terra, il sole, l'aria, la luce, il vento, la pioggia, non sono cose che esso non sia. All'uomo, invece, nascendo è toccato il triste privilegio di sentirsi vivere' (*Spsv* 155) repeats this. In George Lakoff and Mark Johnson's influential study of the fundamentally metaphorical nature of human thought, one of the metaphors isolated as basic to our understanding of reality and culture is that of ideas as organisms (either people or plants): thus Pirandello has taken a very conventional metaphor, exaggerated and stylized it, and reinserted it into a context of literalism. Lakoff and Johnson, *Metaphors We Live By*, 47.

57. Examples of such metaphors of selfhood are frequent in Pirandello's narrative: see his description of Nocio Pigna in *I vecchi* as 'come una rocca assediata che di tutto ciò aveva dentro si fosse fatta arma e puntello per resistere agli assalti di fuori, e dentro fosse rimasta vuota' (*Tr* II, 172); in 'L'avemaria di Bobbio', Bobbio says that 'ciò che chiamava coscienza è paragonabile alla poca acqua che si vede nel collo d'un pozzo senza fondo' (*Na* I, 507); most interesting is the projection of the subject's unknowable 'mondo dentro' into external forms in the 1918 *novella* 'La morte addosso', in which the narrator remarks how he loves to watch shop assistants wrapping parcels because: 'mi sembra di essere, vorrei essere veramente quella stoffa là di seta... quante cose immagino! Mi serve... Attaccarmi così, dico con l'immaginazione... attaccarmi alla vita, come un rampicante, attorno alle sbarre d'una cancellata' (*Na* I, 57).

58. It is impossible to paraphrase a metaphor, as J. R. Searle points out: 'without using a metaphorical expression we will not reproduce the semantic content which occurred in the hearer's comprehension of the utterance'; 'Metaphor' in A. Ortony (ed.), *Metaphor and Thought* (Cambridge: Cambridge University Press, 1981), 92–123 at 123.

59. Clodagh Brook has examined the use of the prepositional complement in the poetry of Montale, a device which is, she notes, derived from Symbolism. For her the prepositional complement 'when acting as a metaphor, has a level of tension equivalent to that of the copula'; *The Expression of the Inexpressible in Eugenio Montale's Poetry* (Oxford: Oxford University Press, 2002), 54.

60. See the 1908 *novella* 'Il guardaroba dell'eloquenza' (*Na* III, 159–84). Pirandello's use of this metaphor seems to parody traditional rhetorical concepts of language as 'a dress which thought puts on', as Richards puts it: Richards points to a less 'wretchedly inconvenient metaphor' (and one which is more pertinent to Pirandello's metalinguistic discourse), saying: 'we shall do better to think of a meaning as though it were a plant that has grown'; *Philosophy of Rhetoric*, 17.

61. 'Un critico fantastico' (*Spsv* 377); much of this essay was later reused in 'L'umorismo', where Pirandello writes of the 'speciale fisionomia psichica' of *umorismo*, which 'non permette più al sentimento ingenuo di metter le ali e di levarsi come un'allodola perché lanci un trillo nel sole, senza ch'essa la trattenga per la coda nell'atto di spiccare il volo' (*Spsv* 138). Pirandello was possibly influenced in his use of the prepositional complement by Cantoni's own predilection for it: the titles of some of his *racconti* include 'Il demonio dello stile' and 'L'altalena delle antipatie'. In the short story 'L'altalena delle antipatie' occurs the phrase 'le ginocchia della mente' which may have inspired Pirandello's use of this construction. 'L'altalena delle antipatie', in *Il demonio dello stile: tre novelle* (Milan: Lombardi, 1987), 51–111 at 59. See the phrase in the *novella* 'Il professor terremoto' (1910), 'la saettella di trapano del loro raziocinio' (*Na* I, 687); see also the metalinguistic musings on the art of comparison in the 1923 *novella* 'Un po' di vino' (*Na* II, 399–404).

62. Aristotle, *'Art' of Rhetoric*, 3. 2. 9–10, Loeb Classical Library 22 (London: Heinemann, 1975).

63. In *Il fu Mattia Pascal* there is a use of this construction in an extended and audacious sequence which is both metalinguistic and intertextually parodic as Mattia describes his recounting of his life: 'a poco a poco, superati gli scogli delle prime domande imbarazzanti, scansandone alcuni coi remi della menzogna, che mi servivan da leva e da puntello, aggrappandomi, quasi con tutte e due le mani, a quelli che mi stringevano più da presso, per girarli pian piano, prudentemente, la barchetta della mia finzione poté alla fine filare al largo e issar la vela della fantasia' (*Tr* I, 454). The 'barchetta della mia finzione' of course recalls and parodies Dante's 'navicella del mio ingegno' from *Purgatorio*, 1, symbol of the poetic imagination itself; in *I vecchi e i giovani*, the description of the hypocrisy of Corrado Selmi's enemies verges on self-parody in its hyperbolic excess: 'egoisti meschini e miopi, diligenti coltivatori dell'arido giardinetto del loro senso morale, cinto tutt'intorno da un'irta siepe di scrupoli, la quale non aveva poi nulla da custodire, giacchè quel loro giardinetto non aveva mai dato altro che frutti imbozzacchiti o inutili fiori pomposi' (*Tr* II, 195).

64. *The Rule of Metaphor*, 193; Ricoeur's comments on the 'opacity' of figurative language are worth quoting here, as he remarks that 'in poetic language the sign is looked at, not through: in other words, instead of being a medium or route crossed on the way to reality, language itself becomes "stuff"', like the sculptor's marble'; p. 209.

65. In the 1890 essay 'Prosa moderna', Pirandello described the renovatory power of modern journalism in destroying outdated prose styles,using a vivid metaphor: 'il contegno austero, da edifizii ambulanti, delle matrone periodesse è spezzato' (*Spsv* 879). The spatializing tendency of metaphor, taken to its absurd conclusion by Pirandello, is defined by Derrida as a property of figurative language: 'every metaphorical enunciation spatializes as soon as it gives us something to imagine, to see or touch'; 'White mythology: metaphor in the text of philosophy', in *The Margins of Philosophy*, trans. Alan Bass (Brighton: Harvester, 1982), 207–71 at 227.

66. See Vicentini, *L'estetica di Pirandello* (1985 edn.), 31–3 on Pirandello's assimilation of Marchesini's 'finzione' to his own 'illusione'. Pirandello uses 'finzione' and 'illusione' interchangeably in his two 'discorsi' on Verga: 'sono in fondo una medesima illusione quella dell'arte e quella che comunemente a noi tutti viene

dai nostri sensi'; 'Discorso di Catania' (1920) (*Spsv* 419); 'sono in fondo una medesima finzione quella dell'arte e quella che a noi tutti viene dai nostri sensi'; 'Discorso alla Reale Accademia d'Italia' (*Spsv* 399). See Milone, 'Prefazione' to 'L'umorismo', pp. lxii–iii for more details on Pirandello's adaptation of Marchesini; more generally see Giorgio Lanaro, 'La critica alle *Finzioni dell'anima* nella cultura italiana del primo Novecento', *Rivista critica di storia della filosofia* 37 (1982), 430–42.

67. On the common practice of late nineteenth-century borrowings of language and metaphors between literary and scientific texts, see Gillian Beer, *Darwin's Plots* (London: Routledge and Kegan Paul, 1983), 6–8.

68. *Le finzioni dell'anima* (Bari: Laterza, 1905), 8 (author's italics).

69. Although he acknowledges the specific contribution which Marchesini's book made to his essay in a footnote ('Mi avvalgo qui di alcune acute considerazioni contenute nel libro di Giovanni Marchesini, *Le finzioni dell'anima*' (*Spsv* 147)), this ambiguously worded acknowledgement fails to declare exactly how much of the book is incorporated into Pirandello's text and passed off as his own: in particular, pages 147–50 of his essay are almost a verbatim transcription of Marchesini.

70. An example of this technique is when Pirandello plagiarizes a passage from Marchesini, ending with the words 'rifuggiamo da quell'analisi che, svelando la vanità, ecciterebbe il morso della coscienza e ci umilierebbe di fronte a noi stessi' and follows it up with 'Ma quest'analisi la fa per noi l'umorista, che si può dar pure l'ufficio di smascherare tutte le vanità e di rappresentar la società, come fa appunto il Thackeray, quale una *Vanity Fair*' (*Spsv* 149).

71. 'Intervenivano le esoteriche formulazioni del Leadbeater a spiegare come la forza del pensiero può dar vita non solo a forme e fisime immaginarie, ma anche ad esseri effettivamente reali e percettibili. Di particolare interesse pirandelliano, nel volumetto del teosofo inglese sul piano astrale [*The Astral Plane*], si discorre degli abitanti di quel piano detti "elementali formati inconsciamente".' Illiano, *Metapsichica e letteratura in Pirandello*, 63.

72. This metalinguistic *mise en abyme*, in which each figure recessively points to or contains another, is typical of the metaphors of metaphor, as Paul Ricoeur points out: 'Metaphor has been compared to a filter, a screen and a lens, in order to say that it places things under a perspective and instructs us to "see as". Yet it is also a mask that disguises'; *The Rule of Metaphor*, 252.

73. Pavel, *Fictional Worlds* (Cambridge: Harvard University Press, 1986), 63.

74. Parker, 'The metaphorical plot', 155.

CHAPTER 2

The Unrepeatable Repeated:
Epiphany and Self-Plagiarism

> Il vero dell'arte, il vero della fantasia, non è il vero comune.
>
> PIRANDELLO, 'Arte e scienza' (1908)

> Il valore dell'atto ch'io compio può essere stimato e apprezzato
> solamente da quei pochissimi, a cui la vita si sia rivelata come
> d'un tratto s'è rivelata a me.
>
> PIRANDELLO, 'La carriola' (*Na* III, 554)

The relations and exchanges which I have so far traced between
Pirandello's theory and fiction are embedded in a subtext which is not
merely metaphorical, but which is, as I have pointed out, predicated
on the particularity of Pirandello's concept of humoristic insight: in
this moment of superior insight, the unreliability of the visible and the
uncertainty of language are fused. In terms of metaphor, this is the
narrative moment in which unlikely similarities are perceived or
created: 'ogni immagine, ogni gruppo d'immagini desta e richiama le
contrarie' (*Spsv* 133). Recurring patterns of metaphor, as I noted,
organize and structure Pirandello's narrative, creating intertextual
links between theory and fiction and between fictions: in this chapter
I will examine the analogous function performed by the recurring
moments of silent revelation which litter Pirandello's narratives, the
'momenti di silenzio interiore' which 'L'umorismo' outlines. These
'epiphanic' moments also become, in Pirandello's narrative, structuring devices, whose repetition and patterning implies a complex
authorial and narrative game of textual recall, echo and autointerpretation. I will argue that such moments are often, ultimately, like
the metaliterary poetics embodied in Pirandello's narrative use of the

mirror, shadow and tree metaphors, metafictional moments whose positioning in his narratives enact different types of narrative revelation, and which are vital for an understanding of Pirandellian narrative poetics. These revelatory moments need to be resitutated outside of the context in which they are usually discussed: criticism has normally discussed them as pantheistic moments of dissolution of the self into the eternal when the narrative presents 'nella sua piena ed enigmatica espressione "l'altra" dimensione'.[1] Instead I focus on epiphany as a crucial element of Pirandello's narrative technique, which calls into question the idea of narrative chronology itself. These moments are, I will argue, both intertextual and metatextual elements, which enact and reflect humoristic poetics and institute a dialogue between narrator, character and reader. As 'interruptions' to individual texts they pose vital questions about the nature of narration and diegesis, and by repeating these moments more or less exactly, Pirandello also intriguingly foregrounds his own practice of self-plagiarism and forces the reader to confront issues concerned with repetition and textual memory in the Pirandellian narrative corpus.[2]

Literary Epiphany from Romanticism to Modernism

Literary epiphany is a vast topic, which I will treat briefly here and explain why I feel it is a valuable concept to apply to my discussion of Pirandello's narrative. The *Oxford English Dictionary* defines epiphany as 'a manifestation or appearance of something divine or super-human', deriving from the Greek verb *phanein*, to 'make visible' or 'bring to light'. The original context of its usage was in describing appearances of gods to men, and it is used in the New Testament to refer to the appearance of Christ: however, more recent critical work has focused on it as a characteristic of Romantic lyric poetry, pin-pointing the Wordsworthian 'spots of time' as a lyric description of the moments of illumination which enable the subject to penetrate and transcend the veil of visible reality, emphasizing the characteristics of suddenness, achrony and repetition which define these moments.[3] In the late nineteenth century, the epiphany moves from the context of the Romantic sublime and makes its appearance in the novel, influenced by contemporary interest in experimental psychology and spiritualism, finding its apotheosis in the modernism of Joyce, Woolf and Proust among others.[4] It was Joyce who codified modernist epiphany as a moment of illumination arising from a disproportionately trivial incident or object, in *Stephen Hero* (1904–6), the first draft of *A Portrait of the Artist as a Young Man*. In *Stephen Hero,* Stephen Daedalus overhears an insignificant fragment of conversation in the street: 'This triviality made him think of collecting many such moments together in a book of epiphanies. By an epiphany he meant a sudden spiritual manifestation, whether in the vulgarity of speech or of gesture or in a memorable phase of the mind itself.'[5] The idea of epiphany as lyrical fragment or interlude in a narrative is significant as it rewrites the Romantic sublime as a prose moment in which, instead of the poetic mind's encouragement to transcend the phenomenal by a sight of intense beauty, 'the ordinary is rendered remarkable by the imaginative transformation of experience'.[6] Thus the disjunction between the moment or flash or epiphanic revelation and the process of its registration (a disjunction which is always already present in writing about the sublime or ineffable) is heightened.[7] In the deliberate fragmentation and incompleteness of modernist epiphany, in Joyce's fragments of recorded life, or Virginia Woolf's 'matches struck unexpectedly in the dark',[8] the spiritual and sublime experience of the Romantics is broken down, and we have a 'new form of meaning in which the moment of inspiration is absolute and determinate, while the significance provided by the epiphany is relative and indeterminate'.[9]

The reason I am applying this term to Pirandello's 'momenti eccezionali', in the wake of critics like Barilli and Debenedetti, is precisely to exploit this quality of modernist epiphany, whereby the subject's reaction to the experience is out of proportion to its perceived significance.[10] It is in this dual aspect that I wish to explore epiphany in Pirandello, examining it both as a momentary insight and as recorded aesthetic fragment. Pirandellian epiphany is part of a metaliterary poetics which inscribes his theory within his narrative and is at the heart of his discussions of artistic creativity: in these discussions an awareness of the potential inadequacy of language and the recurring crises of articulation on which *umorismo* is founded are countered by the liberating power of *fantasia*.

Humoristic Epiphanies: The 'Momenti di silenzio interiore'

In a famous passage in Part II of 'L'umorismo', Pirandello writes of the hypersignificant moments which occur when the flux of life threatens to overwhelm the individual, who has a sudden, often chilling revelation of the fictions of social life which are abruptly stripped away:

In certi momenti di silenzio interiore, in cui l'anima nostra si spoglia di tutte le finzioni abituali, e gli occhi nostri diventano più acuti e più penetranti, noi vediamo noi stessi nella vita, e in se stessa la vita, quasi in una nudità arida, inquietante; ci sentiamo assaltare da una strana impressione, come se, in un baleno, ci si chiarisse una realtà vivente oltre la vista umana (*Spsv* 152).[11]

This passage first appeared in identical form under the title 'Deserti del cuore' in the 'Taccuino segreto di Luigi Pirandello' (1889–93), and parts of it will be echoed in later Pirandello works, especially in *Suo marito*, the exactitude of its replication making the reader aware from the start just how important the linguistic composition of such moments will be to Pirandello.[12] These moments of superior vision or insight are represented as supremely humoristic moments in which empirical sight becomes humoristic insight ('occhi più penetranti'), a humoristic insight which is, as I pointed out in the last chapter, predicated upon the unreliability of the visible in the work of the *umorista*.[13] As Lone Klem points out, the assumption of the unreliability of the visible world is not the sole prerogative of the humorist: 'un certo grado di perspicacia psicologica è obbligatorio ad ogni artista; infatti, nemmeno a quelli "ordinari" è lecito fermarsi all'apparenza'.[14] However, for Pirandello the process of vision is a permanent negotiation between empirical perception and subjective fantasy, a shifting of frames between what is there and what is absent or potential, between denotation and connotation, and it thus acts as a metaphor for narrative practice itself. The model of humoristic perception, represented by the 'vecchia signora', is, as I noted in Chapter 1, a model which subordinates the 'error' of ordinary perception to the liberating potential of invention or fantasy, which overwrites the earlier vision and uses the visible as a pretext for fantastic speculation.

The exactitude of the replication of the description of the 'momenti di silenzio interiore' in 'L'umorismo' is consistent with, indeed emblematic of, Pirandello's overall narrative praxis, in which the transposition and recontextualization of passages from text to text serves to blur the boundaries between them; such exact replication reaches its apotheosis in the repeated descriptions of these epiphanic moments in Pirandello's narrative. The repetitive, imitative quality of Pirandello's epiphanies raises the question of whether such theoretically unrepeatable moments have a constant value or function, or whether the fact of their appearance in a new context is automatically sufficient to assign a new value to them.

We can crudely categorize Pirandello's narrative epiphanies as having two kinds of valorizations: the first is the positive kind, in this example from the 1917 *novella* 'La mano del malato povero', in which the revelatory moment is endowed with positive values:

Eppure è raro che almeno una volta, in un momento felice, non sia avvenuto a ciascuno di vedere all'improvviso il mondo, la vita, con occhi nuovi; d'intravedere in una subita luce un segno nuovo delle cose; d'intuire in un lampo che relazioni insolite, nuove, impensate, si posson forse stabilire con esse, sicché la vita acquisti agli occhi nostri rinfrescati, un valore meraviglioso, diverso. (*Na* III, 241)

The unnamed first-person narrator uses the language of revelation, the lexicon of light derived from mysticism, to convey the exceptional status of such an awareness;[15] significantly, the story is about the power of fantasy to construct alternative hypothetical versions of reality based on scraps of evidence, in this case the hand glimpsed on the other side of the hospital curtain, from which metonymic symbol the narrator/ protagonist constructs an imaginary life for its owner, overcoming the limitations of his own restricted knowledge and point of view and demonstrating the power of narrative fantasy in Pirandello. Salvatore Battaglia, in reference to this *novella*, talks of 'la gratuita e lussuosa presenza della fantasia',[16] in which what is seen triggers off an imaginative and creative process which itself frequently becomes a narrative within the main narrative.[17]

To the positive view of the narrative potential embodied in the 'narrating epiphany', Pirandello opposes a frequent negative one, in which the moment is perceived in images of violence and rupture ('strappo', 'guasto', 'squarcio'), as in the continuation of the original description in 'L'umorismo': 'Lucidissimamente allora la compagine dell'esistenza quotidiana, quasi sospesa nel vuoto di quel nostro silenzio interiore, ci appare priva di senso, priva di scopo [...] il vuoto interno si allarga, varca i limiti del nostro corpo, diventa vuoto intorno a noi, un vuoto strano' (*Spsv* 152–3).[18] This potential threat to selfhood will be examined in more detail in the chapter on *Suo marito* (in which this passage is repeated verbatim), but it is significant that the images of revelation and suppression which characterize the humoristic poetics are also enacted narratively in the threat of disruption felt by the protagonists, their fear of revelation, which I will examine later.[19]

Intertextuality and Authorship

Pirandello's practice of autocitation, or self-plagiarism, in the form of passages duplicated throughout his work, takes on a particular significance in the (anti)descriptive segments which form his epiphanic moments: these moments constitute, so to speak, the signature lexical elements whose presence acts almost as a guarantee of Pirandello's authorship (though, as I will discuss, their endless repetition creates an almost self-parodic hyper-Pirandellianism).[20] The following key words and syntagms reappear over and over again: 'silenzio attonito', 'infinita lontananza', 'stupore', 'arcano', 'sgomento'.[21] Likewise, Pirandello's physical landscapes in these moments are distinguished by their static and unchanging linguistic components, with ever-present elements such as 'fritinnìi di grilli', 'alberi assorti' and a Leopardian moon, as in this example from the conclusion of the 1904 *novella* 'Il "fumo"': 'I grilli, tutt'intorno, salutavano freneticamente quell'alba lunare [...] E guardò attorno agli alberi, con la gola stretta d'angoscia: quegli olivi centenarii [...] immobili, come assorti in un sogno misterioso nel chiarore lunare' (*Na* I, 92–3).[22] In such moments, both protagonist and the natural elements of the landscape are often implicated in the 'stupore' or 'attonimento' of the moment, and such repetitive moments lack the transfiguring power of other narrative moments which, rather than the 'tempi morti' which constitute a pause or hiatus in the narration, as is the case here, open up the possibilities of narrative itself.[23]

In a sense, the isolated moment of recognition or revelation in Pirandello's texts is emblematic of what occurs to the reader who is familiar with his entire oeuvre: he or she is constantly waiting for the next moment of recognition, and such passages provide a sense of familiarity and continuity which often offsets their sense of estrangement. Palmira de Angelis argues that, as a narrative technique, epiphany operates on two levels: 'uno interno che interessa i personaggi e uno esterno che interessa il lettore', as both character and reader are united in the exegetic act.[24] I will discuss this further in Chapter 4, but I would argue that the Pirandellian practice of imitation of Romantic models of epiphany, as well as his imitation of himself in these moments of insight, foregrounds the linguistic composition of the epiphany in a way that produces a different kind of epiphanic revelation, one that suggests that for Pirandello a kind of humoristic 'sublime' moment can be achieved by an almost magical incantation, by the fetishistic attachment to the same groups of words.[25]

The descriptive economy of Pirandello's epiphanic landscapes is based on the rigid, recycled and limited lexicon used to express these seemingly unrepeatable moments. This dichotomy between the singular unrepeatable 'attimo' and its plural discursive representations also highlights the seemingly gratuitous status of such passages, their function as narrative 'excess'. These isolated ekphrastic passages seem to violate the conditions of relevance attached to storytelling, offering the reader, in the words of Renato Barilli, 'la valorizzazione di brani di vita di oggetti e di eventi al di fuori di ogni evidente ragione economica e utiliaria'.[26] Pirandello can also be said to be engaged in a modernist redefinition of what is to be considered trivial in narrative, as his epiphanic representations privilege the fragmentary over the complete, both thematically and formally. As he says in 'L'umorismo':

> Nella realtà vera le azioni che mettono in rilievo un carattere si stagliano su un fondo di vicende ordinarie, di particolari comuni. Ebbene, gli scrittori, in genere, non se n'avvalgono, o poco se ne curano, come se queste vicende, questi particolari, non abbiano alcun valore e siano inutili e trascurabili. Ne fa tesoro invece l'umorista [...] Ma l'umorista sa che le vicende ordinarie, i particolari comuni, la materialità della vita in somma, così varia e complessa, contradicono poi aspramente quelle semplificazioni ideali [...] E l'impreveduto che è nella vita? E l'abisso che è nelle anime? Non ci sentiamo guizzar dentro, spesso, pensieri strani, quasi lampi di follia, pensieri inconseguenti, inconfessabili finanche a noi stessi? (*Spsv* 159)

Again, Pirandello takes a vocabulary essentially derived from another discipline (psychology), and translates it into a metaliterary context. As I pointed out, it is the process of representation itself that is here foregrounded, as what is actually revealed in such 'momenti ecce-zionali' is inevitably unclear or incomplete, as in this example from the *novella* 'I due compari' (1912): 'E quel ronzio e questo canto dei grilli e il frusciare degli alberi non rompevano, anzi rendevano più attonito lo stupore della natura'(*Na* II, 417). The use of 'attonito' seems to designate a deliberate failure of meaning here, as if the landscape is at the same time hyper-significant and deliberately meaningless, assimilated to every other Pirandellian landscape in its generic lack of differentiation—hence most of the 'revelations' experienced by Pirandello's protagonists are indeterminate, marked by vague nostalgia or numbness, and they acquire extra significance through repetition. They are also sharply differentiated from the narrating epiphanies which I will discuss at the end of the chapter.

Epiphany, as I noted, is both a moment of illumination and a verbal strategy: it is both the trivial, everyday experience and the recording or narrativization of that experience, and in this sense there is a fundamental contradiction inherent in any attempt to represent it. As Martin Bidney remarks, 'mere rhetorical description is not epiphany, nor is discursive psychological analysis'. To take his point even further, there is a sense in which rhetorical description cannot be epiphany, the epiphanic experience necessarily being of a different nature from its registration.[27] Even in the modernist epiphany, something is always 'missed', something eludes definition and the complete revelation is infinitely deferred. In this sense, the epiphanic moment can also be read as a synecdoche of the process of *umorismo* itself: Pirandello famously defined the *umorista* as a *critico fantastico*, saying that: 'Ogni vero umorista non è soltanto poeta, è anche critico, ma—si badi—un critico *sui generis*, un critico fantastico: e dico *fantastico* non solamente nel senso di bizzarro o di capriccioso, ma anche nel senso estetico della parola, quantunque possa sembrare a prima giunta una contradizione [*sic*] in termini' (*Spsv* 133).

The concept of the *critico fantastico* expresses the fundamental dualism at the heart of *umorismo* and at the heart of Pirandellian epiphany: that is, the creative moment is also always an interpretative one, as the Pirandellian articulation is always immediately anatomized.[28] The sudden 'showing forth' of epiphany, its irruption into the ordered world of the work of art and the world of the character, is paralleled in the actions of the 'critico fantastico'. It is significant to note that both epiphany and fantasy derive from the same etymological root: 'phanein', to 'make visible', to 'show', as both work to make evident what was previously obscure. I mentioned in the last chapter that *umorismo*'s fundamental dynamic is one of revelation and suppression, and I would suggest that it is in the Pirandellian revelatory moment that this union of epiphany and *fantasia* becomes clear.

I will argue that tracing epiphanies at a thematic and formal level provides an interpretative key to Pirandellian narrative poetics: the endless repetition and transposition of one text into another tells us much about the nature of *umorismo*, which is a rewriting, both figuratively (in the humoristic questioning of rewriting of conventional plots and norms) and literally. Epiphanies are both privileged moments and also moments or points of stress: it is particularly in these moments that Pirandello's practice of self-plagiarism becomes obvious. His exactly repeated moments thus involve the reader in a process of intertextual 'plotting'—only the 'competent' reader, who is familiar with most or a large part of Pirandello's oeuvre, receives the full revelation of the identical nature of these discrete segments and also recognizes that in Pirandello the moment of artistic creation is paralleled with the moment of retouching or transposition.[29]

In their withdrawal from denotation (or rather, in their incessant repetition, the sameness of which seems to defer revelation), Pirandello's epiphanic moments centre on the power of the text to articulate itself and on the ability of the reader to interpret its meaning. In Lia Guerra's definition of the 'reader's epiphany', which is a parallel experience in the reader to the one undergone by the character, this technique of textual fragmentation, through which the reader reassembles the fragments and fills in the gaps, is an occasion when 'the reader can trigger and activate the meaning of anaphoric or intertextual references or other forms of recovery and reassessment'.[30] Pirandello's readers can trace the passage of epiphanic descriptions from one text to another, their reliability contrasting both with their protagonists' inability to decode them and with the threat which their appearance poses to the text, a point I will discuss later in the chapter. Pirandello's fictions are founded upon these ambiguous and multivalent revelations and recognitions, which arise out of his theory of humoristic perception, his privileging of *sentimento* over *avvertimento*, of the inexpressible over the defined, which produces these aporetic instants of 'indeterminezza della visione'.[31]

Metafiction and Artistic Creativity

My discussion of the epiphanic moment in Pirandello's narrative has centred on the problems of articulation and expression implied in its composition: as I will point out in Chapter 3, the Pirandellian physical landscape becomes an imaginative space where the said and unsaid meet and struggle for supremacy. As such, these 'momenti' form a crucial part of Pirandello's metalinguistic discussions on the creative process, enunciated not only in the essay on humour, but throughout his narrative. The agonistic struggle for expression of the Pirandellian

individual and his author reaches its apex in these moments: I have
already discussed Pirandello's linguistic borrowings from other authors
and his self-plagiarism, but I would like to point out another aspect of
this intertextual and metatextual process which occurs as Pirandello
seems to transpose and recuperate his own early lyric persona in these
moments. Gösta Andersson briefly notes, in his study of influence and
aesthetics in Pirandello, the source of Pirandello's later ecstatic or
sublime moments in the lyric 'I' of his early poetry, quoting the poem
'Momentanee' from Pirandello's first collection of poetry, the humoristically titled *Mal giocondo* (1889):

> Non memorie, non dolori. Sono in preda
> a un confuso stupor vago,
> levemente di lontani dolor conscio,
> di lontani desiderî.
>
> E un fantastico stupor di sogni strani
> ho negli occhi, e parmi al guardo
> una luce fresca e mite alberghi il cielo
> oltre i limiti visivi. (*Spsv* 491)

Andersson notes this 'forma visionaria' and places it firmly within
Pirandello's metaliterary discussion of the creative process, isolating
the word 'stupore' and calling it 'una parola a Pirandello assai cara',
which 'prepara la fase immaginativa che qui poi si trasforma in mite
contemplazione, sentimento di dolce rapimento'.[32] The anti-
cognitive significance of 'stupore', its meaning as both an index of
inexpressibility and of the self-forgetfulness which accompanies both
the creative moment, in Pirandello's articulation of it, and the aphasic
epiphanic moment, will be central to my reading of *Suo marito*, where
the word is used in the context of Pirandello's conception of the
Romantic ecstasy of creation and of Silvia Roncella's construction of
herself as a writer.[33] This moment in which intellectual apprehension
is superseded by creative fantasy thus seems to me a crucial one: *Mal
giocondo*, Pirandello's highly derivative poetic exordium and juvenile
manifesto, is full of such moments of 'stupore', as the poet struggles
to find his own voice, and his 'stupore' seems to me the silent still
point at the heart of this negotiation between feeling and expression,
between influence and originality, between the absolute conven-
tionality of his poetic vocabulary and his desire to transpose that
vocabulary into his narrative.[34] Pirandello's poetic 'stupore' is aware of
its origins whilst trying to forget them and forge a poetic identity of

his own: similarly, the persona of the lyric 'I', as in all poetic *canzonieri*, is a self-conscious construction paradoxically predicated upon ideas of spontaneity and immediacy of feeling.

The schematic and derivative nature of Pirandello's epiphanic lexicon is not in question—its connection to the Romantic sublime is obvious, as is evidenced in the repetition of both 'stupore' and 'attonito', two key words in the vocabulary of the sublime, as Edmund Burke points out:

The Romans used the verb 'stupeo', a term which strongly marks the state of an astonished mind, to express the effect either of simple fear, or of astonishment; the word 'attonitus' ('thunderstruck') is equally expressive of the alliance of these ideas: and do not the French 'étonnement' and the English 'astonishment' and 'amazement' point out as clearly the kindred emotions which attend fear and wonder?[35]

Another element of the derivative and self-parodic hyper-Pirandellianism visible in these moments is the schematic repetition of the following Leopardian moment in Pirandello's prose (from the *novella* 'La cattura'), where the deliberately ponderous description is at slightly bathetic odds with the lack of revelation finally offered: 'Solo, tra gli alberi e con la distesa sterminata del mare sotto gli occhi, come da un'infinita lontananza, nel fruscio lungo e lieve di quegli alberi, nel borboglio cupo e lento di quel mare s'era abituato a sentire la vanità di tutto e il tedio angoscioso della vita' (*Na* III, 18).[36]

This passage evokes both Leopardi's 'A se stesso' ('infinita vanità di tutto') and also identical passages in other works by Pirandello, in a way which seems deliberately designed to draw attention to the passage: in a sense passages like this one embody the other meaning of *fantasia*, its musical sense meaning 'improvisation on a theme'—within the tightly controlled lexical space of epiphany, Pirandello inserts the lyric persona, where it comes to symbolize both creativity and its limitations.

The moments of silent encounter between the subject and nature, so central, for example, in *Suo marito* to Silvia's construction of herself as a writer whose 'originality' comes from works which are also Pirandello's, are also moments of fictional visions of the self, when the self becomes for characters an object as well as a subject of perception. The discourses of character and narrator are confused as the characters assume the standpoint of the narrator, opening up another level of narration within the text, inaugurating a new form of telling as well as seeing. In certain situations, Pirandello posits the epiphanic moment as a metanarrative one, in which the character becomes uneasily aware of the possibilities of other narratives, as in this extreme example from 'Il treno ha fischiato' when Belluca has an epiphanic vision: 'pareva che i paraocchi gli fossero tutt'a un tratto caduti, e gli si fosse scoperto, spalancato d'improvviso all'intorno lo spettacolo della vita' (*Na* I, 664). His vision introduces him to what the protagonist of 'La morte addosso' calls 'il piacere dell'immaginazione' (*Na* II, 59), as his world opens up to the potential for storytelling: 'a un uomo che viva come Belluca [...] la cosa più ovvia, l'incidente più comune [...] un ciottolo per via [...] possono produrre effetti straordinari' (*Na* I, 666), as his babbling 'delirio' is an effect of this 'immaginazione risvegliata' by his momentary revelation. The potential in Pirandello's narratives (especially in the 'metaracconti') for storytelling characters to use their epiphanies as a source or spring-board for imaginative creativity and narrativity is embodied in Belluca, in Silvia, and in the unnamed narrators of 'La carriola' and 'La mano del malato povero'.

Epiphany as Narrative Strategy in the *Novelle*. 'Vedersi': Narration as Second Sight

The moment of humoristic revelation is therefore a self-reflexive one in which the subjects not only pierce the fictions of social life, but also the fictions that contain them ('tutte le nostre fittizie relazioni consuete di sentimenti e d'immagini si sono scisse'), as Pirandello makes clear in the passage immediately preceding the 'certi momenti di silenzio interiore' one: 'Oh perché proprio dobbiamo essere così, noi—ci domandiamo talvolta allo specchio,—con questa faccia, con questo corpo?—Alziamo una mano, nell'incoscienza; e il gesto ci resta sospeso. Ci pare strano che ce l'abbiamo fatto noi. *Ci vediamo vivere*' (*Spsv*, 152, author's emphasis).

These irrevocably dissociative visions are the product of a confusion between the discursive positions of narrator and character, as I said, framed by the schematic form of the epiphany. Nigel Parke writes that such an awareness of the self occurs when 'momentarily, a version of the self experiences the defamiliarizing circumstance of an extra-narrative position'.[37] This occurs most prominently in *Suo marito*, in the episodes in which Silvia's relentless 'fantasticare' projects her out of the time and space she occupies: 'Avrebbe voluto rimanere laggiù presso al suo mare, nella casa ov'era nata e cresciuta, dove si vedeva ancora, ma con l'impressione strana che fosse un'altra, quella là, sì, un'altra *se stessa* ch'ella stentava a riconoscere. Le pareva di vedersi proprio, così da lontano, con occhi d'altri' (*Tr* I, 643).

The link between creative fantasy and epiphany is not merely an etymological one: I mentioned that, in Pirandello's narrative, vision becomes a metaphor for narrative practice itself, the 'vedersi' of the moment of epiphany bringing with it a correlative transformation in narrative positions. The transformative power of memory and fantasy in Pirandello's characters, triggered in these moments of revelation, concurs with Giacomo Debenedetti's view of epiphany as a 'feno-meno di seconda vista per cui la cosa, percepita nell'oggettività materiale, naturale, del suo apparire, invita a scorgere ed effettiva-mente fa scorgere qualcosa d'altro'.[38] 'Second sight', in Pirandello's narrative, operates as an embedding of narratives within narratives, as the protagonists take on the narrating function in third-person stories. I will give some brief examples of how the characteristic techniques of Pirandello's narrative, specifically prolepsis and analepsis, are produced by this metaphorical equivalence between vision and writing. Genette calls the alternative modes of narration constituted by analepsis and prolepsis 'second narrative', saying that 'every anachrony constitutes, with respect to the narrative into which it is inserted—onto which it is grafted—a narrative that is temporally second, subordinate to the first'.[39] The first example is from Piran-dello's first novel, *L'esclusa* (1901), and the shifting of perspective gives the impression of past and present being confused, moving in and out of focus, as Marta, the heroine, revisits analeptically the scene of her earlier 'fall':

Lì, con gli occhi chiusi, volle rifarsi lucidamente i minimi particolari della giornata [...] Rivide la corte piena di colombi, la scala scoperta. Ecco: se la scala non fosse stata così scoperta, forse non sarebbe salita... Ah, sì, certo! Le si riaffacciò alla mente lo spettacolo dell'ampia chiostra dei monti. Poi provò una strana impressione, suscitata dal ricordo d'aver cercato con gli occhi, dal terrazzo dell'Alvignani, il tetto della propria casa presso il Duomo: le parve di trovarsi ancora a guardare da quel terrazzo e di vedersi com'era adesso, lì, nella sua camera, con la fronte su i vetri del balcone. (*Tr* I, 159)

The 'fall', the humoristic fulfilment of the general belief at the novel's beginning that Marta had had an affair with Alvignani, is here re-enacted mentally to show how in the Pirandellian suspended moment, past, present and future come together and there is no difference between them; the 'moment' also offers an alternative version of the event already recounted, as in the next example when Marta thinks of her proposed suicide, and the narration is performed through the gaze of the character:

Si era veduta allora in preda a quel vento, lungo la spiaggia deserta, col mare mosso, rabbioso, urlante sotto gli occhi; si era veduta in cerca d'un luogo acconcio per buttarsi a quelle onde torbide, orrende, giù; e mentre con l'animo sospeso seguiva quasi i suoi passi fino all'ultimo, fino al punto di spiccare il salto, era guizzato un lampo, era scoppiato il tuono. (*Tr* I, 187–8)

L'esclusa is structured around the trope of analepsis, in its multiple flashbacks, returning to and reinterpreting the first, non-existent 'fall' which relentlessly determines the future;[40] such recurring analepses are mirrored by the prolepses which dominate entire *novelle*, such as 'L'illustre estinto' and 'Con altri occhi', where the characters' self-figuring suggests infinite possibilities for the plot. In 'L'illustre estinto' (1909), the dying protagonist, a senator, foresees his funeral, narrated through his gaze:

La salma... Sì, meglio tenersi alla salma soltanto. Ecco: la prendevano per la testa e per i piedi. Nella cassa era già deposto un lenzuolo zuppo d'acqua sublimata, nel quale la salma sarebbe stata avvolta [...] Ecco la lastra di zinco da saldare su la cassa; ecco il coperchio da avvitare... A questo punto l'on. Costanzo Ramberti non vide più se stesso dentro la cassa: rimase fuori e vide la cassa, come gli altri la avrebbero veduta... (*Na* III, 147)

As frequently happens in Pirandello, the proleptic 'revelation' is countered by a bathetic reality, as events turn out very differently: 'tutto questo l'on. Costanzo Ramberti immaginò alla vigilia della morte. Un po' per colpa sua, un po' per colpa d'altri, la realtà non corrispose interamente a quanto egli aveva immaginato' (*Na* III, 150).

In his description of the 'momenti di silenzio interiore' in 'L'umorismo', Pirandello describes them as constituting an 'arresto del tempo e della vita' (*Spsv* 153) and this temporal dimension is very much in evidence, both in the analepses and prolepses I have discussed, and in the effects which such moments of hiatus and fracture have upon ideas of narrative linearity and closure. In his essay Pirandello claims that 'è stato tante volte notato che le opere umoristiche sono scomposte, interrotte, intramezzate di continue digressioni' (*Spsv* 133) and the role of digression in Pirandello's narrative has been documented.[41] I would argue that the epiphanic moment can be profitably explored by keying it into a reading which emphasizes its relation to Aristotelian anagnorisis (recognition) and peripeteia (reversal), as well as to nineteenth-century narrative and dramatic conventions, in order to demonstrate its function in Pirandellian narrative. This can best be seen by examining several *novelle* by Pirandello which feature the narrative epiphany.

'Tutto per bene' and 'Il viaggio': The 'Scandal' of Revelation

The first examples I will discuss are the *novelle* 'Tutto per bene' (1906) and 'Il viaggio' (1910). In 'Tutto per bene', a *novella* narrated in the third person, there is a strong progressive and linear movement in the narrative, a movement from the protagonist Martino Lori's ignorance to his acquisition of knowledge at the story's end. The plot has a clearly naturalistic character, centring on the classic theme of the revelation of paternity, with Lori's final realization that his daughter is in fact the daughter of his best friend, who had had an affair with his now dead wife years before.[42] At the end of the *novella*, Lori experiences a moment of revelation, in which the significance of narrated events which had previously been unclear is revealed:

Non sapendo più che pensare, riandava, riandava con l'anima smarrita il passato... Tutt'a un tratto, senza saper perché, il pensiero gli s'appuntò in un ricordo lontano, nel più triste ricordo della sua vita. Ardevano in quella notte funesta quattro ceri, e Marco Verona, con la faccia affondata nella sponda del letto, su cui giaceva Silvia morta, piangeva. Fu all'improvviso come se, nella sua anima scombuiata, quei ceri funebri guizzassero e accendessero un lampo livido a rischiarargli orridamente tutta la vita, fin dal primo giorno che Silvia gli era venuta innanzi, accompagnata da Marco Verona. (*Na* I, 379)

The earlier funeral scene now takes on a different aspect, as Lori's revelation transforms retrospectively the earlier narration into a prelude to this moment of anagnorisis. The recognition scene has here an analeptic function, as the events of the past are brought into the clearer light of the present, and earlier enigmas explained: 'Più di vent'anni c'eran voluti perché comprendesse. E non avrebbe compreso, se quelli con la loro freddezza, con la loro noncuranza sdegnosa non gliel'avessero dimostrato e quasi detto chiaramente' (*Na* I, 380). The humoristic twist in the tale is that Lori realizes that his daughter and friend assumed he had known the secret of her paternity all along, and had been performing a typical Pirandellian masquerade, so the revelation is a double one, revealing his daughter's paternity, and also the part he has unwittingly played for years, that of the willingly cuckolded husband.[43] Terence Cave explains how revelation is a plot device which foregrounds the impact of new and shocking information on the characters in a drama: 'Recognition is a scandal. The word may seem excessive, but it is appropriate even in its most ordinary, vulgar sense, since recognition plots are frequently about scandal—incest, adultery, murder in the dark, goings-on that characters ought to know about but usually don't until it is too late.'[44]

It is useful to make a brief comparison of the revelation scene in 'Tutto per bene' with its counterpart in the stage version, first performed in 1919. Anna Laura Lepschy has demonstrated the influence on the play of the Venetian dramatist Giacinto Gallina's *La famegia del santolo* (1892), strengthening the reliance of both play and story on nineteenth-century concerns of paternity and also emphasizing their structural dependence on the nineteenth-century denouement.[45] In the dramatic text, the revelation occurs when Lori is informed of the truth by his daughter: Pirandello confronts the difficulties inherent in dramatizing the kind of epiphanic moment quoted above from the *novella* (the dramatization providing a kind of second-order counterpart to the problems of narrativizing epiphany itself) by having Palma, the daughter, explicitly tell Lori he is not her father. The stage directions at this point read 'come a un baleno' (*Mn* II, 475), and Lori relives the past and realizes he has failed to read the clues properly: 'Non m'ha tradito nessuno! Non m'ha ingannato nessuno! Io, io, non ho visto... ma sì, ma sì, tante cose' (*Mn* II, 472). The stage directions echo the narrative version: 'd'un tratto sorpreso da una visione lontana che lo fa fremere tutto', and Lori narrates the revelation which the narrator had performed in the story: 'che cosa sto vedendo... Senti, morta, io ero come un insensato [...] lui era lì, con la faccia affondata nella sponda del letto, su cui giaceva lei tra i quattro ceri' (*Mn* II, 475) and Lori concludes this retrospective revelation (the stage directions tell us he is 'trasfigurato') with the announcement 'Apro gli occhi adesso!'

In the case of both *novella* and play, the moment of anagnorisis is accompanied by a peripeteia, a reversal or change which comes out of the recognition:[46] in the story Lori is exiled from the company of his daughter and her father, while in the play Palma's scorn turns to pity after she realizes his ignorance and he is integrated into their company at the expense of Manfroni. The epiphanic moments of revelation described above have clear analeptic functions, constituting a return to the past of the narrative and recasting it in the knowledge of the present, emphasizing the absolutely conventional nature of both narratives, as the anagnorisis functions on a thematic and formal level to fill in the gaps and mysteries of the earlier narration.[47] Terence Cave, in his work on anagnorisis, emphasizes its heterodox nature, saying that 'it is a means of knowing which is different from rational cognition. It operates surreptitiously, randomly, elliptically and often perversely, seizing on precisely those details that from a rational point of view seem trivial. And so it tends to be outlawed, or at least relegated to an inferior status in the hierarchy of knowledge.'[48]

A study of the recognition topos in Pirandello's fictions is outside the remit of the present work, although such a study would have a rich and diverse body of material with which to work, from failed recognition ('Amicissimi', 'I nostri ricordi', 'La morta e la viva', *Il fu Mattia Pascal, Come tu mi vuoi*) to the humoristic parody of climactic recognition scenes (*Così è se vi pare*) as well as the variety of ways the past returns metaphorically to shock protagonists.[49] However, as well as the naturalistic use of the topos, there is an equally typical function of Pirandellian revelation or epiphany, one in which such retrospective knowledge is either inaccessible or inexpressible, where the meaning of what is revealed cannot be deciphered by the protagonist, or cannot be communicated by him to anyone else; this function is one which is closer to modernist epiphany, as I described it, while still appearing in a relatively conventional narrative and thematic context. A good example of this is the *novella* 'Il viaggio', which, like 'Tutto per bene', has a resolutely linear structure, indicated paratextually by the title, and set up by the opening of the novella's insistent repetition of the words 'morte' and 'morta'. Adriana Braggi, the widowed protagonist, sets off on a journey from Sicily in the company of her brother-in-law to consult a doctor, and the reader is made aware from the outset that the journey will, in all likelihood, be one-way only.[50] The sentimental plot, in which Adriana inevitably falls in love with her brother-in-law, and its progressive movement towards a predeter-mined end is interrupted by two epiphanic moments, both in Palermo, after Adriana's final prognosis. In the first, she is looking out at the Foro Italico and experiences a typically dissociative Pirandellian vision, in which the physical landscape is dissolved and reconstituted as a purely imaginative space, a space of reverie: 'si sentiva lontana, lontana anche da se stessa, senza memoria né coscienza né pensiero, in un'infinita lontananza di sogno' (*Na* III, 223). The very imprecision of this moment represents the irruption of the synchronic into the diachronic, an effect heightened by the following moment, when, on gazing at the fountain of Hercules (it is no coincidence that both moments occur in the presence of visual remains of a lost classical past), Adriana suddenly and unpredictably experiences a (wholly predictable) Pirandellian epiphany:

subito a quel soffio un gran silenzio di stupore le allargò smisuratamente lo spirito; e, come se un lume d'altri cieli le si accendesse improvviso in quel vuoto incommensurabile, ella sentì d'attingere in quel punto quasi l'eternità, d'acquistare una lucida, sconfinata coscienza di tutto, dell'infinito che si nasconde nella profondità dell'anima misteriosa, e d'aver vissuto, e che le poteva bastare, perché era stata in un attimo, in quell'attimo, eterna. (*Na* III, 224)

Here, the 'stupore' is connected to the time-filled timelessness of the experience: Frank Kermode's reading of narrative revelation through Augustine and the New Testament is relevant, as he discusses the two different conceptions of time, *chronos* or 'passing time' which becomes *kairos* in the moment of revelation—*kairos* is the New Testament time which is a fulfilment of the past, time that is 'charged with a meaning derived from its relation to the end'.[51] Thus, in narrative, 'that which was conceived of as simply successive becomes charged with past and future: what was *chronos* becomes *kairos*', as the sense of an ending casts retrospective meaning on the earlier events. I would argue that Pirandello's 'momenti eccezionali', whilst being moments saturated with the sense of an ending, also contain their own origins and resist conclusion, while pointing to it, representing a time of becoming as well as a time of fulfilment. Instead of a naturalist revelation which offers some kind of vital information (as in 'Tutto per bene'), this is a revelation which, in its gratuitousness, cancels time and information: it is anagnorisis without peripeteia and the plot resumes its naturalistic drive towards the convention of Adriana's suicide.[52] It is tempting to assume that Pirandello inserts such lyrical achronies (and it is their status as inserted, grafted or foreign elements, signalled both by their randomness and irrelevance to concerns of plotting which interests me) into his texts as 'signature' elements. It is these moments, of explicit Romantic derivation, drawn from Pirandello's earlier poetic persona, which challenge and interrupt the codes of naturalist fiction which many of his texts, on the surface, evoke. In this way, the epiphanic moment can be seen to bear an important narrative function: in 'Il viaggio', it is clear that the epiphanic moments run counter to the conventions and themes of popular fiction (sexual awakening, naturalist portrayal of individual decline) which dominate the rest of the story: this practice will reach its apotheosis in *Uno, nessuno e centomila*.[53]

Losing the Plot: 'La carriola'

The idea of revelation as casting a retrospective light on an enigma, as in 'Tutto per bene', or as highlighting, by means of its randomness, the rigid structure of the rest of the plot, as in 'Il viaggio', is opposed by the more radical and more humoristic reworking of the revelation plot in which the epiphanic moment is not merely an interlude but takes over the entire narration and itself provides the mode of narration. A good example of this is the *novella* 'La carriola', narrated by an unnamed first-person protagonist, as an 'epilogue'—the narrator is telling the story in the retrospective light afforded him by his revelation. The moment of anagnorisis is here a specifically humoristic one, in the sense that it can only be a recognition of the protagonist's alterity, of the self-as-other, and it occurs when the narrator, a bourgeois lawyer, looks at his office name-plate:

> Io vidi a un tratto, innanzi a quella porta scura, color di bronzo, con la targa ovale, d'ottone, su cui è inciso il mio nome, preceduto dai miei titoli e seguito da' miei attributi scientifici e professionali, vidi a un tratto, come da fuori, me stesso e la mia vita, ma per non riconoscermi e per non riconoscerla come mia. Spaventosamente d'un tratto mi s'impose la certezza, che l'uomo che stava davanti a quella porta [...] non ero io, non ero mai stato io. (*Na* III, 556)

Several critics have commented on the Pirandellian 'metaracconto',[54] and have agreed that the first-person *novella* is the privileged space in Pirandellian narrative for the kind of metanarrative strategies I have discussed.[55] I argued earlier that in the epiphanic moment the character assumes the standpoint of a narrator and the worlds of the diegesis and narration collide. This can be seen perfectly in 'La carriola', as the anagnorisis is followed by the peripeteia (a wholly interior one, however), in this case the lawyer's descent into the repetition of a random act of insanity.

It might also be useful to note the parallels between 'La carriola' and the overtly metafictional 'La tragedia d'un personaggio' (1911): Giovanni Macchia has written of the lawyers' offices common to Pirandello's fictions that they are analogues of the writer's study in 'La tragedia' and *Sei personaggi*.[56] The invasion of the scene of private, solitary writing in 'La tragedia', when the narrator is assailed by his fictional creations,[57] is equated with the lawyer's assertion in 'La carriola' that 'sono affidati a me la vita, l'onore, la libertà, gli averi di gente innumerevole che m'assedia dalla mattina alla sera per avere la mia opera, il mio consiglio, la mia assistenza' (*Na* III, 553). The entire story is narrated in retrospect, with the narrator-protagonist having gained insight into his fictional condition after the revelation quoted above. The narrator has managed, in the epiphanic moment, to see himself as if from outside, which has thrown him into a 'tetro, plumbeo attonimento' (*Na* III, 555), and his narration is now imbued with a weary knowledge of his fictionality:

Chi vive, quando vive, non si vede: vive... Se uno può vedere la propria vita, è segno che non la vive più, la subisce, la trascina [...] Solo si conosce chi riesca a veder la forma che si è data o che gli altri gli hanno data, la fortuna, i casi, le condizioni in cui ciascuno è nato [...] vedo che non sono mai stato vivo, vedo la forma che gli altri, non io, mi hanno data, e sento che in questa forma, una mia vera vita non c'è stata mai. Mi hanno preso come una materia qualunque, hanno preso un cervello, un'anima, muscoli, nervi, carne, e li hanno impastati e foggiati a piacer loro, perché compissero un lavoro, facessero atti, obbedissero a obblighi, in cui mi cerco e non mi trovo. (*Na* III, 558–9)

In this case the revelation based on the sight of his name has moved the character to an awareness of his fictionality, of his very own 'tragedia d'un personaggio' ('Ora, la mia tragedia è questa!' (*Na* III, 558)) and it is in an act of resistance to the predestined plot of his life that the protagonist performs the act of madness at the end of the story, lifting his dog's hind legs up like the wheelbarrow of the title, and anticipating the similar crisis of self and fictionality experienced by Moscarda in Pirandello's last novel: 'vi assaporo, tremando, la voluttà d'una divina, cosciente follia, che per un attimo mi libera e mi vendica di tutto [...] Giacché, se scoperto, il danno che ne verrebbe, e non soltanto a me, sarebbe incalcolabile. Sarei un uomo finito. Forse m'acchiapperebbero, mi legherebbero e mi trascinerebbero, atterriti, in un ospizio di matti' (*Na* III, 553).

The metafiction of 'La tragedia' of course anticipates that of *Sei personaggi in cerca d'autore*, in the 1925 preface of which Pirandello wrote of his serving-girl, 'Fantasia': 'È da tanti anni a servizio della mia arte (ma come fosse da ieri) una servetta sveltissima e non per tanto nuova sempre del mestiere. Si chiama Fantasia [...] E si diverte a portarmi in casa, perché io ne tragga novelle e romanzi e commedie, la gente più scontenta del mondo, uomini, donne, ragazzi, avvolti in casi strani da cui non trovano più modo a uscire' (*Mn* II, 653). I wrote in the last chapter of how Pirandello grounds his metaphors in the knowable and bourgeois world: the creative process is thus domesticated and explained in his own terms. The etymological doubling I established between epiphany and fantasy suggests that the domestication of fantasy, its subordination to the linear plot, is always open in Pirandello to the rupturing power of epiphany, just as the schematic, rigid and highly codified formulae of his epiphanies are always shot through with the liberation offered by another kind of narration.

In 'La carriola', the act of 'liberation' and 'revenge' is a narrative one: the narrator is caught up in a process of endless narrating in which the 'scandal' revealed is a very different one from that of the naturalistic or melodramatic plot. The furtive act of madness is a product of a narration which has been unable to provide itself with a conclusion: its epiphany is the consequence of a humoristic interrogation of the very ability of the subject to narrate. Pirandello describes the humoristic epiphany as an irrevocable fracture or rupture, both of the subject's illusions of coherence and of the possibility for the subject to narrate their subjectivity, saying that after the 'arresto' occasioned by the epiphany: 'con uno sforzo supremo cerchiamo allora di riacquistar la coscienza normale delle cose, di riconnetter le idee, di risentirci vivi come per l'innanzi, al modo solito [...] Ma a questa coscienza normale, a queste idee riconnesse, a questo sentimento solito della vita non possiamo più prestar fede' (*Spsv* 153).

The previous self cannot be recuperated and, in similar terms, the narrating subject cannot join together present, past and future to form a coherent narration: instead, we have a perpetual present of narrating which is also full of analepses (as in the flashbacks to normal life before the revelatory moment) and prolepses. The narration, like that of the finale of *Uno, nessuno e centomila*, cannot end, as the narrator experiences epiphany after epiphany, provoking change after change in his perception of himself, and the logic of sequentiality is shattered, as is the logic of narrative relevance. In the same way that Cave suggests that 'recognition scenes in literary works are by their nature "problem" moments rather than moments of satisfaction or completion',[58] I would argue that Pirandello's narrative epiphanies are also 'problem' moments as both their momentary nature and their repetitiveness seem to paradoxically both contain and challenge ideas of resolution.

Paul Ricoeur emphasizes the importance of restraint in the use of peripeteia, noting 'the reader's expectation that some form of consonance will finally prevail. This expectation implies that not everything will be a peripeteia, otherwise peripeteia itself becomes meaningless, and our expectation of order would be totally frustrated.'[59] I have suggested that Pirandello's use of epiphanies, as well as being an obvious subversion of chronological norms, is also an attempt to reconstitute them, or to construct an alternative mode of ordering narration.[60] The 'patterns of epiphany' (to quote the title of Martin Bidney's book) enable Pirandello to reconstitute narrative temporality as a parodic and exaggerated version of naturalism, and, through their intertextual and imitative echoes of earlier texts, they act as metaphors of the analeptic practice of rewriting which criss-crosses his work.[61] In the novels which I will examine, epiphany is also a metatextual moment, a moment of the protagonist's self-figuration, in which the sense of an ending, which is, according to Kermode, what drives our reading forward, is really the sense of an ending without end, a revelation whose meaning is incessantly deferred.

Notes to Chapter 2

1. Maria Argenziano Maggi describes Pirandello's epiphanies thus in her study *Il motivo del viaggio nella narrativa pirandelliana* (Naples: Liguori, 1977), 31.

2. Several critics have written on Pirandellian 'epiphany': the most extensive contribution to the subject is that of Renato Barilli, beginning with his *La barriera del naturalismo* in 1964, which institutes a parallel between Pirandello's 'momenti di silenzio interiore' and Joycean epiphany, pp. 39–42 in the second edition (Milan: Mursia, 1980); see also his general study of epiphanic moments in twentieth-century literature, *L'azione e l'estasi* (Milan: Feltrinelli, 1967), esp. pp. 70–7, for comments on Pirandello, as well as his *La linea Svevo-Pirandello*, 153–74. Giacomo Debenedetti is the other major critic to have devoted significant space to this topic in Pirandello, in his *Il romanzo del Novecento*, 288–435. Julie Dashwood discusses the epiphanies or 'momenti eccezionali' in a Nietzschean context in 'I momenti eccezionali di Pirandello: *umorismo*, novelle e "paradiso terrestre"', in E. Lauretta (ed.), *Pirandello e l'oltre* (Milan: Mursia, 1991), 169–78. Lone Klem provides a useful history of the 'momento' in Pirandello in 'Certi momenti di silenzio interiore', ibid. 313–24. Maria Argenziano Maggi writes on the epiphanic journey in Pirandello (which I will discuss in the last section of the chapter) in 'Il viaggio come possibilità di epifanizzazione' in her *Il motivo del viaggio*, 31–8.

3. *The Prelude* (1850 version), Book XII, 208–21:

> There are in our existence spots of time
> That with distinct pre-eminence retain
> A renovating virtue [...]

> A virtue, by which pleasure is enhanced,
> That penetrates, enables us to mount,
> When high, more high, and lifts us up when fallen.
> This efficacious spirit chiefly lurks
> Among those passages of life that give
> Profoundest knowledge to what point, and how
> The mind is lord and master

Morris Beja refers to this passage as 'almost [...] a theory of epiphany', and argues that epiphany 'seems essentially a Romantic phenomenon'; *Epiphany in the Modern Novel* (London: Peter Owen, 1971), 32–3; see also M. H. Abrams on the Romantic poets' emphasis on 'the intersection of eternity with time' in such moments of illumination, in *Natural Supernaturalism: Tradition and Revolution in Romantic Literature* (London: Oxford University Press, 1971), 385–408. Abrams's view that in Wordsworth 'the object itself suddenly becomes charged with revelation' (p. 388) is important to a discussion of twentieth-century epiphany, as is Thomas Weiskel's observation that Wordsworth 'aggrandized the everyday', in *The Romantic Sublime: Studies in the Structure and Psychology of Transcendence* (Baltimore: Johns Hopkins University Press, 1976), 169; see also Wim Tigges's useful introductory chapter, 'The significance of trivial things: a typology of literary epiphanies', to his volume *Moments of Moment: Aspects of the Literary Epiphany* (Amsterdam and Atlanta, Ga.: Rodopi, 1999), 11–35.

4. On the shift from Romantic to modernist poetics of insight, see Beja, *Epiphany*, 47–8; Charles Taylor, *Sources of the Self: The Making of the Modern Identity* (Cambridge: Cambridge University Press, 1989), 456–93; Ashton Nichols, *The Poetics of Epiphany* (Tuscaloosa: University of Alabama Press, 1987), 1–34.

5. James Joyce, *Stephen Hero* (London: Panther, 1977), 188. Joyce in fact collected 'epiphanies', jottings and fragments in his notebooks, which are published in Robert Scholes and Richard Kain (eds.), *The Workshop of Daedalus: James Joyce and the Raw Materials for A Portrait of the Artist as a Young Man* (Evanston, Ill.: Northwestern University Press, 1965); see Giorgio Melchiori's preface to the Italian edition in which he writes of the epiphany as a 'breve lirica in prosa' and comments that there are two stages in epiphany: firstly, the 'espressione drammatica' of the instant, and secondly, the 'teorizzazione dell'attimo di intuizione' when Joyce 'passa ad una forma che si esita a chiamare narrativa in quanto non presenta continuità nel tempo e tuttavia vuole creare una rete di parole e di immagini nella quale cogliere la rivelazione dell'istante'; *Epifanie (1900–1904)*, ed. by G. Melchiori (Milan: Mondadori, 1982), 9–22 at 14. I will return to this point later of epiphany as both a spiritual manifestation and the material registration of that manifestation, bearing in mind Palmira De Angelis's definition of Joycean epiphany as designating 'sia un'esperienza di illuminazione interiore, "spirituale", causata da un evento fortuito, sia il componimento letterario volto a raccogliere e a riprodurre tale esperienza'; *L'immagine epifanica: Hopkins, D'Annunzio, Joyce. Momenti di una poetica* (Rome: Bulzoni, 1989), 11.

6. Nichols, *The Poetics of Epiphany*, 21.

7. See Bruce Kawin, *The Mind of the Novel: Reflexive Form and the Ineffable* (Princeton: Princeton University Press, 1982), 5–35 for a discussion of these problems of representation.

8. 'The great revelation had never come. The great revelation perhaps never did come. Instead there were little daily miracles, illuminations, matches struck unexpectedly in the dark; here was one.' *To the Lighthouse* (London: Penguin, 1992), 175–6.

9. Nichols, *The Poetics of Epiphany*, 1.

10. See Palmira De Angelis's description of the 'scarto significativo tra il momento dell'esperienza e quello della sua espressione' in twentieth-century epiphany, in *L'immagine epifanica*, 59.

11. There is a similar passage a few pages earlier, in which Pirandello inserts the following observation between a quote from Binet and a passage lifted from Marchesini on the stratification of consciousness: 'E tante e tante cose, *in certi momenti eccezionali*, noi sorprendiamo in noi stessi, percezioni, ragionamenti, stati di coscienza, che son veramente oltre i limiti relativi della nostra esistenza normale e cosciente' (*Spsv* 150). Italics mine.

12. 'Taccuino segreto di Luigi Pirandello' was published in the *Almanacco letterario Bompiani*, 16 (1938) devoted to Pirandello, with a 'commento' by Corrado Alvaro, now reprinted in Leonardo Sciascia (ed.), *Omaggio a Pirandello* (Milan: Bompiani, 1987), 14–15.

13. See Marinella Cantelmo's persuasive reading of 'L'umorismo' in this key, where she argues that the 'retorica dello sguardo' in 'L'umorismo' produces a deconstructive gaze which undermines realism from within; 'Vedere, far vedere, essere visti', 126. See also Novella Gazich's '"Con occhi nuovi": modalità narrative nelle *Novelle per un anno*', *Rivista di studi pirandelliani*, 11 (1997), 29–34: she refers to *umorismo* as a 'condizione percettivo-conoscitiva, che fa cogliere l'ambiguo, il doppio, il relativo, il negativo' (p. 30). Renato Barilli also links epiphany with explicitly humoristic insight, calling the 'atteggiamento umoristico' a 'visione del mondo che insegna a mantenere una continua apertura e disponibilità verso le manifestazioni più varie e impensate cui può dar luogo la realtà'; *La barriera del naturalismo* (1980 edn.), 39.

14. '*Umorismo* in atto: accenni ad una interpretazione integrale dei *Sei personaggi in cerca d'autore*', in Enzo Lauretta (ed.), *Il teatro nel teatro di Pirandello* (Agrigento: Centro Nazionale di Studi Pirandelliani, 1977), 39–52 at 48.

15. De Angelis asserts an intimate connection between the mystical experience and the epiphanic one, saying that 'non è un caso che dalla tradizione della letteratura mistica la poetica dell'epifania abbia ripreso l'apparato metaforico di luce e di fiamma con cui rappresenta il fulgore estetico'; *L'immagine epifanica*, 34; the link between superior vision and a higher order of knowledge is a direct one here, as in much of Pirandello's writing about illumination, and is one that is authorized by theological and philosophical tradition, as Richard Sennett remarks of St Augustine's idea in *City of God* that 'the Christian who follows his or her eyes will find God [...] for Augustine the eye was an organ of conscience, as it was for Plato; indeed, the Greek word for theory is *theoria*, which means "look at", "seeing" or—in the modern usage that combines physical experience of light with understanding—"illumination"'. *The Conscience of the Eye* (London: Faber, 1990), 8.

16. Salvatore Battaglia, 'Pirandello e la requisitoria del vivere', in *I facsimile della realtà* (Palermo: Sellerio, 1991), 280–6 at 285.

17. 'Mi misi a contemplare con curiosità amorosa quella mano, e da essa a poco a

poco *mi feci narrare la favola che vi dirò*' (*Na* III, 243; emphasis mine). Giovanna
Cerina's analysis of this *novella* as a 'metaracconto' is interesting, although she
does not attribute special significance to the epiphany: her description of the
'autore in cerca del personaggio' institutes a doubling between narrator and
author: 'si tratta di [...] un personaggio *ex novo*, tutto da "inventare" sulla base di
un dettaglio, "una mano", che sigla il procedimento costruttivo del personaggio
per metonomia'; *Pirandello, o, la scienza della fantasia: mutazioni del procedimento
nelle Novelle per un anno* (Pisa: ETS, 1983), 84.

18. Here, as elsewhere, Pirandello's language betrays the influence of the
experimental psychology of Alfred Binet: see *Alterations of Personality* (London:
Chapman and Hall, 1896), pp. ix–x for Binet's account of the rupture in the
unity of consciousness, and 279–84 for his discussion of his observation of optical
hallucination in patients ('the subject sees what does not exist, he does not see
what does exist', 283). Casella points out that Pirandello's access to Binet's work
occurs by means of his reading of Gaetano Negri's *I segni del tempo* (1892);
Casella, *L'umorismo di Pirandello*, 135.

19. There are obvious parallels between the moments of epiphanic suspension and
the fantastic as a genre: the 'hesitation' felt by the reader of the fantastic,
produced by the fantastic's play between the referential and the illusory, is
certainly close to that experienced by the Pirandellian *character*, especially in his
later *novelle*. See Tvetzan Todorov, *The Fantastic*, trans. R. Howard (Ithaca:
Cornell University Press, 1975), 25. For the fantastic in Pirandello's late *novelle*
see Neuro Bonifazi, 'L. Pirandello, dall'umorismo, alla realtà del sogno', in *Teoria
del fantastico: il racconto fantastico in Italia: Tarchetti–Pirandello–Buzzati* (Ravenna:
Longo, 1982), 109–39; Bonifazi concludes that 'l'umorismo è sempre a un passo
dal fantastico' (p. 116).

20. Barilli writes persuasively of the repetition of epiphanic moments in Pirandello
that it forms part of a 'narrativa "retorica", volta a persuaderci circa una
particolare interpretazione della realtà'; he notes the 'sommarietà' of the
descriptive language employed in these passages and says that they must be
examined together, in their capacity as representing 'un preciso ruolo persuasivo
di possibilità "altre" di vita e di comportamento', but he fails to interrogate the
precise narrative functions that such repeated rhetorical excurses perform. *La
linea Svevo-Pirandello*, 168.

21. The examples of these are too vast to enumerate, so I will limit myself to a few
examples selected for their typicality: 'Lo spirito mi s'era quasi alienato dai sensi,
in una lontananza infinita, ove avvertiva [...] il brulichio d'una vita diversa, non
sua, non qua, non ora, ma là, in quell'infinita lontananza'; 'La carriola' (*Na* III,
555); 'E, all'improvviso, un silenzio, un gran silenzio gli s'era fatto dentro; e
anche fuori, un gran silenzio misterioso, come di tutto il mondo'; 'L'avemaria di
Bobbio' (*Na* I, 511); 'stanco, s'era sdraiato per più ore su l'erba d'un prato [...]
sentendosi perduto come in una lontananza infinita [...] il silenzio profondo,
quasi attonito, era lì presso, però, non rotto'; 'Il coppo' (*Na* I, 769–71).

22. The recurring 'grilli' betray the influence of Pascoli on Pirandello's landscapes;
see in particular Pascoli's *Nuovi poemetti*, *Primi poemetti* and *Canti di Castelvecchio*,
which are full of them. Luciana Salibra's lexical study of the *novelle* discusses
Pirandello's silences only briefly, saying merely 'è possibile che *silenzio attonito* sia
ricalcato sul *silenzio intento* dannunziano, di una delle prime raccolte di poesie,

La chimera [...] In generale, comunque, è da tener presente che nell'ambito letterario e poetico [...] il silenzio è frequentemente adoperato come ricevitore di immagini'; *Lessicologia d'autore*, 86.

23. I have borrowed this term from Franco D'Intino, who talks of the 'vuoti che sono intercalati agli attimi, tempi morti che costituiscono la misura della scansione'; *L'antro della bestia: le Novelle per un anno di Luigi Pirandello* (Caltanissetta: Sciascia, 1992), 14.

24. De Angelis, *L'immagine epifanica*, 138.

25. Giovanni Carchia argues that it is in the recognition of the 'familiarità dell'estraneo' embodied in the 'sentimento del contrario' that the humoristic sublime is possible: 'l'umorismo qui, allora, non è già un sublime rovesciato, bensì quasi il solo punto a partire dal quale, per noi, il sublime stesso è accessibile'; *La retorica del sublime* (Bari: Laterza, 1990), 183–4.

26. Barilli, *La barriera del naturalismo*, 41; such passages almost seem to belong to the type of narrative 'luxury' that Roland Barthes ascribes to realist description— Pirandello's 'luxury' passages take on, however, a predictable and *economic* linguistic form. Roland Barthes, 'The reality effect', in *The Rustle of Language* (Oxford: Blackwell, 1986), 141–8 at 141.

27. Martin Bidney, *Patterns of Epiphany* (Carbondale: Southern Illinois University Press, 1997), 4.

28. Giovanna Cerina's definition of the 'critico fantastico' as one who is 'impegnato nella contestazione delle vecchie forme, non meno che nella creazione fantastica' covers the uses of the epiphany which I examine here: its interruption of traditional plot structures and its role as imaginative tool. *Pirandello, o, la scienza della fantasia*, 53. I would also agree with Olga Ragusa's opinion that '*umorista* and *critico fantastico* are interchangeable synonyms for Pirandello, and it is interesting to speculate whether if the language had offered him an "ism" from the root that gives "fantasy", "fantastic" or "phantasm" he might not have preferred it to *umorismo*'; *Pirandello* (Edinburgh: Edinburgh University Press, 1980), 36–7.

29. See Corrado Donati's mention of the 'lettore accorto' in Pirandello, in *La solitudine allo specchio*, 10.

30. Lia Guerra, 'Fragmentation in *Dubliners* and the reader's epiphany', in Rosa M. Bosinelli (ed.), *Myriadminded Man: Jottings on Joyce* (Bologna: CLUEB, 1986), 41–9 at 44.

31. Roberto Salsano, *Pirandello novelliere e Leopardi* (Rome: Lucarini, 1980), 41.

32. Andersson, *Arte e teoria*, 54.

33. I will return to this topic in Ch. 4, where I will discuss the influence of the arguments of Séailles on Pirandello's concept of the creating genius; here, I will merely cite Pirandello's 'Scienza e critica estetica' (1900), which Andersson has shown to be a calque of Séailles's essay: 'Quante volte l'artista non si stupisce egli stesso di quel che ha fatto!', repr. in the appendix to Andersson, 225–9 at 229.

34. 'Stupore' appears many times in 'Mal giocondo', including the following examples: 'Se non che tosto, come sogno lieve / che a poco a poco si sciolga da i sensi, / stupor mesto lasciando'; 'Romanzi' II (*Spsv* 441); 'Ora egli sta ne la gran selva chiuso, / de le verdi serpi, de i rami, de i fiori, / de lo stupor, de le spine in potere, / tutto tenuto' (*Spsv* 441); 'allor balzai, da lo stupor compreso / del sogno ancora' (*Spsv* 448); 'Stupor novo, qual d'epici sogni meravigliosi, m'invade i sensi, e sol negli occhi ho vita' (*Spsv* 481).

35. Edmund Burke, 'The sublime' (1757), in I. Kramnick (ed.), *The Portable Enlightenment Reader* (London: Penguin, 1995), 329–33 at 330.

36. This description is repeated in 'Canta l'epistola' (*Na* I, 484–5) and *I vecchi e i giovani* (*Tr* II, 42).

37. Nigel Parke, 'Stifled cries and whispering shoes: rites of passage in the modern epiphany', in Tigges (ed.), *Moments of Moment*, 207–32 at 213.

38. *Il romanzo del Novecento*, 288.

39. Gérard Genette, *Narrative Discourse*, trans. Jane E. Lewin (Oxford: Blackwell, 1980), 48.

40. *L'esclusa*'s analeptic structure is derived from its exaggeration of naturalist determinism, as Pirandello's dedicatory letter to Luigi Capuana, prefaced to the 1908 edition, indicates: 'qui ogni volontà è esclusa, pur essendo lasciata ai personaggi la piena illusione ch'essi agiscono volontariamente [...] una legge odiosa li guida' (*Tr* I, 881).

41. On digression in Pirandello's narrative, see Giancarlo Mazzacurati, *Pirandello nel romanzo europeo* (Bologna: Il Mulino, 1987), 277–89; also Olivia Santovetti, 'Digressive art as humorous art?', *Pirandello Studies* 20 (2000), 117–34.

42. The theme of paternity and the bourgeois triangle is a recurrent one in Pirandello's narrative and drama, notably in *novelle* such as 'Il lume dell'altra casa', 'La fedeltà del cane', 'Pena di vivere così', 'Il nido' (which I discuss in detail in Ch. 4), 'Al valor civile', 'In silenzio', 'L'altro figlio', 'Tutt'e tre', 'L'ombra del rimorso' and dramas including *Il berretto a sonagli*, *La morsa*, *La ragione degli altri*.

43. The figure of the cuckold who pretends not to know of his wife's infidelity is memorably embodied in Quaqueo in 'Certi obblighi' (1912) and Tararà in 'La verità' (later Ciampa in *Il berretto a sonagli*): in his trial for the murder of his adulterous wife, Tararà's response to the judge when asked if he was aware of her infidelity exemplifies the nature of social knowledge as opposed to the intimate and self-stating revelation of epiphany: 'E la verità è questa: che era come se io non lo sapessi!' (*Na* I, 750).

44. Terence Cave, *Recognitions: A Study in Poetics* (Oxford: Clarendon Press, 1990), 1.

45. Anna Laura Lepschy, 'Gallina's *La famegia del santolo* and Pirandello's *Tutto per bene*', *Yearbook of the British Pirandello Society* 6 (1986), 19–35.

46. In the *Poetics*, Aristotle says of 'anagnorisis' that 'a "discovery" [...] is the change from ignorance to knowledge [...] A discovery is most effective when it coincides with reversals [...] There are also other forms of discovery, for what we have described may in a sense occur in relation to inanimate and trivial objects'; he describes peripeteia as the 'change of the situation into the opposite', and says that the best plot is one in which anagnorisis is accompanied by peripeteia; *Poetics*, 1452^a26–35. It is interesting to note that Aristotle uses as his paradigm of this *Oedipus Rex*, and specifically its themes of the revelation of paternity.

47. Peter Brooks considers the Aristotelian plot (and his own Freudian reading of it) as manifesting a desire for the end which would be constituted by 'full predication, completion of the codes in a "plenitude" of signification [...] It is at the end—for Barthes as for Aristotle—that recognition brings its illumination, which then can shed retrospective light'; *Reading for the Plot* (Cambridge, MA: Harvard University Press, 1992), 92.

48. Terence Cave, *Recognitions*, 3.

49. Novella Gazich's insistence upon Pirandello's 'utilizzazione esasperata [...] di

espedienti tipici della tradizione novellistica (coincidenze, simmetrie, figure di doppi, scambi di persona, ecc)' and his 'uso instrumentale dell'intreccio' can thus be inserted into the context of a discussion of recognition and epiphanies as humoristic appropriations of typically naturalistic devices. 'Con occhi nuovi', 31.

50. This impression of a teleological movement is heightened by Adriana's fear of crossing the Straits of Messina and leaving Sicily: 'poteva ella confessargli l'oscuro presentimento che la angosciava alla vista di quel mare, che cioè, se fosse partita, se si fosse staccata dalle sponde dell'isola [...] non sarebbe più ritornata alla sua casa, non avrebbe più rivalicato quelle acque, se non fosse morta?' (Na III, 226).

51. Frank Kermode, The Sense of an Ending (Oxford: Oxford University Press, 1968), 47.

52. Other naturalist models for Adriana's disease and suicide include Madame Bovary, Verga's early novels such as Una peccatrice, Eros and Tigre reale, Wharton's The House of Mirth and Pirandello's novelle 'La veste lunga', 'Scialle nero' and 'Spunta un giorno' as well as Vestire gli ignudi.

53. Cave discusses the use of recognition as a 'low' or somehow unliterary device, drawing attention to its links with melodrama: 'Recognition in melodrama is frequently and flamboyantly recognition of persons: false or disguised identities abound' (Recognitions, 212). See also Peter Brooks's excellent study of melodrama, The Melodramatic Imagination: Balzac, Henry James, Melodrama, and the Mode of Excess (New York: Columbia University Press, 1984), cited by Cave, for a discussion of the role of recognition in melodrama, pp. 24–55. It is significant to bear in mind the use Pirandello makes of the melodramatic plot as the 'base' element in his metatheatrical trilogy, Sei personaggi, Ciascuno a suo modo and Questa sera si recita.

54. See Novella Gazich, 'Per una tipologia della novella pirandelliana', Otto/Novecento 5 (1992), 43–56 and the chapter 'Il metaracconto' in Giovanna Cerina's Pirandello, o, la scienza della fantasia, 49–94.

55. Gazich says that 'Pirandello impiega la formula dell'"io narrante" per personaggi depositari di un sapere privilegiato, critico, ed è proprio questa prerogativa che consente all'autore di investirli spesso di un ruolo de portavoce della sua stessa visione del mondo (come ad esempio nella celeberrima "La carriola"'), '"Con occhi nuovi"', 54 n.12. Pirandello's distinction between 'romanzo', 'racconto' and 'novella', in which 'racconto' is any first-person narration, is relevant here: in his 1897 article 'Romanzo, racconto, novella' he says that 'racconto insomma diventa il romanzo, quando la favola in essa racchiusa venga esposta per dir così descrittivamente, o riferita dall'autore o da un personaggio che parli in prima persona, più che rappresentata o messa in azione'; 'Romanzo, racconto, novella', partly reprinted in Paolo Sipala, Capuana e Pirandello: storia e testi di una relazione letteraria (Catania: Bonanno, 1974), 35–7 at 36; see also Ann Caesar's discussion of this article, where she argues that the 'racconto' 'catches the action in its making, the story is related from within its own frame of reference'; Characters and Authors in Luigi Pirandello (Oxford: Clarendon Press, 1998), 23.

56. Macchia's comments are in relation to the novella 'La casa del Granella': 'E la posizione dello scrittore non è diversa da quella di un avvocato [...] che interroga, prende nota, su nomi, condizioni, sentimenti, aspirazioni, prima di rispondere se quel caso è abbastanza strano perché possa interessarlo'; 'Luigi Pirandello', in Cecchi and Sapegno (eds.), Storia della letteratura italiana, ix. 387–435 at 401. See

also Giancarlo Mazzacurati's exposition of the dramatic and narrative protagonists of Pirandello as defendants in a 'forma metaforica del processo'; 'Il
personaggio: l'imputato di turno', in Stefano Milioto (ed.), *Gli atti unici di
Pirandello (tra narrativa e teatro)* (Agrigento: CNSP, 1978), 181–8 at 188. The
'studio' in the *novella* 'Visita' has a similar function, as the narrator says of his
cameriere: 'Gente in casa senza preavviso me n'ha introdotta tanta; ma che
ora m'abbia fatto entrare anche una morta non mi par credibile'; 'Visita'
(*Na* III, 696).

57. 'È mia vecchia abitudine dare udienza, ogni domenica mattina, ai personaggi
delle mie future novelle [...] Non so perché, di solito accorre a queste mie
udienze la gente più scontenta del mondo, o afflitta da strani mali, o ingarbugliata
in speciosissimi casi, con la quale è una vera pena trattare'; 'La tragedia d'un
personaggio' (*Na* I, 816).

58. Cave, *Recognitions*, 489.

59. Paul Ricoeur, *Time and Narrative*, 3 vols. (Chicago: University of Chicago Press,
1988), ii. 25.

60. 'Rejecting chronology is one thing, the refusal of any substitute principle of
configuration is another. It is not conceivable that the narrative should have
moved beyond all configuration. The time of a novel may break away from real
time. In fact, this is the law for the beginning of any fiction. But it cannot help
but be configured in terms of new norms of temporal organization that are still
perceived as temporal by the reader, by means of new expectations regarding the
time of fiction'; ibid.

61. Claude Cazalé Bérard points out that in the naturalist model, 'la fine si
contrappone all'inizio come l'ultima tappa di un processo irrreversibile'; 'Effetti
di una storia interrotta: strategie dell'esito nelle *Novelle per un anno* di L.
Pirandello', *Rivista di studi pirandelliani* 6/7 (1991), 51–71 at 56. However, in
novelle such as 'La carriola', the epiphanic moment irrevocably transforms the
narrating subject, and the ending of the story is opposed to its beginning by
being of a radically altered order.

PART II

CHAPTER 3

Metaphors of History:
I vecchi e i giovani

Ci sono certi scrittori [...] di natura più propriamente storica.
Ma ve ne sono altri che [...] sono di natura più propriamente
filosofica. Io ho la disgrazia d'appartenere a questi ultimi.

PIRANDELLO, 'Prefazione' to *Sei personaggi in cerca d'autore*

Introduction

Pirandello's historical novel *I vecchi e i giovani*, 'romanzo della Sicilia
dopo il 1870, amarissimo e popoloso romanzo, ov'è racchiuso il
dramma della mia generazione', was first published in 1909, a year
after 'L'umorismo'.[1] The novel has traditionally been regarded by
Pirandello criticism as a problematic text for two specific and connected reasons, firstly for its seemingly anachronistic position in Pirandello's oeuvre, coming as it does after the narrative experimentation
of *Il fu Mattia Pascal*. The second reason concerns its relation to the
historical novel genre, with Pirandello criticism broadly divided as to
whether the novel functions by appropriation of the generic codes of
the historical novel or by their subversion, and thus as to whether it
should be read as a reversion to an earlier genre, or as a radical
experiment.[2]

More recently, the novel was re-evaluated by Vittorio Spinazzola in
his influential 1990 monograph, *Il romanzo antistorico*, in which he
asserted the centrality of the novel to Pirandello's narrative production. Spinazzola linked *I vecchi* with De Roberto's *I vicerè* and
Lampedusa's *Il gattopardo* as examples of 'antihistorical novels':
historical novels which display a lack of faith in historical progress and
intend to 'demistificare icasticamente la vacuità della credenza in un
flusso di progresso inarrestibile'.[3]

In this chapter I suggest that such problems regarding the critical classification of the text can be illuminated by an examination of the narrative and structuring roles performed by the elements of *umorismo* examined in Part I, namely metaphor and epiphany. In *I vecchi e i giovani* the dual functions of the historical novel genre—the possibility of the recovery of the past as a lesson for the present and the mapping of the individual onto society and history—are complicated precisely through the use of epiphany and metaphor as metahistorical and metanarrative devices. *I vecchi* takes the relationship between the individual and the environment, an opposition which is central to the historical novel genre, and complicates it: through epiphanic moments, the landscape, which in the locus classicus of the Italian historical novel, Manzoni's *I promessi sposi*, was a space of history, is transformed into a space of atemporal and ahistorical reverie, or into a site where the past is read and interpreted in varied and competing ways by the novel's characters. The relationship between history and place is further complicated by the novel's use of recurring natural metaphors, metaphors which are already familiar from 'L'umorismo', which simultaneously describe and complicate the status and meaning of historical events. Such questioning of the status of the discourse of history is paralleled with the palimpsestic text itself, which, with its use of concealed historical sources and documents, adopts a complicated and 'humoristic' attitude towards the referential illusions of the historical novel.

The Text

I vecchi e i giovani has always proved an enigmatic text for Pirandello criticism to deal with: Walter Geerts, pointing to the critical silence which greeted it (and which lasted until Salinari's *Miti e coscienza del decadentismo* in 1960) says that 'si può [...] sostenere che la critica pirandelliana italiana abbia spesso maltrattato *I vecchi e i giovani*'.[4] The novel is still routinely excluded from studies of Pirandello's narrative and the reason for this exclusion seems to derive from two kinds of critical readings of Pirandello: the first (and largest group) is one which attempts to map the novel onto a *pirandellismo* defined by the twin 'milestones' of *Il fu Mattia Pascal* and 'L'umorismo'. This generalized critical anxiety regarding the positioning of the novel in Pirandello's oeuvre has wider implications, as it implicitly ascribes to his narrative a retrospective trajectory of maturation or progression from naturalism or realism to an experimental *telos*. Giovanni Macchia's famous definition of the novel as a 'passo indietro', implying that Pirandello's literary career is a metaphorical journey, has been echoed by other critics who share the view of the historical novel as being inherently tied to realism, a mode which Pirandello has now left behind.[5] In my opinion, this critical view has been influenced by Croce's 1940 essay on Pirandello.[6] Such an assumption also overlooks the complexity of the referential games played by the historical novel.[7] Issues of a Pirandellian 'progression' will be discussed more fully in the next two chapters, by examining in more detail the practices of self-quotation and self-plagiarism which problematize critical ideas of a purely diachronic authorial movement. Here I will merely point out that the second edition of the novel came out in 1913, when Pirandello had already started working on *Uno, nessuno e centomila* and was close to publishing *Si gira!* Also, large chunks of the novel are repeated *verbatim* in *Uno, nessuno e centomila*, consistent with Pirandello's analeptic and proleptic compositional techniques.

The second type of critical reading of *I vecchi*, the first example of which was Carlo Salinari's 1960 essay on the novel, sees it as an exposition of the theory of *umorismo* elaborated in the essay, yet there has been no serious attempt to ascertain exactly the nature of this relation, apart from noting that the novel (like all of Pirandello's novels) is full of quotations from the essay.[8]

I vecchi e i giovani deals with the post-Risorgimento generation, Pirandello's own, in the years 1893–4, moving between events in Sicily (the formation of the Socialist *Fasci*, the mobilization and subsequent repression of the Sicilian sulphur miners) and the financial scandals in Rome which brought down the government of Francesco Crispi. The indictment of the failure by the members of the generation of the Risorgimento to create lasting change in Sicily is interspersed with the personal narratives of the protagonists, and to the traditional dialectic enacted in the historical novel genre between the time of events and the time of their reproduction is added a third time, that of the heroic past of the Risorgimento, which underlies and haunts the novel.

Whilst thematically, as Croce and Spinazzola pointed out, the novel bears similarities to Federico De Roberto's novel of post-Risorgimento stasis and corruption in Sicily, *I vicerè*, its major influence, and the model against which I will read it, is undoubtedly Manzoni's *I promessi sposi*, especially with regard to the two crucial issues I will discuss: the use of documentation in relation to the referentiality of the text and the function of space and place in the novel.

In 'L'umorismo', Pirandello discusses the the the scepticism of the *umorista*, which places in doubt the ability of the historian or novelist to retrieve or reconstruct the past in a coherent form: 'L'umorista sa che cosa è la leggenda e come si forma, che cosa è la storia e come si forma: composizioni tutte, più o meno ideali, e tanto più ideali forse, quanto più mostran pretesa di realtà: composizioni ch'egli si diverte a scomporre' (*Spsv* 158). Such scepticism inevitably privileges an awareness of the contingency of historical representations over the 'empiricist epistemology' of the historical novel, countering and undermining Manzonian attempts to separate historical truth from fiction.[9] Pirandello's 'scomposizione' of the historical novel, I will argue, takes the form of a decomposition (and transformation through metaphor) of the notion of place and space as unproblematic geographical and historical markers.[10]

Manzoni and the Mapping of the Historical Novel

Nineteenth-century narrative production in Italy was dominated by the historical novel, at least until the post-Risorgimento period:[11] the polemic which had surrounded its rise gave way to its triumphant acquisition of the status of 'ufficialità',[12] and its civic function as 'portatore privilegiato dell'ideologia nazionale'.[13] Against the use of the past to glorify a civic present by the likes of Guerrazzi, D'Azeglio and Cantù, Manzoni 'inaugurates the modern critical discussion of the status of fiction and historical knowledge' in his 1850 essay 'Del romanzo storico e, in genere, de' componimenti misti di storia e invenzione'.[14] In the essay, he terms the historical novel 'una specie d'un genere falso, quale è quello che comprende tutti i componimenti misti di storia e d'invenzione', and argues that this mixture is doomed to failure because of the impossibility of distinguishing between fact and fiction: 'la realtà, quando non è rappresentata in maniera che si faccia riconoscere per tale, né istruisce, né appaga'.[15] Thus Manzoni, in rejecting the fusion of fiction which he had accomplished ten years earlier in *I promessi sposi*, also addresses both epistemological and ontological problems inherent in the historical novel: if the author of the historical novel does not mention that an event is real, then, says Manzoni, it is a 'bell'operazione dell'arte, che consistesse non nell'ideare cose verosimili, ma nel lasciar ignorare che le cose

presentate da essa sono reali' (p. 1062). The author of the historical
novel is warned that he must 'circostanziare gli avvenimenti storici,
coi quali abbia legato la sua azione ideale' and 'dovrà mettere insieme
e circostanze reali, cavate dalla storia o da documenti di qualunque
genere; e circostanze verosimili, inventate da lui' (p. 1060). At the
heart of this mixture of fact and fiction is an epistemological problem
regarding the status of the historical event and its narrative
representation. Manzoni's renunciation of the historical novel takes
this problem into consideration, but is still predicated upon a belief in
the possibility of reproducing historical events, concluding that what
is needed is a historical discourse in which there is no ontological
break between fiction and 'truth': only historiography, he argues, can
remedy the oversights of historiography, and it is necessary that the
new history 'frughi ne' documenti di qualunque genere [...] faccia,
voglio dire, diventar documenti anche certi scritti, gli autori de' quali
erano lontani le mille miglia dall'immaginarsi che mettevano in carta
de' documenti per i posteri, scelga, scarti, accozzi, confronti, deduca
e induca' (p. 1069). The question of documentation, its status as a text
within a fictional text, its veracity and *literalness*, and also its mediating
function, will be a central one to both Manzoni and Pirandello.[16] The
tensions between historiography and fiction and their epistemological
goals remain a subject of much critical debate: such debate centres on
the problems of the different kinds of knowledge and certainty
involved in each.[17] The question of fictional worlds again raises its
head: where are the points of rupture between the real, historically
documented world and its fictional 'equivalent'? This is a point which
I will discuss in more detail in relation to *Suo marito* and it is one
which is fundamental to a discussion of *I vecchi e i giovani*.[18]

   In addressing these issues, a comparison of the incipits of *I promessi
sposi* and *I vecchi e i giovani* is instructive for what it reveals about both
texts' approach to the question of fictional worlds. *I promessi sposi* is,
of course, framed by a double incipit, the first part of which is the
'Introduzione'. The 'Introduzione' begins with what is ostensibly a
quotation from the manuscript which the narrator is in the act of
transcribing before he stops and decides instead to tell the story in his
own words—thus the narrative immediately discloses itself to be a
pastiche, revealing its source to be a quotation through the use of
which it verifies itself. This complex play between primary and
secondary sources and texts also sets up a divide between narrative and
historical 'truth'. The opening of the chapter is revealed to be a

discussion of historiographical method: Michel De Certeau discusses the role of the quotation in historical discourse which is one, he claims, of 'accrediting discourse': 'the quotation introduces a necessary outer text within the text. And reciprocally, the quotation is the means of attaching the text to its semantic outer surface, of letting it appear to play a role in culture, and of thus giving it the stamp of referential credibility.'[19] This 'stamp of referential credibility' extends to the trope of the 'manuscript trouvé', and its foregrounding, as Umberto Eco points out, substitutes one 'resoconto verbale' of the past for another, both of which claim equal historical accuracy. As Eco states, 'al di sotto di questo discorso (verbale) [of the manuscript] traspaia una "storia così bella" (e una storia è *fabula*, sequenza di fatti o, come avrebbe detto Aristotele, imitazione di una azione, cosa non verbale)'[20] and this ordering process (or *narrativization* as Hayden White calls it)[21] is implicit in the narrator's idea that he might simply 'prender la serie de' fatti da questo manoscritto e rifarne la dicitura'.[22]

Manzoni's seemingly unproblematic transformation of this raw material will be supplemented by his use of the authentic 'gride' of the period as well as his consultation and extensive quotation of the historiography of Ripamonti. Even while acknowledging the hiatus between historical documents and fictional invention, Manzoni still implies a certain continuity between historical events, historical documents and their narrative representations, a continuity which conceals the ontological disparity between fiction and reality.[23]

Pieter de Meijer was the first critic to uncover the hidden sources of *I vecchi e i giovani* in a 1963 article, which demonstrated how Pirandello transcribed large excerpts of his text from an 1896 book by the Sicilian Socialist writer and politician Napoleone Colaianni, *Gli avvenimenti di Sicilia e le loro cause*.[24] De Meijer lists a series of verbatim textual appropriations from Colaianni, consisting of Colaianni's own eyewitness reports and his quotations from contemporary journalistic accounts; indeed, Pirandello audaciously even has Colaianni appear in the novel under the name Spiridione Covazza, with Covazza's speeches taken directly from Colaianni's text! It would appear from a comparison of the two texts that a substantial proportion of the descriptions of events of public history, for example, the revolt of the women of Milocca (Pt. II, ch. 3) and the rebellion at S. Caterina Villarmosa (Pt. II, ch. 7), after which Lando visits the scene, is a repetition or rewriting of Colaianni and his sources.[25] Pirandello thus has his own hidden 'Anonimo', Colaianni: however, while Manzoni painstakingly asserts the difference between his own text and his sources by his quotation of Ripamonti and the 'gride'—as well as his playful hypothetical quotation from his 'manuscript trouvé', Pirandello denies or suppresses this difference. Pirandello's text attempts to erase the distance between himself and his source and also that between the realms of history and narrative.[26] While Manzoni feigns an untroubled narrativization of history, Pirandello actually accomplishes it, and in doing so, relegates the issue of history itself and its veracity to a marginal or peripheral position, in the process assuming the kind of authority possessed by the writer of history. The convention of false sources exploited by Manzoni in the topos of the 'manuscript trouvé' inserts itself into a well-worn self-reflexive procedure of self-authorizing: Pirandello's (overly) faithful copy of sources paradoxically lessens the 'authenticity' (in Manzonian terms) of his own historical sequences, because the reader simply does not know that they are true. This fits in with Manzoni's statement that 'la realtà, quando non è rappresentata in maniera che si faccia riconoscere per tale, né istruisce, né appaga'.[27] Pirandello offsets this plagiarism (for that is, ultimately, what his practice of unacknowleged copying amounts to) against his minimal use of documents in the text. His 'faithful' rendering of history, his mapping of the historical onto the geographical, is actually a faithful copy of Colaianni's copy, virtually unmediated except in the act of transposition into Pirandello's narrative, and a comparison of the passages indicates that for Pirandello there is seemingly no difference between narrative and historiography.[28]

Pirandello's plagiarism addresses another fundamental problem. Critics have long noticed the novel's imbalance between the public and private, which the traditional historical novel had purposefully held in equilibrium: in *I vecchi e i giovani* the emphasis is very much on the latter.[29] Pirandello borrows or copies descriptions of the events of 'official' history, and then concentrates on what really interests him, the private and essentially unknowable subjectivity of the individual. Manzoni's narrator occasionally admits the gaps in his knowledge ('Quel che facesse precisamente non si può sapere, giacché era solo e la storia è costretta a indovinare. Fortuna che c'è avvezza'; *PS* 246), but Pirandello's attempts to plumb the psychology of his characters and to situate the individual in society, and particularly in the physical landscape, are more problematic. In fact, his attempts to map the individual onto the landscape—an exercise whose complexity is compounded by the difficulty inherent in mapping the blank spaces of epiphany—can be contrasted to Manzoni's as representing different models of referentiality.

In 'Del romanzo storico', Manzoni articulated the viewpoint of those opposed to the historical novel's mixing of fact and fiction, inventing an imaginary hostile address to the author of historical fiction: 'La storia che aspettiamo da voi non è un racconto crono-logico di soli fatti politici e militari [...] ma una rappresentazione più generale dello stato dell'umanità in un tempo, in un luogo, naturalmente più circoscritto di quello in cui si distendono ordinariamente i lavori di storia' ('Del romanzo storico', 1055). It is significant that Manzoni then uses the metaphor of the map as a vehicle to express this opposition between the topographic detail afforded by the 'romanzo storico' and the larger scale of 'lavori di storia':

Corre tra questi e il vostro la stessa differenza, in certo modo, che tra una carta geografica, dove sono segnate le catene de' monti, i fiumi, le città, i borghi, le strade maestre d'una vasta regione, e una carta topografica, nella quale, e tutto questo è più particolarizzato (dico quel tanto che ne può entrare in uno spazio molto più ristretto di paese), e ci sono di più segnate anche le alture minori, e le disugualianze ancor meno sensibili del terreno, e i borri, le gore, i villaggi, le case isolate, le viottole.[30]

Leaving aside the trickery of this prosopopeia, Manzoni's use of the map metaphor is suggestive: it is predicated upon a view of the map as an unproblematically realistic and descriptive tool, which somehow equates the representational function of the map with the detail of the historical novel.[31] Manzoni's theory, which proposes the geographical space as a space which should somehow narrate and signify history faithfully, is one which, I will show, underpins I promessi sposi, in which the clear relationship between landscape and history is central.

Manzoni strengthens the geographical metaphor in the passage of the essay in which he discusses the need for the historian to draw distinct boundaries between the real and the verisimilar:

Infatti per poter riconoscere quella relazione tra il positivo raccontato e il verosimile proposto, è appunto una condizione necessaria, che questi compariscano distinti. Fa, a un di presso, come chi, disegnando la pianta d'una città, ci aggiunge in diverso colore, strade, piazze, edifizi progettati; e col presentar distinte dalle parti che sono, quelle che potrebbero essere, fa che si veda la ragione di pensarle riunite. ('Del romanzo storico', 1067)

This strict division between what actually happened and what could have happened is thus rendered not just as a conflict between fiction and fact, but between real and hypothetical or imaginary spaces. Landscape and historical representation are here intertwined: historical events, Manzoni suggests, can be mapped out or traced in the physical landscape, which becomes a stage for the encounter between the individual and the forces of historical progress, in a way which Pirandello's novel will not allow.

The second incipit of *I promessi sposi* actualizes the metaphor of the map, as the geographical sweep of history is particularized in the physical details of the topography: the geographical expansion from the immediacy of the famously deictic 'Quel ramo del lago di Como' (*PS* 9) out towards the environs of Lecco initiates a process by means of which the individual and the historical, the factual and the fictional, intersect. The description of the 'strade e stradette' which 'correvano, e corrono tuttavia' through the landscape, emphasizing its timelessness (*PS* 10), is intersected by the fictional 'historical' journey of Don Abbondio: 'Per una di queste stradicciole, tornava bel bello dalla passeggiata verso casa, sulla sera del giorno 7 novembre dell'anno 1628, don Abbondio' (*PS* 11).[32] Manzoni's mapping gives us the exact historical coordinates of this event, and there is seemingly no rupture between the historical and the invented. His combination of the historical date and the proper name further strengthens the chapter's cartographic exactitude, and elides the question of historical and fictional referentiality.[33] Such an effective illusion of referentiality reinforces the Manzonian idea of the text as a map capable of situating the individual in his proper relation to a known, empirically defined nature.[34]

Manzoni's linking of narrative and landscape extends to his conception of the authorial role, which he describes by using the ancient metaphor of the narrative as journey: 'A questo punto della nostra storia, noi non possiam far a meno di non fermarci qualche poco, come il viandante, stracco e triste da un lungo camminare per un terreno arido e salvatico, si trattiene e perde un po' di tempo all'ombra d'un bell'albero, sull'erba, vicino a una fonte d'acqua viva' (*PS* 407). The teleological implications of this metaphor are evident, as the narrator represents the narrative as a journey towards a desired ending through a terrain which, although wild, is also familiar. Manzoni thus inscribes his characters into a landscape which is completely known, in which there are no blank spaces (apart, ironically, from the suppressed place name itself). In Pirandello's novel, the idea of the map as standing for a realistic mode of representation, or a narrative journey through already-plotted territory, is set to come apart because the referential stability and certainty of proper names and toponyms are constantly transformed and refigured in epiphanic moments, which are, by their very nature, random.[35] Pirandello will attempt, in his characters' epiphanic moments, to inscribe the unknown into the known, and to create new imaginary and internalized topographies, destroying the idea of a coherent topography or of the narrative as a linear journey, and replacing it with a series of relativistic, impressionistic renderings of landscape through his characters' eyes.

I vecchi e i giovani and the Space of Figuration

The incipit of *I vecchi e i giovani* appears at first sight to be similar to that of Manzoni's novel, depicting a character undertaking a fictional journey through an ostensibly 'real' landscape: however, Pirandello's landscape is a highly anthropomorphized one, and sets up a very Pirandellian mode of mapping the real, which is to render the physical space at once real and symbolic, as a 'space of figuration'.[36] As Paolo Archi says, in Pirandello's novels 'l'immagine naturale diventa metafora della propria esistenza' and so the landscape is consistently rendered as an imaginative space, a space in which the self and other meet.[37] *I vecchi e i giovani* opens with the journey of Captain Sciaralla through the countryside outside Girgenti, a journey which is essentially a metahistorical movement between the two estates which dominate the landscape, Colimbètra, the palace of Don Ippolito, the Bourbon prince who clings to the pretence that the Bourbon monarchy is still in place, and Valsanìa, the textual double of Pirandello's birthplace Caos, home of Don Cosmo, the sceptical philosopher who dismisses any belief in history or progress as human illusion.[38] Thus the journey through a landscape which the narrator describes as 'fuori della storia' (*Tr* II, 19) is also an allegorical movement between two equally evasive ways of thinking about history and, as such, appears to be a commentary on history, closer to Manzoni's 'Introduzione' than to his opening description. Pirandello attempts to map history onto geography in the oversymbolic, descriptive excursus of the first few pages, in which the 'vuoto del tempo senza vicende' (*Tr* II, 5) is conveyed by the accumulation of pejorative and anthropomorphized terms such as 'il guasto delle intemperie appariva tanto più triste, in quanto, qua e là, già era evidente il disprezzo e quasi il dispetto della cura di chi aveva tracciato e costruito la via per facilitare il cammino tra le asperità di quei luoghi', 'alba livida', 'su quel lembo di paese emergente or ora, appena, cruccioso, dalle fosche ombre umide della notte tempestosa'. This pejorative meaning attributed to the physical landscape will be emphasized by the metaphorical use of 'fango' to denote corruption at the beginning of Part II, the Roman segment of the novel, a specular strategy which retrospectively (over)determines the initial physical landscape.[39]

As in *I promessi sposi*, the landscape is at first empty, before the narrative zooms in on the figure of Sciaralla. His human presence 'reads' and seeks to interpret it as a commentary on the historical period, as a deterministic, naturalist landscape:

L'accidia, tanto di far bene quanto di far male, era radicata nella più profonda sconfidenza della sorte, nel concetto che nulla potesse avvenire, che vano sarebbe stato ogni sforzo per scuotere l'abbandono desolato, in cui giacevano non soltanto gli animi ma anche tutte le cose. E a Sciaralla parve di averne la prova nel triste spettacolo che gli offriva, quella mattina, la campagna intorno e quello stradone. (*Tr* II, 12)

In his essay 'Sicilian epiphanies', Gian Paolo Biasin comments on how Pirandello's landscape becomes in this way a sort of historical 'proof', 'a desolate and squalid vista that communicates the historical dismay of the author vis-à-vis the failure of the Risorgimento'.[40] Biasin refers to the 'emblematic' status of Pirandello's landscape in this incipit, and attributes to it a declarative value, asserting that Pirandello uses anthropomorphism to 'declare (even to cry out) the meaning of the signs in the landscape'.[41] Thus for Biasin, the landscape speaks, 'communicating' and 'declaring' its historicized status. His interpretation, however, which does not refer to epiphany in the sense in which I am discussing it, could and should be taken much further: as I will show, Pirandello's landscape is not merely an unproblematically reflectionist map which bears the marks of history and nature, but a map of increasing complexity which at times seeks to erase those marks.[42]

In fact, *I vecchi* contrasts various modes of reading the landscape, the primary contrast being that between the epiphanic and the 'historical', or between the irrevocably personal and the public. As I have stated before, epiphany in Pirandello is a moment in which the individual, in a moment of enhanced perception, loses his or her sense of selfhood. It is also atemporal and unrepeatable: the individual, rather than being rooted in the landscape, becomes unmoored from it. One such example occurs near the beginning of the novel, when Don Cosmo's gaze passes from his sleeping dogs to the trees outside and produces the imitative, hyper-literary epiphany discussed in the last chapter: 'Guardò gli alberi, davanti alla villa: gli parvero assorti anch'essi in un sogno senza fine, da cui invano la luce del giorno, invano l'aria smovendo loro le frondi tentassero di scuoterli. Da un pezzo ormai, nel fruscìo lungo e lieve di quelle fronde egli sentiva, come da un'infinita lontananza, la vanità di tutto e il tedio angoscioso della vita' (*Tr* II, 42).[43]

Although in the novel epiphanies occur in the natural landscape, they are also moments of interiority, a movement between internal and external which inevitably involves silence and loss of meaning, in a dissolution of the public and transcendence of the private, a transcendence which is, however, doomed to failure as it can only happen in solitude and involves no sense of communion or fraternity with others. A good example of this is Dianella's moment of 'silenzio interiore' in which, after reflecting upon recent events in her mind, she experiences a moment of otherness as she sits outside:

Dianella non poté più frenare le lacrime e si mise a piangere silenziosamente, con amara voluttà in quella solitudine. Ma il silenzio attorno era così attonito, e così intenso e immemore il trasognamento della terra e di tutte le cose, che a poco a poco se ne sentì attratta e affascinata. Le parvero allora gravati da una tristezza infinita e rassegnata quegli alberi assorti nel loro sogno perenne, da cui invano il vento cercava di scuoterli. Percepì, in quella intimità misteriosa con la natura, il brulichìo delle foglie [...] e non sentì più di vivere per sé; visse per un istante quasi incosciente, con la terra. (*Tr* II, 138)[44]

In the last chapter I argued that in epiphanic moments such as this one, *chronos* becomes *kairos*: such 'lyrical achronies', in their gratui-tuousness and 'timelessness', can be interpreted as a challenge to history and chronology and in fact seem to institute an alternative chronology. The random and unpredictable nature of these moments acts as an implicit critique of the possibility of a linear, chronological representation of history. The 'real', historical, time frame which underlies the novel is thus subordinated to a series of fragmented moments in which characters experience a sense of 'timelessness' or imaginative escape from their present surroundings. In Dianella's subsequent epiphany, it is significant that the historical does enter the moment of reverie, albeit indirectly, in the form of her interpretation of the natural signs of the landscape as reminders of the political ferment outside Valsanìa:

Nel vuoto angoscioso, fissando l'udito, senza volerlo, nel fitto continuo scampanellìo dei grilli, le parve ch'esso nel silenzio diventasse di punto in punto più intenso e più sonoro; pensò ai tumulti d'Aragona e di Comitini; e quel fervido concento divenne allora per lei, a un tratto, il clamore lontano, indefinito d'un popolo in rivolta, di cui Aurelio, ribelle, andava a farsi duce e vendicatore. (*Tr* II, 159)

The Pascolian 'grilli', identified in the last chapter as a staple of Pirandello's epiphanic, atemporal landscapes, are here momentarily historicized as signs of unrest and misrule rather than ahistorical and timeless images of poetic imitation and repetition, and the epiphanic moment subtly opens up to point to the historical. The bloody events at Aragona, which will later take centre stage when Aurelio and Nicoletta are killed there by the angry mob, are anticipated and mediated by the natural environment. History thus enters the novel indirectly, in transformations of this sort, whether by way of Colaianni's suppressed text or by way of the anthropomorphization of nature.

In contrast to the idea of the landscape as the site of imaginative and ahistorical retreat, Mauro Mortara, the Risorgimento veteran, is a character who consistently reads the signs of nature as historicized echoes of the Risorgimento past: yet his reading is equally escapist. When he is planning his departure from Valsanìa, disgusted by the profanation of the new Italy by the banking scandals in Rome and the arrest of Roberto Auriti and intent on taking up arms to combat the civil unrest whipped up by the *Fasci*, the physical environment surrounding him presents itself as a dramatic reminder of similar confrontations of the past: 'Tutta la notte era stato fuori, per la campagna, farneticando. La voce del mare era quella del Generale; le ombre degli alberi erano quelle degli antichi congiurati di Valsanìa; e quella e queste seguitavano a incitarlo a partire' (*Tr* II, 492). The space of the present becomes at the same time an imaginative space in which the present no longer exists and an alternative temporal sequence is superimposed. The 'voce del mare' can also be interpreted as an intertextual echo of Manzoni's 'mormorio' of the Adda, which Renzo hears when he arrives back in Lecco after the turbulent events in Milan. In Manzoni's novel, characters read the landscape and use it to orient themselves in a world in which human institutions are ranged against them. In that case, the Adda which meandered through the opening description reappears as a textual and geographic marker, a sign that Renzo has returned home and that the plot is also coming back on itself, as well as progressing: 'cominciò a sentire un rumore, un mormorìo d'acqua corrente. Sta in orecchi; n'è certo; esclama:— è l'Adda! fu il ritrovamento d'un amico, d'un fratello, d'un salvatore' (*PS* 641). It is, above all, a voice which ascertains and establishes Renzo's exact location while, in Pirandello's text, the similarly anthropomorphized voice of the sea is not speaking of itself but rather of what it is not.[45]

Mauro's only reference point is the Risorgimento, which for him is reduced to a series of stock phrases and images, and all of his readings are subjugated to that: 'Cammino qua per Valsanìa, vedo i fili del telegrafo, sento ronzare il palo, come se ci fosse dentro un nido di calabroni, e il petto mi s'allarga; dico, "Frutto della Rivoluzione!" Vado più là, vedo la ferrovia, il treno che si caccia sottoterra, nel traforo sotto Valsanìa, che mi pare un sogno; e dico: "Frutto della Rivoluzione!"' (*Tr* II, 151–2). This identification of past history with present landscape reaches its apotheosis in Mauro's bathetic death: denied the possibility of re-enacting his heroics at Milazzo, he is shot by government troops, ironically at the exact moment when his identification of himself with Sicily's heroic past is at its peak: 'Sentì veramente in quel punto di esser la Sicilia, la vecchia Sicilia' (*Tr* II, 514).

Possibly the novel's most significant example of this kind of sublimation of the public and social to the personal and psychological is the extended sequence describing the thoughts of Lando Laurentano, the key figure emblematizing the transition from the Risorgimento generation to the next one—Lando, son of Don Ippolito, has broken away from his father's Bourbon principles to become a Socialist, but is still atavistically tied to his family's aristocratic status. His interior monologue, with its repeated use of free indirect speech, which mediates between the narrator's description and Lando's own thoughts, becomes a critique of historiography and the historical novel itself:

Ma, leggendo, era tratto irresistibilmente a tradurre in azione, in realtà viva quanto leggeva; e, se aveva per le mani un libro di storia, provava un sentimento indefinibile di pena angosciosa nel veder ridotta lì in parole quella che un giorno era stata vita, ridotto in dieci o venti righe di stampa, tutte allo stesso modo interlineate con ordine preciso, quello ch'era stato movimento scomposto, rimescolìo, tumulto. Buttava via il libro. (*Tr* II, 310–11)

For a text so reliant upon historiography, the novel displays a deep mistrust of it. Lando chooses, instead of reading historical accounts, to interpret the natural signs which provide him with the direct link with public history that historiography cannot provide:

> Dalle due finestre basse, che davano sul giardino, entrava il passeraio fitto, assiduo, assordante, degl'innumerevoli uccelletti che ogni giorno si davano convegno sul pino là, palpitante più d'ali che di foglie. Paragonava quel fremito continuo, instancabile, quell'ebro tumulto di voci vive, con le parole racchiuse in quei libri muti, e gliene cresceva lo sdegno. Composizioni artificiose, vita fissata, rappresa in forme immutabili, costruzioni logiche, architetture mentali, induzioni, deduzioni—via! via! via! (*Tr* II, 311)

The artificial and fictitious nature of historiography is contrasted with Lando's desire for a 'natural' rhetoric which will be equivalent to action. However, this rhetoric produces not a call to arms but rather a solipsistic yearning for a Pirandellian epiphany, defined as a moment in which the internal will negate the external, in language taken almost verbatim from 'L'umorismo':

> Dentro quel suo stesso corpo, intanto, in ciò che egli chiamava anima, il flusso continuava indistinto, sotto gli argini, oltre i limiti ch'egli imponeva per comporsi una coscienza, per costruirsi una personalità. Ma potevano anche tutte quelle forme fittizie, investite dal flusso in un momento di tempesta, crollare, e anche quella parte del flusso che non scorreva ignota sotto gli argini e oltre i limiti [...] poteva in un momento di piena straripare e sconvolger tutto. Ecco, a uno di questi momenti di piena egli anelava! (*Tr* II, 312)[46]

Lando's observation that 'ora era il tempo delle parole' (*Tr* II, 309) was not, then, merely an expression of disgust at the way in which the idealized heroic past of the Risorgimento had become a time of indecision and filibustering. It was also a metahistorical commentary on the problem of the historical novel itself, its dialectic between the time of action and the time of writing. If Manzoni's image of the river or road implies a narrative which can be retraced and the past recuperated and its moral (or 'sugo') inferred, for Pirandello the images which sum up his thoughts on writing the past are rather the 'lampo', 'strappo' or 'baleno' of *umorismo*. In the 'baleno' the relation between past and present is written as not recoverable or traceable, but rather as a sudden, unpredictable and inexplicable moment of revelation, which is represented as being somehow a truer, private history of the individual, even if it is necessarily inaccessible and inexpressible to others.[47] The metatemporal nature of the epiphanic revelation which, as I have discussed before, involves loss, not gain or accretion, counters the 'libri di storia' or any narration (such as the historical novel) which would attempt to make of the past an ideal *paideia*.[48]

The disjunction between the time of events and the time of their retelling (which for Pirandello is also a symbolic gap between the long-gone days of the Risorgimento and the present disillusionment) is thematized in the novel by the figure of Mauro, the veteran of Garibaldi's 'Mille', who continues to retell the story of those glorious days, over and over, and by the 'camerone' of the General, Lando's grandfather, which is preserved exactly as he had left it. Mauro's idealized history of the Risorgimento is shown by Pirandello to be fallacious when Mauro retells the story to Don Cosmo and exclaims 'Ve le siete scordate, voi, queste cose? Io le ho tutte qua in mente, come in un libro stampato!', and Don Cosmo muses to himself that Mauro and his unofficial chronicle are mistaken:

Parecchie volte era stato sul punto di far intendere a Mauro che a Gerlando Laurentano suo padre non era mai passata per il capo l'idea dell'unità italiana, e che il Parlamento siciliano del 1848, nel quale suo padre era stato per alcuni mesi ministro della guerra, non aveva mai proposto né confederazione italiana né annessione all'Italia, ma un chiuso regno di Sicilia. (*Tr* II, 39)

The significance of this mistrust of the act of recording or writing history can be explained by the fact that *I vecchi*, in its guise as 'anti-historical novel', consistently asserts the experiential and ontological *béance* between what Barthes calls 'paper time', or the time of discourse, and the time of the event which is its subject.[49] Instead of relying on the written word, considered incapable of rendering history, characters prefer to experience history through their own, idiosyncratic, readings of the landscape, a landscape which is read variously as escape from or site of historical meaning. If landscape constitutes a 'space of figuration' in the novel, a site of ahistorical or metahistorical epiphanic reverie for Pirandello's characters, this 'space of figuration' can also refer to the recurring use which characters make of figurative language, drawn from Pirandello's theory, to visualize themselves, in a series of organic metaphors which suggestively unite the individual and the historical.

Metaphors of History

In Chapter 1 I argued that Pirandello's texts construct a series of metonymic associations between images, forming a constellation of moments of auto-referential and inter- and intratextual connotation. *I vecchi e i giovani* is a novel which is organized around networks and series of metaphors, which also, at times, comment on their own representational function. They also reaffirm the novel's position as being grounded in the metaphorical discourse of its 'hypotext', 'L'umorismo'. The first, and most significant of these metaphors is that of the vineyard, which appears as part of the long passage I discussed earlier, when Lando experiences a moment of humoristic dissociation from history and his environment. We are told that Lando 'covava in segreto un dispetto amaro e cocente del tempo in cui gli era toccato in sorte di vivere' (*Tr* II, 307) and, as usual in the Pirandellian narrative, the personal and political are united by figurative means:

> Era, quel suo dispetto, come il fermento d'un mosto inforzato, in una botte che già sapeva di secco. La vigna era stata vendemmiata. Tutti i pampini ormai erano ingialliti, s'accartocciavano aridi [...] Aveva dato il suo frutto, il tempo. E lui era venuto a vendemmia già fatta. Il mosto generoso e grosso, raccolto in Sicilia con gioia impetuosa, mescolato con l'asciutto e brusco del Piemonte [...] raccolto tardi e quasi di furto nella vigna del Signore, mal governato in tre tini e nelle botti, mal conciato ora con tiglio or con allume, s'era irrimediabilmente inacidito. Età sterile, per forza, la sua, come tutte quelle che succedono a un tempo di straordinario rigoglio. (*Tr* II, 308)

I have quoted this passage in full because it is typical of Pirandello's deliberate strategy of extension and exhaustion of metaphor, almost to the point of saturation. The vineyard metaphor, with its obvious biblical connotations, contains the idea of the sacred nature of the *patria*, to which Pirandello adds the image of time as regression and involution rather than progress, and also the idea of Lando as a product of this vineyard—his 'dispetto' is the lees of the acidic wine of the Risorgimento.[50] This image must also be read through that of the literal vineyard earlier tended by Mauro Mortaro, a real space which is also a metaphor for Mauro's life: 'Ah, la sua bella vigna! Forse il vino di quell'anno lo avrebbe ancora bevuto, ma quello dell'anno venturo?' (*Tr* II, 121), and through the later reference to Mauro's vineyard as a nostalgic signifier of a patriotic past: 'Più volte, dalla porta aperta, i lunghi filari della vigna [...] gli avevano ricomposto per

un momento la visione quasi lontana di quel mondo, per cui fino a
poco tempo addietro vagava nei dì sereni, gonfio d'orgoglio, da
padreterno, lisciandosi la barba' (*Tr* II, 489).[51]

Lando's figurative 'vigna', recreated in the free indirect mode,
inserts itself into the matrix of natural metaphors which constitute the
figurative economy of the novel, as well as of 'L'umorismo', of which,
as noted in Chapter 1, organic metaphors form the subtext. Pirandello's rhetoric of anti-rhetoric, his critique of the imitative,
formalizing tendency of rhetoric in 'L'umorismo', is cast in metaphors
of growth and fructifying: he writes that 'l'opera d'arte è il germe [...]
ma la nascita e lo sviluppo di questa pianta debbono essere spontanei'
(*Spsv* 134), an image which is contrasted with the involution and
regressive nature of rhetoric: 'La coltura, per la retorica, non era la
preparazione del terreno, la vanga.' The humoristic technique of using
a recessive and ultimately self-referential language seals the failure of
the Pirandellian subject to construct him or herself in any terms other
than figurative ones.[52]

Another example of how Pirandello's novel is structured around
complex metaphoric chains is through the metaphor of fire.[53] This
image echoes constantly throughout the novel, in varying contexts,
but is always a metaphor which comments on the process of historical
representation, due to its double use in the text as both metaphor of
political struggle and unrest and metaphor for the individual's capacity
for rhetorical self-expression. For example, in rendering the thoughts
of Lando, the narrator tells us of his desire that:

Un solo fuoco, una sola fiamma avrebbe dovuto correre da un capo all'altro
d'Italia per fondere e saldare le varie membra di essa in un sol corpo vivo. La
fusione era mancata per colpa di coloro che avevano stimato pericolosa la
fiamma e più adatto il freddo lume dei loro intelletti accorti e calcolatori.
Ma, se la fiamma s'era lasciata soffocare, non era pur segno che non aveva in
sé quella forza e quel calore che avrebbe dovuto avere? Che nembo di fuoco
allegro e violento dalla Sicilia sù sù fino a Napoli! Ancora da laggiù, più tardi,
la fiamma s'era spiccata per arrivare fino a Roma... Dovunque era stata
costretta ad arrestarsi, ad Aspromonte o su le balze del Trentino, era rimasto
un vuoto sordo, una smembratura. (*Tr* II, 309–10)

Again, the extension of the metaphor is typical of Pirandello as the
cumulative effect of each part of the passage builds up into a multiple
metaphor which contains the image of the Risorgimento as a blow-
torch welding the *disiecta membra* of the Italian body politic together.

As well as extension, one of the salient characteristics of these metaphors is iteration: the metaphor is repeated again and again with slight but significant alterations, most spectacularly when Pirandello uses it to describe the uprisings sweeping the island. The task of narrating the state of the island is given to Flaminio Salvo and revolves around the metaphor of the tinderbox:

> Prese a raccontare, con atteggiamento di grave costernazione, i fatti avvenuti di recente in Sicilia [...] i quali provavano come in tutta l'isola covasse un gran fuoco, che presto sarebbe divampato; e a rappresentar la Sicilia come una catasta immane di legna, di alberi morti per siccità [...] poiché la pioggia dei benefizii s'era riversata tutta su l'Italia settentrionale, e mai una goccia ne era caduta su le arse terre dell'isola. Ora i giovincelli s'erano divertiti ad accendere sotto la catasta i fasci di paglia delle loro predicazioni socialistiche, ed ecco che i vecchi ceppi cominciavano a prender fuoco [...] E il peggio era questo: che il Governo, invece d'accorrere a gettar acqua, mandava soldati a suscitare altro fuoco col fuoco delle armi. (*Tr* II, 366–7)[54]

The fire metaphor is a significant one in the rhetorical mythography of the Risorgimento, as the image of Sicily as ablaze with activity was a common one.[55] It is significant that, as used in the reactionary rhetoric of Flaminio Salvo, it is also one of the metaphors of the civil unrest of the 1890s which indicates the failure of the Risorgimento uprisings. Here again, Pirandello draws on Colaianni, as Rita Baldassarri shows, in whose text the image occupied a significant space.[56] The fire is both literal and metaphorical, as it anticipates the novel's climax in Favara where the town hall is burnt down.

These kinds of metaphorical sequences are rooted in 'L'umorismo''s subtext of linguistic multivalence: even the use of the fire metaphor is not restricted to its significance as a political metaphor, but it is also used to connote the individual's capacity for expression and, as such, performs a metalinguistic function. An example of this is in the description of the Socialist agitator Nocio Pigna, whose loss of speech typifies the progressive exhaustion of the verbal which pervades the novel:

> Più parlava e più le stesse parole accrescevano la sua persuasione e la sua passione. Ma a furia di ripetere sempre le medesime cose, col medesimo giro, questi alla fine gli s'erano fissate in una forma che aveva perduto ogni efficacia; gli s'erano, per dir così, impostate su le labbra, come bocche di fuoco che non mandavano più fuori se non botto, fumo e stoppaccio. (*Tr* II, 172)

This ties in with the description of Mauro, mouthpiece of Risorgimento idealism, as a 'fiamma accesa' (*Tr* II, 305), and with Agrò's 'parole di fuoco' (*Tr* II, 241), and causes us to reread the other, political, metaphors of fire as also having this connotation of linguistic expressiveness. The image links individual discourse with that describing broader political and historical events and again demonstrates the complex relations between the self and history which the novel articulates.

Complementing the use of the fire metaphor to signify civil unrest we have Don Ippolito's recollection of the siege and sack of ancient Akragas by the Carthaginians in 406 BC, and the defiance of Gellias who burnt down the temple of Athena rather than see it profaned by the invaders: 'Solo Gellia non fugge! Spera d'avere incolume la vita mercé la fede, e si riduce al santuario d'Athena. Smantellate le mura, ruinati i meravigliosi edifizii, brucia qua sotto la città intera; e lui dall'alto, mirando l'incendio spaventoso che innalza una funerea cortina di fiamme e di fumo su la vista del mare, vuol ardere nel fuoco della Dea' (*Tr* II, 101–2). There is an obvious parallel here between Don Ippolito's pro-Bourbon conviction, his belief in the nobility of his cause and the 'sack' of Sicily, which he sees as a direct consequence of Garibaldi's fiery invasion. This conviction is obviously linked to Don Ippolito's archaeological pursuits, his attempt to read the historical past of Sicily in the landscape and restore it to the present. His scholarly quest for the acropolis of the ancient city of Akragas is an attempt to persuade the landscape, which has been overwritten by successive colonizers, to surrender its secrets: 'Attendeva ora a tracciare, in una nuova opera, la topografia storica dell'antichissima città, col sussidio delle lunghe minuziose investigazioni sui luoghi, giacché la sua Colimbetra si estendeva appunto dov'era prima il cuore della greca Akragrante' (*Tr* II, 94), Here topography and historiography seem to coincide as the prince attempts to reconstruct what is absent from the landscape, what was prior to it, and history is seen as having left its traces in the physical landscape.[57] Colimbetra now covers the heart of the ancient city, on the site of which flourishes the 'bosco detto perciò ancora della Cività' (*Tr* II, 101); the ironic topography of Don Ippolito's rigidly separated land as a site of *civitas* highlights the opposition between his exaltation of the Greek past and Mauro's devotion to the memory of Rome.[58] Both forms of nostalgia are seen as equally deluded, since Mauro's reading of Rome ignores its present, degraded, status, while Don Ippolito's hopes of restoring the civic pride of the Greek past end in his son Lando's exile for his support of the Socialists.

This archaeological activity is also a misleading metaphor for
Pirandello's own text, which appears at first sight to be a work of
meticulous historical reconstruction, an excavation of the layers of the
past to uncover their source, and yet shows such an ambivalence
towards itself as a historical novel, as a 'carta topografica', and instead
of rooting and fixing itself in time, rather slips away from its
suppressed historical markers, towards the undifferentiated and anti-
descriptive space of wordless epiphany. Similarly, while the incipit of
I vecchi e i giovani seemed to promise that the Sicilian landscape would
act as a register or map onto which historical events could be plotted,
the subsequent use of landscape and the natural is as a site of multiple
and conflicting interpretations, in which the protagonist experiences
dissociation, loss of self or desire for escape, and in which the
personal, the political, and the historical are always profoundly
intertwined and sometimes confused. The transformation of the
present landscape into a space of figuration by Pirandello's characters,
and Pirandello's use of natural metaphors to depict and unite the
personal and the political, illustrate the deeply ambivalent position
which *I vecchi* adopts towards the issues surrounding historical representation and the historical novel itself.

Spinazzola's designation of *I vecchi e i giovani* as an 'antihistorical
novel' derived chiefly from its sense of historical pessimism: however,
it is my argument that it is through the narrative techniques of metaphor and epiphany that the text merges and truly confuses the
historical and the personal, embedding the discussion of historical
events in a network of metaphors related to artistic creativity, and
punctuating and puncturing any sense of chronology, progress or
action with epiphanic reveries.

Similarly, it can be seen that the text's strategies of self-quotation,
self-plagiarism, with passages and ideas borrowed from 'L'umorismo',
and outright plagiarism (in the form of the lifts from Colaianni)
contest long-standing critical assumptions of a linear narrative journey
suddenly complicated by the adoption of a nineteenth-century genre.
In *Suo marito*, such strategies emphatically take centre stage.

Notes to Chapter 3

1. Luigi Pirandello, 'Lettera autobiografica', written in 1912 or 1913, first published
   in the Roman journal *Le lettere*, 15 Oct. 1924, and now repr. in *Spsv*, 1285–8 at
   1288. *I vecchi e i giovani* was composed in 1906–8 and first appeared in serial form
   in the journal *Rassegna contemporanea* in 1909. It was subsequently published by

Treves in 1913 in volume form and was partially revised by Pirandello before its publication by Mondadori in 1931. For further details see Giovanni Macchia's 'Note ai testi e varianti' in *Tr*, 905–7.

2. For example, one of the first studies of Pirandello's work considered *I vecchi* as 'il romanzo più altamente nazionale che onori la tradizione manzoniana dopo *Le confessioni di un ottuagenario* di Ippolito Nievo'; Ferdinando Pasini, *Luigi Pirandello, come mi pare* (Trieste: La Vedetta Italiana, 1927), 279; Vincenzo Paladino argues that 'Pirandello adotta [...] da celebri modelli, il genere del romanzo storico, in quanto tale adozione ratificava, *ante litteram*, le sue ambizioni, narrative e conoscitive, di quella struttura, ottocentesca, canonizzate ed esemplarmente collaudate'; 'L'"altrove" di Pirandello', in *Otto/Novecento* 19 (1995), 53–69 at 60; in contrast, Daniela Bini affirms that 'Pirandello si serve di un genere ormai consacrato, il romanzo storico, per minarlo dal di dentro'; 'La storia come maschera', in Enzo Lauretta (ed.), *Pirandello e la politica* (Milan: Mursia, 1992), 199–207 at 202.

3. Vittorio Spinazzola, *Il romanzo antistorico* (Rome: Riuniti, 1990), 21.

4. Walter Geerts, '*I vecchi e i giovani*: la portata del romanzo storico', in M. Rossner and F.-R. Hausmann (eds.), *Pirandello und die europäische Erzahlliteratur des 19. und 20. Jahrhunderts* (Bonn: Romanistischer, 1990), 50–7 at 51.

5. Giovanni Macchia, 'Luigi Pirandello', in *Storia della letteratura italiana*, 406; Francesco Nicolosi also refers to the novel as a 'passo indietro [...] una frattura, un salto indietro dopo le acquisizioni di contenuto e di stile del *Mattia Pascal*'; 'Su *I vecchi e i giovani* di Pirandello', *Le ragioni critiche* 19–20 (1976), 64–86 at 64. Renato Barilli also calls it a 'passo indietro'; *Pirandello: una rivoluzione culturale* (Milan: Mursia, 1986), 81. Rino Caputo, in his assertion that 'il romanzo smentisce il senso delle operazioni precedenti', also uses the journey metaphor, saying that 'dopo *I vecchi e i giovani* Pirandello riprenderà il cammino interrotto'; Caputo, '*I vecchi e i giovani*: l'occasione "storica" di Pirandello', *Trimestre* 6 (1972), 443–66 at 443–4. In a similar vein, Marziano Guglielminetti asserts that *I vecchi e i giovani* and *Suo marito* 'fuoriescono dal reticolato di motivi e di forme che è stato sinora percorso'; 'Introduzione' to *Uno, nessuno e centomila* (Milan: Mondadori, 1997), p. x. A similar judgement is expressed by Salvatore Battaglia, who calls it a 'parentesi di regressione naturalistica'; 'Palazzeschi e l'arte dell'anacronismo', *Filologia e letteratura* 68 (1971), 501–13 at 507. The critical anxiety surrounding the positioning of the text in Pirandello's oeuvre is noted briefly by both Vitilio Masiello in 'L'età del disincanto: morte delle ideologie e ontologia negativa dell'esistenza nei *Vecchi e i giovani*', in Lauretta (ed.), *Pirandello e la politica*, 67–87 and Enrico Ghidetti, in 'Pirandello, il protagonista "disaiutato"', in *Malattia, coscienza e destino: per una mitografia del decadentismo* (Florence: La Nuova Italia, 1993), 95–116.

6. Benedetto Croce's influential essay on Pirandello calls *I vecchi* 'il migliore dei suoi romanzi' and says that it 'arieggia ai *Viceré* del De Roberto': Croce's comments are part of a broader schema which he proposes of Pirandello's work as moving from an early 'veristic' phase to a 'seconda maniera', marked by *Il fu Mattia Pascal*, a view which has, in my view, heavily influenced modern Pirandello criticism and which also bears upon the critical consensus regarding the novel as somehow 'out of time'; Benedetto Croce, 'Luigi Pirandello', in *Letteratura della nuova Italia*, 359–77.

7. Ruth Glynn, for example, points out that 'all historical novels, even the most traditional, typically involve some violation of ontological boundaries'; 'Presenting the past: the case of *Il nome della rosa*', *The Italianist* 17 (1997), 99–116 at 99.

8. Carlo Salinari, 'La coscienza della crisi', in his *Miti e coscienza*, 249–84; Salinari's view that 'appare legittimo il sospetto [...] che il romanzo e il trattato siano collegati l'uno all'altro' (p. 254) is, however, again inserted into a teleological reading which sees Pirandello's narrative as inevitably giving way to theatre in the 'arco del suo sviluppo' from 'verismo' to 'decadentismo' (p. 269). In this vein have appeared contributions from Riccardo Scrivano, '*I vecchi e i giovani* e la crisi dell'ideologia' in Lauretta (ed.), *Pirandello e la politica*, 41–66; Douglas Radcliff-Umstead, 'Pirandello and the psychoanalysis of history', *Canadian Journal of Italian Studies* 12 (1989), 76–98; however, Marziano Guglielminetti cautions against reading Pirandello's post-'L'umorismo' production as 'riportabile a schemi narrativi rivoluzionari', asserting that 'gl'importa di dimostrare [...] come le intuizioni del suo saggio siano parimenti valide in un contesto narrativo dei più tradizionali'. Guglielminetti ends up subscribing to the 'journey' metaphor of Pirandello's writing career: 'resta [...] incomprensibile il motivo che ha spinto Pirandello a scrivere *I vecchi e i giovani* dopo *Il fu Mattia Pascal*, il romanzo che avrebbe dovuto definitivamente preservarlo dalla tentazione di ritornare alla temperie del romanzo naturalistico'; *Il romanzo del Novecento*, 79–80.

9. 'The historical novel invokes a contract presupposing the reader's endorsement of an empiricist epistemology'; Barbara Foley, *Telling the Truth: The Theory and Practice of Documentary Fiction* (Ithaca: Cornell University Press, 1986), 170.

10. Pirandello devotes several pages of 'L'umorismo' to a rereading of Manzoni, in which, significantly, he considers him not as a historical novelist, but as a digressive *umorista*. See *Spsv* 139–45.

11. On the crisis in the historical novel following the Risorgimento, see Leonardo Lattarulo (ed.), *Il romanzo storico* (Rome: Riuniti, 1978), 20–1.

12. See Arcangelo Leone de Castris, *La polemica sul romanzo storico* (Bari: Cressati, 1959), 1–60 on the rise to 'ufficialità' of the historical novel in Italy (p. 10).

13. Marinella Colummi Camerino, 'Il narratore dimezzato: legittimazioni del racconto nel romanzo storico italiano', in AA.VV., *Storie su storie: indagine sui romanzi storici* (Vicenza: Neri Pozza, 1985), 95–119 at 95; on the crucial role played by the French Revolution in creating awareness among individuals of their own historical destiny, which will then be enacted in the historical novel, see Georg Lukàcs, *The Historical Novel*, trans. Hannah and Stanley Mitchell (London: Merlin, 1962), 23–4; also Stefano Calabrese, 'Etica dell'azione e intreccio nel romanzo storico italiano', *Rivista di letterature moderne e comparate* 46/1 (1993), 47–67 at 47–8.

14. Cristina Della Coletta, *Plotting the Past: Metamorphoses of Historical Narrative in Modern Italian Fiction* (West Lafayette, Ind.: Purdue University Press, 1996), 19.

15. Alessandro Manzoni, 'Del romanzo storico', in *Opere*, ed. R. Bacchelli (Milan: Ricciardi, 1953), 1053–1114 at 1073 and 1061. Page references are to this edition.

16. For more on this perspective on Manzoni's essay see Della Coletta, *Plotting the Past*, 19–69; see also Sandra Bermann's introduction to the English translation of the essay, *On the Historical Novel* (Lincoln: University of Nebraska Press, 1984), 1–59. On the generally perceived literalness of documents in fiction and history,

see Hayden White, *Metahistory: The Historical Imagination in Nineteenth Century Europe* (Baltimore: Johns Hopkins University Press, 1985), 53.

17. Della Coletta points out that 'historical fiction problematizes our relationship with the historical referent and yet refuses to abolish it altogether'; *Plotting the Past*, 20. Barbara Foley argues that 'historical and fictional discourse do not adopt equivalent representational procedures or constitute equivalent modes of cognition'; Foley, *Telling the Truth*, 35. It is this fluid yet vital border between these two types of discourse which both Manzoni and Pirandello attempt to negotiate.

18. As Ann Rigney expresses it, in historical discourse both writer and events are part of the same fictional world: 'The connection between the discourse and the historical events it represents is not only that of historical succession, that is, of the fact that the discourse follows the events in time. By definition there is also an *ontological* connection between them: both the discursive act and the events represented are posited as belonging to the same historical world. This means that there is no transgression of any diegetic boundary, no shattering of any fictional illusion'; *The Rhetoric of Historical Representation* (Cambridge: Cambridge University Press, 1990), 26.

19. Michel De Certeau, *The Writing of History* (New York: Columbia University Press, 1988), 94.

20. Umberto Eco, 'Semiosi naturale e parola nei *Promessi sposi*', in G. Manetti (ed.), *Leggere I promessi sposi* (Milan: Bompiani, 1989), 1–16 at 2. On the tradition of the preface to the historical novel as *fictio* as well as site of narrative contract, see Colummi Camerino, 'Il narratore dimezzato', 100.

21. See Hayden White's 'The Narrativization of Real Events', *Critical Inquiry* 7 (1981) 793–8.

22. Alessandro Manzoni, *I promessi sposi* (Florence: La Nuova Italia, 1978), 6. All references to the novel will be given after quotations in the text with the abbreviation *PS*.

23. For a useful study of the relations between fiction and historical elements such as the 'gride' in *I promessi sposi* which addresses some of the epistemological and narrative problems they raise, see Elena Parrini, *La narrazione della storia nei Promessi sposi* (Florence: Le Lettere, 1996), esp. 179–244.

24. Pieter de Meijer, 'Una fonte dei *Vecchi e i giovani*', *La rassegna della letteratura italiana* 67 (1963), 481–92.

25. Riccardo Scrivano also discusses this use of Colaianni and points out that: 'dei casi che la storia e la realtà forniscono all'artista questi si può ben servire: essi costituiscono un materiale greggio che sta lì pronto per essere sfruttato da lui; ma se su di essi egli non interviene, non li modella secondo le sue esigenze, non li altera come la diegesi richiede [...] manca al suo scopo'; '*I vecchi e i giovani* e la crisi dell'ideologia', 50.

26. The only recent critic to have extensively examined Pirandello's borrrowings from Colaianni is Rita Baldassarri: her articles 'Una fonte per *I vecchi e i giovani* di Luigi Pirandello: *Gli avvenimenti di Sicilia* di Napoleone Colaianni', *Ipotesi 80* 18–19 (1986–7), 26–54 and '*I vecchi e i giovani* e le varianti: riecheggiamenti della scrittura di Colaianni', *Ipotesi 80* 21–2 (1987–8), 19–40, provide detailed comparison of the passages lifted from the book, as well as examining the ideological shifts Pirandello operates upon Colaianni's text. The plagiarism from

Colaianni is still little known by most critics: it is not mentioned in Mario Costanzo's 'Note ai testi e varianti' to the Mondadori edition of the novel, or, indeed, in Spinazzola's monograph.

27. 'Del romanzo storico', 1061.

28. Elio Di Bella discusses *I vecchi e i giovani* as a valuable document of local history and notes that 'Calogero Ravenna [a Pirandello scholar of the 1940s from Agrigento] 'annoverava Pirandello tra gli storiografi di Girgenti per la sua indiscutibile corrispondenza tra i personaggi e gli eventi del romanzo e quelli della vita dello scrittore'; *Risorgimento e anti-Risorgimento a Girgenti: mezzo secolo di lotte politiche nella realtà storica e nella narrativa pirandelliana* (Agrigento: Edizioni Centro Culturale Pirandello, 1988), 5.

29. 'The historical novel is an intersection of individual praxis with forces beyond individual agency'; Foley, *Telling the Truth*, 169; this relationship is central to Lukàcs's consideration that the historical novel should 'depict the concrete interaction between man and the social environment in the broadest manner'; *The Historical Novel*, 40. In *I vecchi*, on the other hand, Vittorio Spinazzola notes the profound 'scissura fra atti pubblici e sentimenti privati', '*I vecchi e i giovani*', in AA.VV., *Studi in memoria di Luigi Russo* (Pisa: Nistri-Lischi, 1974), 423–55 at 432.

30. Manzoni, 'Del romanzo storico', 1056. It is useful in this context to consider Hayden White's work on the narrative and figurative elements of historical texts, which he claims 'presuppose figurative characterizations of the events they purport to represent and explain', in 'The Historical Text as Literary Artifact', in *Tropics of Discourse* (Baltimore: Johns Hopkins University Press, 1978), 81–100. See also White's 'Introduction' to *Metahistory*, 1–42 for a discussion of metaphor and emplotment in historical narratives.

31. Geoff King has discussed the qualities of realism and objectivity which the map is traditionally seen to offer, and has questioned the representational assumptions inherent in discussions of the idea of mapping: 'There is and can be no such thing as a purely objective map, one that simply reproduces a pre-existing reality [...] Maps inevitably distort reality, as most cartographers concede. But the notion of distortion is misleading, suggesting as it does the possibility of some kind of pure, undistorted representation'; *Mapping Reality: An Exploration of Cultural Cartographies* (London, Macmillan, 1996), 18.

32. See Parrini, *La narrazione*, 53, on this moment as linking the spaces of history and fiction.

33. De Certeau points out the referential distinction between proper names in fiction and historiography, a distinction which is significant in considering *I vecchi's* conflation of real and fictional characters: 'While the novel must slowly fill with predicates the proper names (such as Julien Sorel) that it poses at its beginning, historiography receives proper names already filled (eg 'Robespierre') and is satisfied with working on a referential language'; De Certeau, *The Writing of History*, 95.

34. The illusory nature of such an enterprise is highlighted by Geoff King, who points out how 'maps tend, if not always to fill in, at least to enclose what might otherwise remain blank spaces', and further writes of the 'impossibility of reproducing exactly the curved surface of the globe on a flat sheet of paper'; King, *Mapping Reality*, 63.

35. In Pirandello's fictions the map is already a highly problematic form of representation: see the 'metamap' of 'Rimedio: la geografia' and the fantastic geography of 'Mondo di carta'.

36. The phrase is De Certeau's and its use refers to the relation of historical narrative to the place of writing (De Certeau, *The Writing of History*, 86). I am using it here in the dual sense of the authorial figuring of the past from the time of the present, and of the protagonists' figuring of the visual either as nostalgic metaphors for the past or as incitement to present action.

37. Paolo Archi, *Il tempo delle parole* (Palermo: Palumbo, 1992), 65.

38. See Vincenzo Consolo's description of this passage in his 'Album Pirandello', in *Di qua dal faro* (Milan: Mondadori, 1999), 149–52, which calls Girgenti 'una città dove è morta la storia' and refers to Colimbètra and Valsanìa as 'luoghi di utopia, diversi e speculari, ai margini, fuori da quella città morta' (p. 150).

39. The bipartite structure of the novel emphasizes this specular move from literal to metaphorical 'fango', with the anaphoric description of the banking scandals which have rocked the government: 'Dai cieli d'Italia, in quei giorni, pioveva fango, ecco, e a palle di fango si giocava [...] Diluviava il fango' (*Tr* II, 273). On the image of 'fango' see particularly Baldassarri, who describes Pirandello's reworking of it from Colaianni; 'Una fonte per *I vecchi e i giovani*', 52–3; it is worth remembering, however, that in 1888, before Colaianni's book was published, Pirandello had published a poem entitled 'Dalle "Elegie della città" IV', which offers a straightforward epanaleptic contrast between the heroic past of Rome and her inglorious present:

> Pervenni a Roma, che era notte. In mente
> Rivolgea glorïose fantasie,
> Ma sotto i pie' guazzavami un torrente
> Di fango [...] Oh sì, quel fango la severa
> Bellezza de le vie mi conturbava;
> Quel fango, sì, mi facea brutto giuoco.

Cited in *Epistolario familiare giovanile*, ed. Elio Providenti (Florence: Le Monnier, 1986), 18–19.

40. G.-P. Biasin, 'Sicilian epiphanies', in *Italian Literary Icons* (Princeton, Princeton University Press, 1985), 78–114 at 96.

41. Ibid. 96.

42. Other critics have agreed with Biasin's interpretation of the landscape in *I vecchi* as simple expression or reflection of historical events: see Franco Zangrilli's view that 'il paesaggio pirandelliano non solo ridà umoristicamente l'ambiente naturale di un periodo storico, ma diventa uno specchio nel quale la storia e la civiltà dell'uomo si rispecchiano'; *Lo specchio per la maschera: il paesaggio in Pirandello* (Naples, Cassitto, 1994), 116. Vitilio Masiello declares that the 'emblemi di rovine, immagini di forme stravolte e distorte', which litter this descriptive landscape are an 'allegoria della condizione di deiezione e d'abbandono dell'esistenza nel tempo vuoto della fine della storia'; 'L'età del disincanto', 78.

43. There are traces here of a Leopardian arcane, in which landscape becomes a repository of meaning, accessible only via distance and memory. This impression is heightened by the later reference to Don Ippolito: 'Aspettava che spuntasse la

luna piena [...] per rinnovare in sé una cara impressione. Gli pareva ogni volta che la luna piena [...] ancora dopo tanti secoli restasse compresa di sgomento e di stupore, mirando giù piani deserti e silenziosi dove prima sorgeva una delle più splendide e fastose città del mondo' (*Tr* II, 438). Archi glosses this passage by commenting that 'mirare [...] è sinonimo che accentua la durata sconvolta dello sguardo e trasporta, leopardianamente, l'immagine dell'*ubi sunt* alla luna che osserva'; Archi, *Il tempo delle parole*, 67.

44. Carla Chiummo comments that this passage invokes a 'natura contigua a una storia-mito', which is contrasted with the landscape of the novel's incipit, which connotes a 'storia-decadenza'; '"Nel vuoto di un tempo senza vicende": natura e storia ne *I vecchi e i giovani*', *Studi e problemi di critica testuale*, 62/1 (2001), 173–97 at 191.

45. Several critics have also commented on the obvious echo of the farewell to Lecco in *I promessi sposi* in the episode in which Mauro is retelling his nostalgic and mythicizing account of the Risorgimento, when he says: 'Le lagrime mi cadevano su le mani. Ero come una creatura di cinque anni; e ne avevo trentatré! Addio, Sicilia; addio, Valsanìa; Girgenti che si vede da lontano, lassù, alta; addio, campane di San Gerlando' (*Tr* II, 147). Spinazzola remarks that 'la pagina si apre, inattesamente, a risonanze affettive di derivazione manzoniana'; '*I vecchi e i giovani*', 429. Gaspare Giudice agrees, saying that Pirandello 'tenta un azzardo estremo: misura la propria impotenza lirica direttamente su un grande modello'; *Luigi Pirandello*, 195. It is also tempting to read in Pirandello's nostalgic 'voce del mare' a reprise of the famous ending of Verga's *I Malavoglia*: at the end of Verga's novel the voice of the sea is for 'Ntoni a signifier of a lost past which he is about to leave behind forever. 'Così stette un gran pezzo pensando a tante cose, guardando il paese nero, e ascoltando il mare che gli brontolava lì sotto'; G. Verga, *I Malavoglia* (Milan, Mondadori, 1992), 271. Thus Pirandello's landscape is a space which invokes the past, and also nostalgically evokes Verga's own, already nostalgic and ahistorical landscape.

46. Compare with the passage from 'L'umorismo' beginning 'La vita è un flusso continuo' and ending 'in certi momenti di piena strapia e sconvolge tutto' (*Spsv* 151–2).

47. The speech of Flaminio Salvo to Aurelio Costa, again drawing on the language and rhetoric of *umorismo*, makes a similar point: 'Quando siamo vecchi, ci si accendono, così, a lampi, ricordi, visioni lontane di noi stessi quali fummo in certi momenti... e non sappiamo neppure perché quel momento e non un altro ci sia rimasto impresso e, a un tratto, ci si stacchi e guizzi sperduto nella memoria. Era forse un ricordo più ampio, di tutto un brano di vita. S'è spezzato' (*Tr* II, 257). He adds 'Non ti tracciar vie da seguire, figliuolo mio', as if to warn against the idea of life as a linear journey.

48. Such a *paideia* is constituted by Ippolito Nievo's *Le confessioni d'un italiano*, for example, in which the narrator hopes that 'l'esposizione de' casi miei sarà quasi un esemplare di quelle innumerevoli sorti individuali'; *Le confessioni d'un italiano* (Milan: Mondadori, 1996), 5. A similar function is expected of Ugo Foscolo's *Le ultime lettere di Jacopo Ortis*, of which its narrator writes 'potrai forse trarre esempio e conforto'; *Le ultime lettere di Jacopo Ortis*, in *Tutte le opere*, 2 vols. (Turin: Einaudi, 1995), ii. 13.

49. Roland Barthes writes of how 'the entrance of the speech-act into historical

statement [...] complicate[s] history's chronicle time by confronting it with another time, that of discourse itself, a time we may identify as "paper time"'; Roland Barthes, 'The Discourse of History', in *The Rustle of Language*, 127–40 at 130.

50. The vine is a textual metaphor in classical literature, as Ivan Illich points out: 'Pliny had already noted that the word *pagina*, page, can refer to rows of vines joined together [*Natural History*, vol. 5, trans. H. Rackham]: Rackham explains that *pagina* is used here as a term for four rows of vines joined together in a square by their trellis [...] The lines on the page were the thread of a trellis which supports the vines'; *In the Vineyard of the Text: Commentary to Hugh's Didascalion* (Chicago: University of Chicago Press, 1993), 57.

51. Pirandello's 'vigna' can of course be likened to Renzo's famous return to the 'vigna' in Manzoni's novel, where Manzoni's bravura *ekphrasis* is a figurative exposition of the way in which nature, the repository of order and divinely guided harmony, now reflects, in its misrule and disorder, the disjunction between the human and the divine. The difference between the two figurative vineyards is that Pirandello's metaphorization links and almost merges the individual with the historical events, fusing history and its perception or representation through Lando's self-figuring. For the description of Renzo's vineyard, see *PS* 623–4; see M. Stassi on the vineyard as 'metafora della stessa storia'; '"Quel ramo del lago di Como": la natura nei *Promessi sposi*: tra idillio e storia', in G. Barberi-Squarotti (ed.), *Prospettive sui Promessi sposi* (Turin: Tirennia, 1991), 15–42 at 32.

52. There are many other examples of this metaphorical self-construction in the novel but I will cite only two: first, Luca Lizio's anagnorisis when he 'sees' himself in the landscape: 'nella magrezza miserabile del suo corpo [...] s'era veduto simile a quegli alberi che s'affacciavano dalle muricce, stecchiti e gongolanti' (*Tr* II, 23), which provokes in him a moment of epiphanic 'stupore'; second, Donna Adelaide's identification of the signs of the visible world as metaphors of her own condition of suffocation in a loveless marriage: 'E il bello era questo: che dalla soffocazione avvertita da lei, le era parso che dovessero soffrire tutte le cose, gli alberi segnatamente [...] c'era da più di cent'anni un olivo saraceno, il cui tronco robusto, pieno di groppi e di nodi [...] era cresciuto di traverso e pareva sopportasse con pena infinita i molti rami [...] Nessuno aveva potuto levar dal capo a donna Adelaide che quell'albero [...] soffrisse' (*Tr* II, 436).

53. Riccardo Scrivano mentions 'l'importanza che nel linguaggio dei *Vecchi e i giovani* hanno le metafore, il fango appunto, il fuoco, (usata, per la verità in una molteplicità di sensi) [...] la vigna che "era stata vendemmiata"'; '*I vecchi e i giovani* e la crisi dell'ideologia', 51. However, he does not discuss the function of these recurring metaphors within the narrative.

54. Other uses of this metaphor include the description of the mobilization of the *Fasci*: 'E se domani i lavoratori si fossero mossi, tutta la gente siciliana sarebbe stata travolta come da una corrente di fuoco, perché già da lunghi anni covava il fuoco in Sicilia' (*Tr* II, 337), as opposed to the fire of Risorgimento idealism which is spent in Donna Caterina: 'Ma per mantenere l'anima, come voi dite, in codesto stato di fusione, ci vuole il fuoco, caro amico! E quando, dentro di voi, il fornellino è spento?' (*Tr* II, 198).

55. See Giuseppe Bandi, *I Mille*, in *Memorialisti dell'Ottocento*, 3 vols, ed. G. Trombatore (Milan and Naples: Ricciardi, 1953), vol. 1, whose description of

the exploits of Garibaldi's troops makes prominent use of the metaphor: 'non mancò in quei giorni chi ci chiamasse matti e tizzoni d'inferno, e censurasse il generale come uomo irrequieto e pronto sempre a metter legno sul fuoco' (p. 939). Also, 'non avea acconsentito il generale a farsi capo della spedizione per la certezza che gli guarentirono, che troverebbe l'isola in fiamme' (p. 940). See also Giuseppe Cesare Abba's *Da Quarto al Volturno: noterelle d'uno dei Mille* (Bologna: Zanichelli, 1918): 'E che cosa è la Sicilia? Domandavamo noi fanciulli.—E lui: Una terra che brucia in mezzo al mare' (p. 13). See also Carducci's famous myth-making oration for Garibaldi: 'con mille dei suoi s'imbarcò su due navi fatate e conquistò in venti giorni l'isola del fuoco'; 'Per la morte di Giuseppe Garibaldi', in *Prose di Giosuè Carducci* (Bologna: Zanichelli, 1909), 925–39 at 935.

56. Baldassarri notes that 'Colaianni usa, per esprimere tale situazione, l'immagine di un "fuoco serpeggiante che minacciava di propagarsi—assurgendo alle proporzioni di un grande incendio" (*Gli avvenimenti di Sicilia e le loro cause*, 121)', while also noting that 'La fiamma sta, del resto, nel romanzo pirandelliano, a significare le battaglie risorgimentali, verso le quali lo scrittore nutre una delusa e nostalgica ammirazione'; 'Una fonte per *I vecchi e i giovani* di Pirandello', 52. She also quotes contemporary accounts of the unrest which repeat the phrase 'La Sicilia è in fiamme'.

57. Alan Baker makes an interesting comparison here between landscape and text, saying that 'landscape [...] has been described using a great variety of metaphors most of which serve to emphasize the duality of the "apparent" and the "hidden" in landscapes: "surface/depth" figures abound', and concludes that 'landscape is being likened to a *written document* to be read critically as a "deeply-layered text"'; id. and G. Biger (eds.), *Ideology and Landscape in Historical Perspective* (Cambridge: Cambridge University Press, 1992), 9.

58. See Carolyn Springer, *The Marble Wilderness: Ruins and Representation in Italian Romanticism, 1775–1850* (Cambridge: Cambridge University Press, 1987), on the interest in pre-Roman civilizations in nineteenth-century Italy as a way to 'divert attention away from the centralizing image of Rome' (p. 137). Springer also examines the metaphor of archaeology in that period as an ideological tool of both reactionary and revolutionary parties (pp. 1–18).

CHAPTER 4

Authors and Authenticity:
Suo marito

The punctuation and fragmentation of the diegesis effected by the
chains of recurring metaphors, and by the epiphanic moments which
interrupt the text, provided a key to reading *I vecchi e i giovani*, in
conjunction with its layers of concealed sources. In Pirandello's other
'realist' novel of this period, *Suo marito*, such issues take centre stage.
In fact, it is in *Suo marito* that issues of textuality (or the problematic
material status of the text) and epiphany converge; both these issues
have been overlooked by critics, or dismissed as peripheral problems,
instead of being considered more properly as important structural and
thematic devices, not peripheral but central to the novel's form. In
Suo marito, the relation between text and reality is always mediated
through other texts, a relation complicated by the fact that, as a
Künstlerroman, the novel also places the creative process at its heart,
giving the text an overtly metafictional quality. Drawing on ideas of
authorship and originality, I will look at *Suo marito*'s staging of the
conflict between the moment of artistic creation (assimilated to the
epiphanic moment in Pirandello's narrative lexicon) and the processes
of textual production, between the idea of the author as original
creator of an 'organic' text and the self-quotation and plagiarism
which is the reality of Pirandello's narrative praxis. How far can *Suo
marito*, in its layering of texts and in its textual and editorial concerns,
stand as a microcosm of Pirandello's entire narrative oeuvre?

In *I vecchi*, I identified syntagmatic chains of metaphor as the
dominant element in the economy of the text, and argued that such
metaphoric chains take on a decisive metonymic function, patterning
through repetition, whilst commenting on the act of representation.
In *Suo marito*, such metaphoric patterning is much reduced and the
novel is, rather, dominated by a single overarching metaphor, which
is that of procreation as a metaphor for artistic creation. The way in

which this metaphor is used by Pirandello, both in this text and in others, and its significance in terms of the debate which the novel airs on the issue of artistic production, are all crucial to a reading of *Suo marito*. The second phenomenon which I identified in *I vecchi* was the obsessive repetition of the 'momenti di silenzio interiore', which I read as interruptions to the diegesis and to historical chronology, as iterated, imitative and antidescriptive episodes, which are both fragmentary and associative. Examining these moments in *Suo marito*, and their subsequent erasure in the revised version of the text, will cast light on Pirandello's articulation of important themes such as creativity, authenticity and metatextuality. Again, it is in the relation which these 'moments' declare between 'L'umorismo' and *Suo marito* that the complicated movement between essay and narrative should be studied: reassessing these 'moments' allows us to resituate them as fundamental to Pirandello's interpretative and creative process.

It is significant that these moments of epiphany are copied from earlier Pirandello texts, both narrative and poetic: I have already discussed Pirandello's tendency towards self-quotation and the recycling of his work. Pirandello's rereadings of himself, his reusing of earlier material, the way in which he mines himself as a narrative seam of ideas, themes, paragraphs and chapters and metaphors, and inserts old material into new works (in an inversion of the typical process of literary revision), his endless repetition and recycling of his work are intimately connected to the nature and concept of *umorismo* itself. As a collage of quotations and ideas, *umorismo* contains within itself its own response to itself—the *umorista* or *critico fantastico* responds to himself, echoes and anticipates himself. Thus, as Riccardo Scrivano points out, the practice of auto-citation has serious consequences for chronology: 'Autocitandosi, Pirandello, se pur non annulla, modifica ogni problema di diacronia e lo sposta inesorabilmente verso delle prospettive di prevalente sincronia.'[1] This problematizing of chronology to which Scrivano points can be added to the problems of composition and revision which I mentioned in *I vecchi*, and which become more crucial and central in *Suo marito*, as the problem of identifying a stable text or version of the novel is complicated by the numerous kinds of texts contained within it. The confusion of narrators, genres and discourses (exacerbated by the *roman à clef* aspects caused by the 'caso Deledda') creates a *mise en abyme* effect (used by Pirandello not merely in *Suo marito* but also in the metafictional *novella* 'La tragedia d'un personaggio' and its variants) and contributes to this complication of chronology, causing as it does a kind of 'retrospective' reading, as the narratives extend backwards in time towards a possible source or origin. Conventional ideas of both authorship and the readership are brought into question by such techniques and it becomes necessary to find new ways of assessing their roles in creating and interpreting Pirandello's narrative discourse.

Textual Problems

The initial composition of *Suo marito* can be traced as far back as 1905, between the publication of *Il fu Mattia Pascal* and 'L'umorismo', and can be narrated through the novel's paratexts, which are constituted both by Pirandello's letters and by evidence of the editorial stages which *Suo marito* went through. In a letter to Luigi Villari in March 1905, Pirandello wrote: 'Intanto scrivo un altro romanzo umoristico; *Suo marito*. Il marito d'una *grandonna*; marito contabile e segretario. Figuratevi!'[2] The conditions of *Suo marito*'s execution and publication are intriguingly linked to its thematic concerns, which revolve around the transformation of the artistic idea into the literary object, via the difficult and, at times, anguished process of composition. *Suo marito* was completed around 1909 and was published by the Florentine publishing house Quattrini (1911), after being rejected for publication by Emilio Treves, whose company had previously published Pirandello's *L'esclusa* and *Il fu Mattia Pascal*, as well as the collections of *novelle La vita nuda* and *Erma bifronte* (Treves would later publish both *I vecchi* and *Si gira!*).[3] Emilio Treves's refusal to publish the novel, despite having signed a contract with Pirandello, was due to the resemblance between the protagonist, Silvia Roncella, and the Sardinian Nobel prize-winning writer Grazia Deledda.[4] After the novel's first print run, it was withdrawn from publication until Pirandello's partial revision of it in the 1930s, which was interrupted by his death in 1936. In 1941 it was reissued under a new title, *Giustino Roncella, nato Boggiòlo*, in the Mondadori edition of *Tutti i romanzi*. In his 1941 'Avvertenza' to the Mondadori edition, Pirandello's son Stefano confronts the issue of the status of the text after its unfinished revision, as he tackles the empirical problem of which version of the text to publish. He eventually opted to print the later version, up to the 'frattura' at the start of the fifth chapter, where Pirandello's revision ends, and then fuse it with the rest of the 1911 edition. In the 1975 Mondadori edition edited by Giovanni Macchia and Mario

Costanzo the opposite editorial practice is employed: they elect to publish the earlier edition in its entirety, followed by the 1941 edition as an appendix.[5] This solution was rejected by Stefano Pirandello on the grounds that it was 'arido', because, he argued, an appendix would be neglected by readers.[6] This is an interesting point, as the revised text, in the 1975 Mondadori edition of *Tutti i romanzi*, thus becomes a paratext, expelled from the main body of the text.[7] Stefano Pirandello unwittingly highlights a recurring problem in an author as given to revision and rewriting as Pirandello was, that of locating a single, definitive text, and also touches upon an issue which textual scholars and philologists had been debating throughout the twentieth century, regarding the issue of 'varianti d'autore'. Lanfranco Caretti, in his seminal essay 'Filologia e critica', addresses this topic, making a distinction between an 'apparato sincronico' and 'apparato diacronico' of a text's critical edition, where 'apparato sincronico' represents the 'interventi postumi dei trascrittori, lettori e interpreti' and 'apparato diacronico' represents the 'varianti d'autore', whose presence forces the reader to 'rivelare [il testo] per isolamento e nitido distacco reciproco delle sue diverse stratificazioni'.[8] This 'distacco' is difficult to find in Pirandello, as his practice of repetition and self-quotation tends to blur the various textual 'stratificazioni' together. Enrico Malato refers to the idea of the 'apparato diacronico' as the 'documento della storia interna del testo, della sua progressiva formazione': it is therefore possible to identify a narrative within and about the finished narrative and it is this 'storia interna' (and the authority which justifies it) which both Stefano Pirandello and Caretti debate.[9] Caretti, debating whether an earlier or later version of a text should be published, says that if there is a suspicion that the later modifications aesthetically weaken the text, the later version should be 'riprodotto integralmente anche se visibilmente volta *in deterius*, ma sarà preceduto da una riproduzione, pure integrale, di quella redazione anteriore che sarà da considerarsi la vera e schietta espressione della volontà libera e consapevole dell'autore'.[10] This postulating of authorial preference or intention obviously raises as many issues as it claims to answer: although it is clear that *Giustino Roncella, nato Boggiòlo* was written to succeed and supersede *Suo marito*, it is still doubtful—especially given the reasons behind the revision—that this text can be said to represent the final, authoritative manifestation of authorial desire. Stefano Pirandello draws on a similar concept of authorial authority to justify the deliberately hybrid text which he has

overseen, admitting: 'Non mi nascondo che il difetto avvertito dall'A.,
dato così in lettura il romanzo per metà rifatto e il seguito nella prima
stesura, avventerà ancora di più. Ma io so che l'A. stesso, poiché non
era arrivato a eliminarlo, nel suo amore dell'arte, non avrebbe avuto
interesse a coprirlo.'[11]

I have dwelt upon these concerns of textual scholarship because
they are intimately connected with the issues of composition and
creation thematized by *Suo marito*. Malato suggests that such attention
to the tortuous progress and evolution of a text constitutes a 'nega-
zione del mitico concetto dell'arte come intuizione folgorante,
premessa agli assiomi di "poesia" e "non-poesia" di Croce'.[12] Stefano
Pirandello, on the other hand, does not acknowledge the provisional
status of the text, indeed of every Pirandello text, instead aiming to
reconstruct a 'complete' text, whatever the cost. Although some
modern commentators have noted the 'unfinished' status of
Pirandellian texts, seemingly poised between successive revisions, they
have not emphasized the disjunction between the text as physical
object to be worked on (as in Stefano Pirandello's terminology,
describing his father's 'lavoro di rifusione' and 'lavoro di rimaneggia-
mento' as opposed to the act of 'creazione' which is the new part) and
the text as abstract, ideal space or entity.[13] This disjunction will be
figured throughout *Suo marito* as one between art as commodity and
art as disinterested aesthetic pleasure. The dichotomy which
Pirandello sets up within *Suo marito*, between art as moment of
creation and as commercial product, can also be read as a dichotomy
between the Romantic idea of the writer as individual and original
genius and writing as quotation and reuse, a dichotomy central to his
own narrative oeuvre.[14]

Silvia's Epiphanies

In Chapter 2 I looked at the nature and significance of the humorous
'momenti di silenzio interiore' or 'momenti eccezionali', and it is
through an analysis of these moments that I wish to structure my
reading of *Suo marito*—the erasure of Silvia Roncella's moments of
ecstatic contemplation from the 1941 edition of the text provides an
interpretative key to the vexed issues of *umorismo*, creativity and
authorship which permeate the novel at the level of the *fabula*. I will
be working from the 1911 edition and comparing it with the 1941
variants, and my reading will attempt to bring out the suppressed

'storia' of the text's composition and revision, and lay bare the tortuous, serpentine movement inherent in all Pirandellian narrative. Mirroring this textual layering or stratification, there is an equivalent layering at a microcosmic level, effected by the text's recurrent metaphors, self-quotations and epiphanies, which share a common function—one connected with memory, both the text's and the reader's.[15] All three phenomena are forms of textual recall or recollection, which force the reader to reconstruct authorial meaning through his or her own recollection. These metanarrative moments unite author, text and reader in a complex game of allusion and response, as will become clear.

In *Suo marito*, it is significant that recurring metaphors of the kind found in *I vecchi* are infrequent; instead, there is a profound sense in which metaphor becomes linked to epiphany and to the idea of the purely metaphorical status of the character. The epiphanic instant is at the core of issues of subjectivity and creativity, representation and textuality. In Chapter 2, I categorized these as moments of humorous insight, as paradoxically anti-cognitive in content, and unrevealing in their repetitive and imitative qualities; it is important to note that they are also moments of silence, of pure encounter between subject and nature, a collapse of the self in a moment of wordless communion which is connected with the self's capacity or incapacity for expression. They share similar dual qualities to Joycean epiphany, being moments of sudden revelation arising out of the everyday, and also the aesthetic description or recording of such moments. This dichotomy or separation between the immediacy and simultaneity of epiphany (as articulated linguistically in the 'lampo', 'baleno' and 'guizzo' of *umorismo*) and its analytical expression is highlighted by the deliberate and repetitive sameness of Pirandello's 'moments'.

Such a discussion of epiphanies as moments within which are embedded the Pirandellian notions of memory, recall and metanarrative can also be extended to the reader: the sophisticated reader of Pirandello is confronted with endless versions of the epiphanic moment with minor variations and is faced with the task of performing a reading which is always a rereading. In this context, Lia Guerra's notion of the 'reader's epiphany', mentioned in Chapter 2, may be usefully recalled: in her analysis of Joycean epiphany she discusses it as a technique of textual fragmentation, and says that the reader's epiphany occurs when the reader reassembles those fragments and fills in the gaps, as 'the reader can trigger and activate the meaning of anaphoric or intertextual references or other forms of recovery and reassessment'.[16] Bearing in mind the different structure of Joycean epiphany—which is not extended ekphrastic description but rather single words or sentences which are suddenly rendered meaningful— the 'reader's epiphany' can be a useful tool to interpret Pirandello, as it links the concepts of memory, self-quotation and the reader's response to the repetitive nature of Pirandello's 'momenti'. I am not arguing for an authorial meaning which can be reconstructed by the reader out of these fragments: rather, I suggest that these pauses or gaps in the narrative contain *in nuce* a series of discussions about the relation of the Pirandellian character to language: also, it is in the recognition of such repeated passages that the reader 'recovers' earlier Pirandello texts, and thus reassesses the relation of these passages to the Pirandellian oeuvre.

Silvia Roncella is one of the few female protagonists of a *Künstlerroman* in late nineteenth- and early twentieth-century Italian literature, and she is the heroine of a text which is full of writers and narratives.[17] By tracing the epiphanic moments which define her, I will reveal them to be an index of her creativity and of her position as a writer within a series of ambiguously authored texts. The first example occurs in the banquet scene which occupies almost all of the first chapter of the 1911 edition: a luncheon has been arranged for Silvia by Attilio Raceni, 'direttore della Rassegna femminile (non femminista) *Le Muse*' to celebrate the success of her novel *La casa dei nani* (*Tr* I, 589). The scene is preceded by a comic depiction of the most prominent figures of Roman literary society, setting up the text's satirical conflict between the desire for public recognition and the essentially private act of literary creation. Silvia's appearance is instantly marked by a narrative shift into free indirect style, which emphasizes her interiority and alterity in this undignified circus, as she turns her gaze towards the 'verde campagna', seen through the windows, and the 'righe nere delle formiche, che tante volte ella s'era trattenuta a mirare, assorta' (*Tr* I, 620). The extended meditation which follows is represented as Silvia's 'fantasticare', and, as such, the narrative follows her microscopic gaze outside the assembly:

Ci vuol tanto poco perché un uccellino muoia; un villano passa e schiaccia con le scarpacce imbullettate quei fili d'erba, schiaccia una moltitudine di formiche... Fissarne una fra tante e seguirla con gli occhi per un pezzo, immedesimandosi con lei così piccola e incerta tra il va e vieni delle altre; fissar fra tanti un filo d'erba, e tremar con esso a ogni lieve soffio; poi alzar gli occhi a guardare altrove, quindi riabbassarli a ricercar fra tanti *quel* filo d'erba, *quella* formichetta, e non poter più ritrovare né l'uno né l'altra e aver l'impressione che un filo, un punto dell'anima nostra si sono smarriti con essi lì in mezzo, per sempre. (*Tr* I, 620–1)

This 'fantasticare' is attenuated in the 1941 edition, as the body of the passage is unaltered but is presented not as Silvia's internal vision but as a more general narratorial insight: the reader no longer experiences the scene through Silvia's humorous perception of it and therefore the contrast between Silvia as *umorista*, gifted with visual and spiritual insight, and the superficiality of the other guests (who are unable or unwilling to see beneath the surface) is dissipated.[18] Silvia had already been gossiped about by the assembled guests—her work is described as having a 'penetrazione della vita, strana, lucida, per la cura forse troppo minuziosa... miope, anzi, dei particolari' (*Tr* I, 613); this linking of her writing and her personal vision in the later moment is significant as what Rita Guerricchio calls Silvia's 'tracciato interiore' is shown in the earlier version to be the source of her writing.[19]

The later edition's separation of the passage quoted above from the figure of Silvia has other consequences, as it diminishes the parallel which the first edition has instituted with the figure of Dianella, whose reverie is described in *I vecchi* (*Tr* II, 137–8) and with the Verghian Isabella, the daughter of Mastro-Don Gesualdo, whose character provides, I feel, a source for this episode. The section of *Mastro-don Gesualdo* where Isabella is at Mangalvite, reading novels and dreaming of Corrado La Gurna, seems to anticipate Silvia's reverie: 'Tante piccole cose che l'attraevano a poco a poco e la facevano guardare attenta per delle ore intere una fila di formiche, che si seguivano, una lucertolina che affacciavasi timida a un crepaccio [...] La vinceva una specie di dormiveglia, una serenità che le veniva da ogni cosa.'[20] Isabella's reverie continues in a lyrical tone and language which will find echoes in many Pirandellian moments of ecstatic silence, including those of Silvia Roncella: 'fantasticando, guardando il cielo che formicolava di stelle. La sua anima errava vagamente dietro i rumori della campagna [...] Penetrava in lei il senso delle cose [...] lo sgomento delle solitudini perdute lontano per la campagna.' The presence of the motif of the moon, a central presence in *Suo marito*'s Cargiore episode, is also significant: 'Luna bianca, luna bella!... Che fai, luna? dove vai? che pensi anche tu?'[21] In Verga's novel, the description of Isabella is a remnant of *bovaryisme* ('le tornavano sulle labbra delle parole soavi, delle voci armoniose, dei versi che facevano piangere, come quelli che fiorivano in cuore al cugino La Gurna') as her reverie is shown to be derived from her reading; this contrasts with Silvia's lack of reading, which I will discuss later—Silvia's moments of contemplation are centred not around her romantic life but emphatically around her creative one.[22]

Suo marito's second epiphanic moment involves Silvia's uncle Ippolito, whose reflections on the stasis surrounding him begin with his own immobility: 'nel silenzio grave, ch'era come la tetra ombra del tempo, Ippolito Onorio Roncella sentiva quasi sospesa in una immobilità di triste e rassegnata aspettativa la vita di tutte le cose, prossime e lontane' (*Tr* I, 625). This immobility, a familiar topos in Pirandellian narrative, is present also in *I vecchi*, but is derived from 'L'umorismo', and in fact *Suo marito* segues into a borrowing from 'L'umorismo': 'E gli pareva che quel silenzio, quell'ombra del tempo, varcasse i limiti dell'ora presente e si profondasse a mano a mano nel passato, nella storia di Roma, nella storia più remota degli uomini' (*Tr* I, 625).[23] 'L'umorismo' here acts as a hypotext to *Suo marito*'s hypertext,[24] authorizing this borrowing of part of its most famous passage, that which discusses the 'momenti di silenzio interiore' ('Il vuoto interno si allarga, varca i limiti del nostro corpo, diventa vuoto intorno a noi, un vuoto strano, come un arresto del tempo e della vita, come se il nostro silenzio interiore si sprofondasse negli abissi del mistero'; *Spsv* 152–3). As in the previous scene of reverie, in which Maurizio Gueli sparked off Silvia's thoughts by referring to the ancient Romans who are walking amongst them ('Guardi, signora Silvia: vedrà che a un certo punto s'affacceranno di là a guardarci, soddisfatti, gli antichi Romani'; *Tr* I, 618), the past within which such moments of difference inscribe the protagonists is not merely the historical past, but also the past of Pirandello's earlier texts.

The passage quoted above regarding Zio Ippolito also looks back to yet another of the texts which act as hypotexts to *Suo marito*, Pirandello's 1902 *novella* 'Gioventù', and also simultaneously looks forward to a later episode of *Suo marito* (the Cargiore episode). 'Gioventù', a *novella* set in Cargiore in Piedmont, is a source for *Suo marito* and is itself drawn from Pirandello's 'Taccuino di Coazze', his journal of a stay in Piedmont in 1901. The line from 'Gioventù', ' pareva che quel silenzio sprofondasse nel tempo' (*Na* I, 257), is echoed in the passage I have just quoted, and also in the central epiphanic sequence of Silvia's stay in Cargiore. I will discuss this sequence later in greater detail, looking at the paradox by means of which the unrepeatable nature of an emotional experience can seemingly be infinitely replicated in text after text, and singularity is countered by a multiplicity of identical representations.

The fact that the passage describing Ippolito's musing is removed from the 1941 edition, creating a much more straightforward comic scene between Ippolito and Giustino, again attenuates the text's own 'sprofondarsi', its punctuation by these aporias.[25] Also, Ippolito's moment of insight creates a familial affinity between himself and Silvia, united against Giustino's lack of reflective or contemplative qualities.

The displacement of these moments between the 1911 and 1941 editions is most momentous in the next example of epiphany, which begins with the narrator's declaration about Silvia, that 'ella aveva sempre rifuggito dal guardarsi dentro, nell'anima' (*Tr* I, 640), and goes on to describe the disturbing effects of such a practice of 'guardarsi dentro'. These moments of introspection are represented as a threat to Silvia's selfhood and are articulated in long descriptive sequences: 'Quante volte, nell'insonnia [...] ella non s'era veduta assaltare nel silenzio da uno strano terrore improvviso [...] Lucidissimamente allora la compagine dell'esistenza quotidiana, sospesa nella notte e nel vuoto della sua anima, priva di senso, priva di scopo, le si squarciava per lasciarle intravvedere in un attimo una realtà ben diversa' (*Tr* I, 640). The Pirandellian subject is left vulnerable, unprotected, without language—ironically through the linguistic and rhetorical con-struction of these moments of threat—but a close textual examination of this passage reveals the relationship of dependence and filiation between this passage and 'L'umorismo': quotes like 'tutte le fittizie relazioni consuete di sentimenti e d'immagini si scindevano' (*Tr* I, 640), 'si cercava [...] un aiuto qualunque per ricomporsi la finzione squarciata' (*Tr* I, 641–2), 'Tutto, tutto quanto era un apparato di finzioni che non si doveva squarciare' (*Tr* I, 643) demonstrate the position of 'L'umorismo' as a hypotext or subtext to this text, like an already written text or palimpsest which shows through the superimposed text.[26]

The presence of such textual borrowings has been noted by critics, but the precise significance of their appearance at such regular and crucial moments has not been interrogated.[27] I have already demonstrated in Chapter 1 that the 'finzioni abituali', 'finzione spontanea' and 'infingimenti' described in the essay on humour are influenced by and derived from Giovanni Marchesini's ideas on the fictions of everyday life. The parallels which I have argued that

Pirandello sets up between the fictions of life and fictional practice itself ensure that the mediated, indirect presence of Marchesini in *Suo marito* in the passages quoted constructs a link between the epiphanic moment, the interiority of the character and the creative and metafictional activity. In these moments of interior silence, all of these elements are called up and associated and the 'epiphany' itself becomes an associative moment, a synecdoche of the creative process itself: it unites character, narrator and reader in a moment which is both one of creation, and, for the reader, one of interpretation, intertextual recall and association. For the character, this moment is a metafictional one, as the recognition of the falsity of the 'finzioni abituali' becomes also an implicit recognition of his/her fictional status. Thus these moments in *Suo marito* are at the heart of the relation between Pirandello's narrative practice and 'L'umorismo'.

If we examine the passage under discussion, Silvia moves from 'osservazione' to 'meditazione', from a more or less realist position to a humorous one, in which the visible serves only as a pretext for reverie, a reverie which is almost completely constructed out of humorous quotations. The conceptual vagueness of Pirandello's repeated statements, such as 'come se il nostro silenzio interiore si sprofondasse negli abissi del mistero' (*Spsv* 153), is offset by the precision of their almost verbatim transformation into *Suo marito*'s 'improvviso e per fortuna momentaneo sprofondarsi del silenzio negli abissi del mistero' (*Tr* I, 647).[28] Significantly for Silvia, this 'mistero' will actually be the mystery of artistic creation itself as this network of references and quotations frames an explicit thematization of the concept of artistic creativity: Silvia has a 'qualcosa dentro di lei, uno spiritello pazzo', a 'demonietto, demonaccio', which 'voleva [...] rider di certe cose che ella, come gli altri, nella pratica della vita, avrebbe voluto stimar serie' (*Tr* I, 644). This characterization of Silvia as a specifically humorous writer is represented as coming out of these metatextual and intertextual moments of 'meditazione', authored by 'L'umorismo';[29] Silvia's works are described as being 'così spessi violentati da irruzioni improvvise di vita' (*Tr* I, 677) and the reappearance of the key humoristic lexemes, the 'guizzi' and 'lampi', in describing her work confirms the analogy between her works and those of Pirandello: 'C'è negli occhi, c'è qualcosa ... Certi lampi, sì, sì... Perché il grande della sua arte è... non saprei... in alcuni guizzi, eh? non vi pare? subitanei, improvvisi... in certi bruschi arresti che vi scuotono e vi stonano' (*Tr* I, 704). Critical and creative discourses underpin and mirror each other as the actress Laura Carmi adds, in a passage which could be lifted from 'L'umorismo': 'Noi siamo abituati a un solo tono, ecco; a quelli che ci dicono: la vita è questa, questa e questa; ad altri che ci dicono: è quest'altra, quest'altra e quest'altra, è vero? La Roncella vi dipinge un lato, anch'essa: ma poi d'un tratto si volta e vi presenta l'altro lato, subito. Ecco, questo mi pare!' (*Tr* I, 704). There is also an intriguing anticipation of 'L'umorismo' in this extended 'momento eccezionale' when Silvia's fear of introspection is described thus: 'Entrare in sé voleva dire per lei spogliar l'anima di tutte le finzioni abituali e veder la vita in una nudità arida, spaventevole. Come vedere quella cara e buona signora Ely Faciolli senza più il parrucchino biondo, senza cipria e nuda. Dio no, povera signora Ely!' (*Tr* I, 640). This offers a possible source for the famous 'vecchia signora' of 'L'umorismo', the figure of unmasking, interpretation and revelation which is significantly absent from the 1908 edition of the essay and was only added by Pirandello in 1920.

What will become clearer later in the novel (and in this chapter) is that both the epiphanic moment and the concept of *umorismo* which spawns it are not just congruent but are both products of a view of artistic creation which is Romantic in origin, in its emphasis on original genius, the spontaneity of the creative act and the organic nature of the artwork. This view of art is completely at odds with the seemingly antithetical view presented in *Suo marito* of artistic production as a process, as labour and as commercial exchange, and indeed is at odds with the painstaking process of production and publication of this text, as I have outlined it. Silvia's disinterested approach to the art she creates is connected to her characterization by the narrator as a kind of Romantic creator, the hierophant who interprets the 'meraviglie nascoste' of the natural world and whose creations permit access to a private, unknowable part of her: 'quella parte ch'ella stessa, per non apparir singolare dalle altre, voleva tener nascosta in sé e infrenata, che ella stessa non voleva né indagare né penetrare fino in fondo' (*Tr* I, 644). The effect of the removal of this entire passage from the 1941 edition is to weaken this interpretation of Silvia as a humoristic author and character and to occlude the discussion of her creativity and its relation to Pirandellian *umorismo*. Luciana Martinelli talks of these 'momenti eccezionali' as moments which posit a fundamental opposition between the logical, or male, and the irrational, alogical female.[30] While this is undoubtedly true, and while Silvia is described as lacking the 'macchinetta cavapensieri' of logic (*Tr* I, 628), Martinelli goes on to claim that in Pirandello there exists a specifically female language, one which becomes apparent in moments such as Silvia's epiphanies, and which consists of a collection of 'esclamazioni e domande attonite, affastellamento concitato di frasi interrotte, di pause e di sospensioni'.[31] I do not wish to repeat the critical discussions on Silvia Roncella's position amongst Pirandello's female protagonists,[32] but I would point out that this type of fragmentary language is not exclusive to Pirandello's women: rather, it is a product of the use of the free indirect style which produces an elliptical series of anacoluthons, as the free indirect is the vehicle for the linguistic collapse and aphasia which besets all of Pirandello's characters. The 'momenti di silenzio interiore' are moments centring around this crisis of expression: Silvia, as the narrative 'double' of Pirandello, symbolizes the act of artistic creation, which, while rooted in these pre-symbolic moments, is a productive state, from which arises the linguistic or artistic artefact, uniting the character's quest for self-expression with the author's.[33]

The connection between language, silence and artistic creation becomes more explicit in the final moment of 'silenzio interiore', which occurs in Cargiore after Silvia's first artistic triumph with the premiere of *La nuova colonia* and the simultaneous birth of her child. This entire 'Cargiore' episode has several hypotexts, chief amongst them being the 'Taccuino di Coazze' and the *novella* 'Gioventù' mentioned earlier, and this amalgam of genres and styles (the mixture of the diaristic and the lyrical) is absorbed or subsumed into the epiphanic moment. The moment begins with a geographical description of the environs of Cargiore seen from Silvia's point of view, before tracing her internal emotional landscape via the technique of free indirect style. The landscape is then rendered impressionistically: 'Era veramente così pieno di fremiti, come a lei pareva il silenzio di quelle verdi alture? trapunto, quasi pinzato a tratti da zighi lunghi, esilissimi, da acuti fili di suono, da fritinnii' (*Tr* I, 722). This description is a direct transcription and elaboration of the jottings in the 'Taccuino di Coazze': 'fremiti nel silenzio—zighi di grilli—risi di rivoli' (*Spsv* 1238). These images also appear in 'Gioventù' ('un silenzio attonito e pur tutto pieno di fremiti. Erano sottili, acuti fritinnii di grilli, risi di rivoli giù per le zane'; *Na* I, 257). Marziano Guglielminetti has highlighted the lifts from 'Gioventù' and also from the 1903 poem 'Cargiore', but other references have gone unnoticed.[34] These words are transcribed in the first part of

Pirandello's poem 'Cargiore' (the second stanza of which is reproduced in full a few pages later in the novel):

> Tutto pieno di fremiti è il silenzio
> di quelle verdi alture: acuti, esigui
> di grilli fritinnìi, risi di rivoli
> per le zanelle a piè de' prati irrigui.[35]

Similarly, in the 1906 poem 'Laòmache' Pirandello includes the lines 'Zighi sommessi / di lepri in amore, fritinnìi lunghi di grilli'.[36] The lyrical description which follows in the novel, in which Silvia is represented in the classic Pirandellian pose of gazing through a window, looks back to the language describing Zio Ippolito and, before that, to the language of 'Gioventù':

> Ah, che solennità d'attonito incanto! In qual sogno erano assorti quegli alti pioppi sorgenti dai prati che la luna inondava di limpido silenzio? E a Silvia era parso che quel silenzio si raffondasse nel tempo, e aveva pensato a notti assai remote, vegliate come questa dalla Luna, e tutta quella pace attorno aveva allora acquisito agli occhi suoi un senso arcano. (*Tr* I, 723–4)

This passage is almost a direct quotation from 'Gioventù', where the same impressions are recounted in free indirect style through the perception of the old lady Madama Mascetti (who becomes Madama Velia in *Suo marito*).[37] Again, the passage is filtered through Pirandello's poem 'Cargiore', the third part of which is an exact replica of this description (a fact which has passed unnoticed by critics). In the poem, the prose of 'Gioventù' is simply rendered as verse:

> Solenne incanto, attonita quiete!
> [...] I prati di silenzio inondi;
> par quasi che il silenzio si raffondi
> nel tempo, e notti assai remote io penso
> da te vegliate come questa, e un senso
> arcano acquista a gli occhi miei la pace. (*Spsv* 826–7)

The poem even contains the incidental background details of the scene in *Suo marito*, such as the sound of a scythe being sharpened: 'un contadin: gli sento ad ora ad ora / la falce raffilare' (*Spsv* 827) ('Un contadino. Falcia il suo fieno, sotto la luna. Sta a raffilare la falce' (*Tr* I, 724). This act of transposition, of converting poetry into prose with minimal changes (an act identical to that which saw sections of 'Pier Gudrò' inserted into *I vecchi e i giovani*), is also a movement between genres: I will discuss this displacement of material from one text to

another in greater detail with reference to the transition which
Pirandello operates between drama and narrative, but it is interesting
that forms as diverse as the writer's journal of the 'Taccuino di
Coazze', the narrative of 'Gioventù' and the lyrics of 'Cargiore' and
'Laòmache' are subsumed into an episode of *Suo marito*, which is itself
both a lyrical interlude and a *cahier* of Silvia's progress as a writer, as
we shall see. To add yet another layer to this intertextual reading,
the lyrical vocabulary of this segment is infused with an obvious
Leopardian influence: the word 'arcano' is an emblematic Leopardian
lexeme (from 'L'ultimo canto di Saffo', 'Arcano è tutto / Fuor che il
nostro dolor') and it is also an obsessively recurring word in
Pirandello's early poetry.[38]

In Chapter 3 I described the act of the Pirandellian protagonist in
the moment of ecstatic contemplation in *I vecchi* as a 'reading' of the
landscape, saying that landscape is read as a text; in *Suo marito* this idea
of protagonists reading landscapes as text is exaggerated (and almost
literalized), as the nocturnal landscape is figured as a suggestive literary
topos of Leopardian nostalgia and loss, a space waiting to be filled
with memories of other texts, both Pirandello's and those of other
authors. The distinctive quality of Pirandello's 'epiphanic' moments
lies thus in their connection to literary tradition, although they are
also metafictional moments, in their reference to the process of
creation of Pirandello's own texts. The ecstatic moment is emblematic
of Silvia's artistic creativity, a point underscored by the fact that in the
source *novella*, 'Gioventù', there is an identical descriptive passage, yet
the female protagonist undergoes no correlative internal transfiguration: Silvia is described as experiencing a 'specie d'ebbrezza
sonora in cui vaneggiava, accesa, e stupita, poiché le trasformava con
quei vapori di sogno tutte le cose' (*Tr* I, 725). In 'Gioventù' the
moonlit night reminds the dying protagonist of a night many years
previously and she directs her heirs to open a box filled with love-
tokens and a note saying merely 'Notte di luna!' (*Na* I, 267): the
moon has a memorial function but it is of the romantic-sentimental
kind, rather than the anxiety of loss of self experienced by Silvia.
Similarly, in the description of Giustino's moonlit walk home at the
novel's end there is no 'reading' of the landscape by the protagonist
save a purely conventional one, as Giustino experiences merely a
'guardinga ambascia della misteriosa affascinante bellezza della notte'
(*Tr* I, 857) and undergoes no internal transfiguration. Silvia, like
Dianella, reads herself into the landscape, and interprets its natural

signs as emblems regarding the personal and creative choices she must make: 'Là, nella vallata dell'Indritto, che c'era? L'acqua incanalata, saggia, buona massaia, e l'acqua libera, fragorosa, spumante. Ella doveva esser questa, e non già quella' (*Tr* I, 725).[39]

Pirandello's removal of these epiphanic moments alters Silvia's evolution as a writer who has defined herself through this process of introspection and contemplation. It also loosens the connection between the lyric 'I' of Pirandello in his early poetry and that of Silvia, a connection which seemed to decant Pirandello's private poetic self into the female writing subject. It would be interesting to discover if Pirandello intended to remove the episode I have just discussed (his revision terminates just before this episode), as it marks a turning point for Silvia as a writer, after which she becomes a truly humorous writer, one whose *umorismo* is written as a product of these revelatory moments:

Con quel viaggio, tante e tante immagini nuove le avevano invaso in tumulto lo spirito [...] ella notava in sé con sgomento un distacco irreparabile da tutta la prima vita. Non poteva più parlare né comunicar con gli altri, con tutti quelli che volevano seguitare ad aver con lei le relazioni solite finora. Le sentiva spezzare irrimediabilmente da quel distacco. Sentiva che ormai ella non apparteneva più a se stessa (*Tr* I, 724).

The different kinds of narratives present in the text imply a miscellany of narrators and voices, echoes and texts, which destabilize both text and authorial voice. A good example of this is the seemingly random insertion of the poem 'Verrà tra poco, senza fin, la neve', which is a fragment of Pirandello's 'Cargiore', of which, as we have seen, the first and third parts have already appeared as prose in the novel. The poem is, however, presented to the reader as Silvia's creation, thus implicitly doubling the narrator and character, as Silvia is presented as the 'author' of a Pirandello poem which has already appeared as narrative. There is a hint of playfulness in this doubling as the poem is attributed to Silvia by the narrator, although she has no recollection of composing it: 'Ma no! Ma che! Ella finora non aveva mai scritto un verso! Non sapeva neppure come si facesse a scriverne...—Come? Oh bella! Ma così, come aveva fatto! Così come cantavano dentro... Non i versi, le cose. Veramente le cantavano dentro tutte le cose, tutte le si trasfiguravano, le si rivelavano in nuovi improvvisi aspetti fantastici'(*Tr* I, 726). Silvia's 'transfiguration' of Pirandello's verses posits some intriguing questions about authorship and authenticity, quotation, copy and reproduction and the effect these have upon a literary text. The *mise en abyme* of this textual labyrinth brings me back to metaphor and metafiction and their effect on the status of the text.

In Chapter 1, I pointed out that Pirandello's appropriation of the psychological discourse of Marchesini (as well as that of Binet, Séailles and Leadbeater) had led him to a conceptualization of the self as having purely metaphorical status, as existing as a site of humorous, figurative interpretation. I pointed to the images and metaphors which Pirandello derives from these treatises and argued that the 'momenti' are moments of the revelation of the fictional status of the self, akin to a metafictional unmasking. The concept of authenticity assumes a new significance here: Silvia's experience is described as accessing the secret essence of her selfhood, her 'segreta potenza', her creative self which she both yearns for and fears, and yet her creations are 'Pirandello''s, of the historically existing author called Luigi Pirandello. Nino Borsellino argues that, for Pirandello, 'avergli attribuito opere sue, drammi appena concepiti, poesie, riflessioni' serves to 'dimostrare l'istintività del suo lavoro contro i sospetti di mentalismo'.[40] This procedure of Pirandello's, then, would bestow authorial validation on Silvia's works as well as justifying Pirandello's own practice, yet Silvia's 'authenticity', which validates Pirandello's, is contested by the intertextual and metatextual nature of these moments. The reader is immediately brought into contact with the anterior texts which form the subtext of such moments and undergoes a kind of adjustment of perspective or 'arresto' at this perception of the other texts echoed in the novel. Such contact with other texts is crucial to *Suo marito*, as we will see: the fictional 'world' implodes as the 'author-function', narrator and fictional author (Silvia) seem to collide.[41]

To add to the already highly complex status of fictional characters and their discourse within the novel, there is the aspect of the *roman à clef*. The fact that Pirandello drew on Grazia Deledda as a model for Silvia is freely admitted by Pirandello in his private correspondence.[42] One critic who has devoted a significant amount of space to the relationship between Silvia Roncella and Grazia Deledda is Beatrice Alfonzetti. She argues convincingly for a reading of Silvia as Grazia, not just in the obvious biographical parallels between Deledda and her manager husband Palmiro Madesani, but in terms of the thematic and stylistic content of Deledda's work, which she reads as a source of Silvia's work. Alfonzetti implies that Pirandello has based both Silvia's 'works' (i.e. *La nuova colonia* and *Se non così*) and his narratorial depiction of her at least partly on the person and works of Deledda.[43] Yet, if Pirandello is in dialogue with Grazia Deledda as a 'real' person, as he undoubtedly is, he is also and equally in dialogue with himself, with earlier versions of himself and his text, setting up a dichotomy between reality and fiction which runs throughout his work.[44] The confusion between Deledda the person and the writer shifts the relation of Silvia to Grazia from a personal one to an intertextual one, and again confuses implied author with historical person—an analysis of Deledda's fiction as a stylistic source for *Suo marito* is beyond the scope of this chapter, although it would be interesting to trace the way the relation between the closed system of textuality and the extra-textual world fragments in several different directions here. Instead I will concentrate on Silvia Roncella as creator of Pirandello's texts.

Silvia as Creator of Pirandello's Texts

At the beginning of *Suo marito*, the reader is informed that, as well as the novel *La casa dei nani*, Silvia Roncella has already published a volume of short stories, *Procellarie*, of which we know nothing save that Silvia will 'adapt' one of its stories to produce *Se non così*.[45] The first play of Silvia's which is described in the novel is *La nuova colonia*, which will be performed as a Pirandello play in 1928. (In the 1928 version Pirandello changes the end, leading the reader to wonder what a critical edition of Pirandello's *La nuova colonia* would look like: could it include Silvia's 'version'?) In the revised edition of *Giustino Roncella, nato Boggiòlo*, Pirandello changes the title to *L'isola nuova*, possibly to lessen the similarities between the two texts. In the text there is a lengthy synopsis of the plot of *La nuova colonia*, followed by an extended discussion of its rehearsal and staging. The progress from narration of the *fabula* to dramatization (or description of the dramatization) implicitly restates a familiar Pirandellian discussion on the passage from script to representation, which had been enunciated clearly in the essay 'Illustratori, attori e traduttori':

Che impressione avrebbe fatto questo dramma? Quei personaggi, quelle scene ella li vedeva su la carta, come li aveva scritti, traducendo con la massima fedeltà la visione interna. Ora dalla carta, come sarebbero balzati vivi su la scena? con qual voce? con quali gesti? che effetto avrebbero fatto quelle parole vive, quei movimenti reali, su le tavole del palcoscenico, tra le quinte di carta, in una realtà fittizia e posticcia? (*Tr* I, 679)[46]

Similarly, the refusal of the leading actress of the company, Laura Carmi, to perform La Spera's final shriek during rehearsals ('Se lo sento una volta, io stessa, anche fatto da me, addio!! Io ricopio, alla rappresentazione. Mi verrebbe a freddo. No, no! Deve nascere lì per lì'; *Tr I*, 683) anticipates Pirandello's 1920 *novella* 'Il pipistrello', which also discusses the need for spontaneity and simultaneity and the unrepeatable nature of life paradoxically entrapped in the repeatable form of theatre.[47] Such metaliterary concerns are obvious anticipations of the later metatheatrical trilogy, but they also reiterate the point that the *umorista*, the 'critico fantastico' (in this case, both Silvia and Pirandello), is engaged in a constant critique of himself, of his own processes.

The second play within the novel, *Se non così*, has a more convoluted history: it was originally written as a *novella*, 'Il nido', published in *La tribuna illustrata* in 1895.[48] It was then seemingly transformed into a play called *Il nibbio*, between 1899 and 1906, although it was never performed and there is no manuscript or published edition of it in this version. Indeed, the only mentions of Pirandello's *Nibbio*—also the title which Maurizio Gueli suggests to Silvia for *Se non così*, a title she rejects—are several publicity notices announcing its imminent staging. It is interesting to speculate as to the relative status of the 'phantom' play *Il nibbio* and the two not-yet-written Pirandello plays, *Se non così* and *La nuova colonia*: is the status of all three plays equally hypothetical in the year in which *Suo marito* was published? *Se non così*, in particular, has a fascinating publication history: it was first performed in 1915 and published in 1916. Treves published it in 1917, and in 1919 it was performed for the first time as *La ragione degli altri*. Even such a bare outline of this progression of texts gives an idea of the problematic status of the play-within-the-novel and addresses questions of completion, revision and what exactly constitutes a definitive text, adding a metatextual level to the textual concerns which I discussed at the beginning of this chapter. The condition of the text within the novel, before and after the novel, mimics that of the text in *Suo marito* itself, unstable, evolving and generating new versions of itself. The fact that 'Il nido', the *novella*, was not discovered until 1950 means that *Suo marito*, like *I vecchi*, is a text whose sources are concealed, but it is also a text which dramatizes the idea of textual production, the disjunction between the moment of original inspiration and the process and labour of writing and rewriting a text.[49] This coincides with what Enrico Malato says in relation to philological reconstruction of 'varianti d'autore' which reveals texts in their 'lento e a volte tormentato farsi', as 'continuo divenire, una lenta e faticata conquista'.[50]

Attempts at source-hunting in *Suo marito* are also problematized by the way in which the texts and the plots of text recounted within the novel also dramatize both the creative process and notions of authorship and originality. The game of concealed sources takes on another level of significance when Giustino finds an untitled *novella* which Silvia has written, and which, from his reading of it, appears to be the story of an earlier chapter of the novel, the chapter in which Silvia had gone to Cargiore: 'Oh, guarda! Cargiore... don Buti, col suo cannocchiale... il signor Martino... la storia della mamma... il suicidio di quel fratellino del Prever... Una novella strana, fantastica, piena d'amarezza e di dolcezza insieme, nella quale palpitavano tutte le impressioni ch'ella aveva avuto durante quell'indimenticabile soggiorno lassù. Aveva dovuto averne all'improvviso, nella notte, la visione' (*Tr* I, 790). We are told that Silvia had rushed off the *novella* whilst 'ispirata' (*Tr* I, 789), and we see how Pirandello has constructed an evolution for her as a writer, who, after the epiphanic moments experienced in Cargiore, becomes truly and naturally inspired (although the product of such inspiration might 'belong' to another writer). Fiction and metafiction become even more confused when Giustino finds another manuscript of Silvia's, a fragment of a *novella* which contains descriptions taken more or less directly from the earlier chapter, in which the narrator described Silvia's gaze from the window. The fragment written by Silvia runs thus: 'campane, gocce d'acqua in fila su la ringhiera del ballatoio... alberi pazzi e pensieri pazzi... le tendine bianche della canonica, l'orlo sbrindellato d'una veste su una scarpa scalognata' (*Tr* I, 816). In the earlier chapter the narrative presents, in free indirect style, Silvia's impressions as she looks out of the window:

In che strani atteggiamenti da pazzi si storcevano i tronchi ischeletriti degli alberi [...] ella si passava la mano su la fronte e su gli occhi, quasi per levarseli, quegli sbrendoli di nebbia, anche dai pensieri ispidi, atteggiati pazzes-camente, come quegli alberi là [...] Fissava su l'umida imporrita ringhiera di legno del ballatoio le gocce di pioggia in fila [...] vedeva le cinque finestre verdi [della cura] guarnite di certe tendine, che col loro candore dicevano d'essere state lavate e stirate. (*Tr* I, 738)

The status of both text and fragmentary metatext seems to be elided and Silvia appears not just to be writing Pirandello plays, but to be rewriting parts of the novel in which she is a character. Concepts of character, narrator and author-function are confusingly interchanged to the point of parody, as the spontaneity of Silvia's moment of creative 'ispirazione' generates a new text and questions ideas of authorship and originality.

Examining the source text of *Se non così*, 'Il nido', we see how the *novella* also stages these questions: the husband Ercole Orgera is a writer who has published two novels and has now given up writing. He begins to write again: 's'era impegnato con un'importante rivista di letteratura e di scienze per un nuovo romanzo, che andava scrivendo affrettatamente' and becomes carried away by the writing process which the *novella* describes as a mixture of 'estro' and 'enorme fatica' (*Na* III, 939). Silvia's composition of *Se non così* is characterized by a crisis of inspiration, a 'difetto dell'estro', and is a laborious and tortuous process: 'Non aveva mai lavorato così, volendo e costruendo la sua opera. L'opera, appena intuita, s'era sempre voluta invece lei stessa prepotentemente... Ogni opera in lei s'era sempre mossa da sé, perche da sé soltanto s'era voluta' (*Tr* I, 779). This terminology, derived from Gabriel Séailles, and from 'L'umorismo', emphasizes the importance for Pirandello of spontaneity in artistic creation.[51] However, in the text's 'riassunto' of *Se non così*, the role of creativity in the character of Ercole (now Leonardo), is played down. A rereading of the *novella* also emphasizes the gulf between husband and wife, between the 'colto' Ercole and the 'incolta' Livia. Her failure to understand his writing, indeed her disdain for it, will be replicated in *Suo marito* in the positions of mutual incomprehension represented by Silvia and Giustino and by Maurizio Gueli and his lover: 'Ella [Livia] in fondo, non arrivava a comprendere come si potesse pigliar sul serio la professione di scrivere dei libri' (*Na* II, 938). In *Suo marito*, Livia Frezzi's jealousy of Gueli extends to his passion for writing: 'Livia Frezzi era fermamente convinta che la professione del letterato non potesse comportare alcuna serietà; che fosse anzi la più ridicola e la più disonesta delle professioni' (*Tr* I, 798). Her view of art as a 'continuo gioco di finzioni' (*Tr* I, 799) and a 'gioco disonesto' (*Tr* I, 801), her categorization of writing as a dishonourable profession, a 'fingere, fingere, sempre, dare apparenza di realtà a tutte le cose non vere!' (*Tr* I, 799), mirrors that of Livia in 'Il nido', who too late realizes she has let slip a 'volgarità' when she asks her husband scornfully, 'Di' un po', si guadagna forse qualche cosa ammazzandosi così?' (*Na* III,

940). The involvement of Ercole in 'Il nido' with journalism as a method of financial survival (which for Pirandello has strong autobiographical connotations) is amplified in *Suo marito*, both in the reported play-text of *Se non così*, where the first scene is set in the newspaper office, and by the humorous conflict between the literary and paraliterary, exemplified by characters such as Attilio Raceni, Dora Barmis and the critic Baldani. (In the published versions of *Se non così* and *La ragione degli altri*, there is a scene in which Leonardo's newspaper column is accidentally spliced together with part of his novel in an unwitting fusion of the journalistic and the literary.)

The conflict between Giustino and Silvia, who represent competing attitudes to literature, is also and simultaneously a competition for control and authorship of the work of art.[52] Giustino at various points tries to substitute himself for Silvia, regarding himself as the true 'proprietor' of her work, even appropriating her literary voice by impersonating her in writing in the albums sent by her fans:

Vi scriveva lui i pensieri invece della moglie. Non se ne sarebbe accorto nessuno, perché egli sapeva imitare appuntino la scrittura e la firma di Silvia. I pensieri li traeva dai libri di lei già stampati; anzi, per non star lì ogni volta a sfogliare e a cercare, se n'era ricopiati una filza in un quadernetto, e qua e là ne aveva anche inserito qualcuno suo (*Tr* I, 638).

Giustino's operation, by means of which the borders between quotation and original text become blurred, shows a complete lack of understanding of the concepts of originality and the individuality of the artistic creation which underpin this novel: it also has interesting parallels with Pirandello's own procedures of appropriation, which similarly confuse copy and creation. These questions of authorship and ownership are foregrounded by Giustino's self-definition as both 'padrone' of Silvia's work and 'author' of the triumph of *La nuova colonia* ('L'autore, il vero autore di tutto, era lui'; *Tr* I, 690) for his role in marketing the play, and intersect with the idea of legal propriety.[53] The codification of literary property rights in copyright laws is parodied in Giustino's encounter with the artist Nino Pirino: Pirino has done some drawings of scenes from *La nuova colonia*, based on his attendance at a performance of the play.[54] Giustino accuses Pirino of unlawful reproduction of literary material: 'E che è roba di tutti, *La nuova colonia*, scusi? Lei prende così le scene e... e se le appropria... Come? con qual diritto?' (*Tr* I, 710), and insists that, the island being wholly fictional and imaginary, Pirino could not have seen it: 'Esiste forse nella realtà, nella carta geografica quest'isola?' To his assertion of the island's fictionality, Pirino retorts: 'vuol essere Lei soltanto il proprietario dell'isola? il proprietario d'un'isola che non esiste?' (Pirandello in fact retitled chapter 4 of the novel 'Il padrone dell'isola' in the 1941 edition). Giustino's inability to grasp the intellectual issues at stake here ('Esiste, esiste, esiste, sissignore!' 'L'isola?' 'Il mio diritto di proprietà!'; *Tr* I, 711) is mirrored by the text's ambiguity with regard to the status of fictional characters and worlds and their 'existence'. Interestingly, Silvia is also indirectly accused of plagiarism by the journalist Riccardo Betti, who writes that '*La nuova colonia* era "la *Medea* tradotta in tarentino" ' (*Tr* I, 685). The narrator, however, declares that Silvia is innocent because she has not read the play: 'Non sapeva nulla, proprio nulla, lei, della famosa maga della Colchide; aveva sì letto qualche volta quel nome, ma ignorava affatto chi fosse Medea' (*Tr* I, 685). Silvia's ignorance testifies to the absolute originality of her artistic temperament and defends her work (and Pirandello's future work?) against the charges of unlawful appropriation.

The novel elaborates the conflict between the spiritual and economic functions of art in Giustino's simplification of art's processes, and his reduction of it to the material: 'Tu mi dai carta scritta; scrivi per niente, come vuoi; buttala; io la prendo e te la cambio in denari ballanti e sonanti' (*Tr* I, 762), as well as in references to the literary 'market': 'Si giuoca come alla Borsa, al rialzo o al ribasso dei valori. Oggi la Roncella può valere cento, domani zero' (*Tr* I, 1085 (not in 1911 edition)). Pirandello himself was, of course, familiar with the dominance of the economic imperative in publishing, both from his journalistic activities, and also his experience of Treves's rejection of *Suo marito* under pressure from a Nobel prize-winner. But there is also an ambiguity regarding the economic value of art, hinted at by the suggestive metaphor referring to Silvia, spoken by one of her critics: 'una miniera affatto inesplorata, una miniera vergine, una miniera d'oro' (*Tr* I, 740). Whilst Silvia's work is ripe for exploitation, there is a sense in which in Pirandellian narrative words are regarded as a resource, as a seam to be mined and refashioned again and again, as I have demonstrated: the reuse of metaphors and images, of passages mined from the ore of 'L'umorismo', opposes a pragmatic or utilitarian view of literature to one which affirms the chrismatic quality of words, as in Pirandello's passionate statement in 'L'azione parlata' (1899), talking of the unrepeatable nature of the utterance, the need for 'la parola che sia l'azione stessa parlata, la parola viva che muova, l'espressione immediata [...] la frase unica, che non può esser che quella, propria a quel dato personaggio in quella data situazione: parole, espressioni, frasi che non s'inventano, ma che nascono' (*Spsv* 1015–16). Silvia's disinterested approach to literary creation (she insists upon giving away her texts for free, in an act of implicit resistance to her husband's assertion of the economic imperative) is opposed to Giustino's attempt to calculate the exact monetary value of each word: 'È vero che in America i letterati sono pagati a tanto per parola? [...] Scrivo, per esempio, *ohibò*, due lire e cinquanta? [...] da noi, le parole vanno più a buon mercato' (*Tr* I, 664–5).[55]

The idea of words as material resource can be linked to Pirandello's practice of incessant metaphorization which constantly materializes everything, as I discussed in Chapter 1, as well as to his practice of repetition itself. It is possible to identify a continuum between this aspect of language and the practice of recycling (of images, passages and characters)—both contain within them a tension between the economic and creative, between reuse and invention, and the labour-efficient maximization of resources is set against the creation of the new. The idea of characters as a resource whose recycling underlines an authorial ambivalence towards the idea of fictionality can be profitably examined if we look briefly at a *novella* published by Pirandello in the same year as *Suo marito*, 'La tragedia d'un personaggio'.

Fictional Personae: 'La tragedia d'un personaggio'

'La tragedia d'un personaggio' is a story where notions of authorial and fictional *personae*, metafiction, self-plagiarism and recycling intersect. In it are played out the relations between literature and journalism, between fiction and reality.[56] In 'La tragedia', Pirandello uses the metafictional device of the 'udienza' (which he will reprise in *Sei personaggi*), which the narrator holds for fictional characters who wish to be written. The character which the narrator selects, Dr Fileno, is a character in the novel which the narrator had been reading the night before, 'un lungo romanzo inviatomi in dono mi tenne sveglio fino alle tre del mattino [...] ero rimasto a lungo, nel silenzio della notte, con l'immagine di questo personaggio davanti agli occhi, a fantasticare. Peccato! C'era tanta materia in esso, da trarne fuori un capolavoro!' (*Na* I, 818). Dr Fileno himself is an author of an unpublished work of non-fiction, *La filosofia del lontano*, but is unhappy with the way he is portrayed as a character and demands that the narrator rewrite his story. The metatextual dimension of the *novella* is emphasized by the narrative switches between the narrative containing Fileno, and the narrator's description of the novel which Fileno is attempting to write: its intertextual dimension is foregrounded by Fileno's exposition of his *filosofia del lontano*, which involves a metaphorical 'cannocchiale rivoltato', with which to examine the world and its events and make them recede into the past. Pirandello had, of course, already made the 'cannocchiale rivoltato' one of *umorismo*'s central metaphors, and, indeed, at one point the narrator accuses Fileno of plagiarizing him: 'È lei, sì o no, veramente l'autore della *Filosofia del lontano*?' Fileno angrily refutes the charge of plagiarism by accusing 'Pirandello' (i.e. the author of 'L'umorismo') of being the plagiarist: 'È sempre per colpa di quel mio assassino! Ha dato appena appena e in succinto, di passata, un'idea delle mie teorie, non supponendo neppur lontanamente tutto il partito che c'era da trarre da quella mia scoperta del cannocchiale rivoltato' (*Na* I, 823). The slippages between real and imaginary texts (is *La filosofia del lontano* more 'real' than *Se non così*?), between the double optic of the narrator and his metafictional alias, double and triple the text and its viewpoints, spawning myriad 'authors' and making 'La tragedia' into a playful statement of humorous poetics. The recessive *mise en abyme* of Fileno's hypothetical book, within a novel read by the narrator, within a story written by the author, performs a similar function. Pirandello's authorial persona is itself doubled, as the reader is aware of both his 'real' biographical self, alluded to in the narrator's reference to another of 'La tragedia''s characters, Icilio Saporini ('un povero vecchietto arrivatomi da lontano'), who is also the protagonist of the Pirandello *novella* 'Musica vecchia' ('E lo feci morire subito subito in una novelletta intitolata "Musica vecchia"'(*Na* I, 818)), and *also* of his fictional status as narrator. The *novella* also keeps returning to the idea of plagiarism, both in the examples I have mentioned and in the narrator's rather cheeky assertion that he is constantly being plagiarized by other authors: 'Mi è avvenuto non di rado di ritrovare nelle novelle di parecchi miei colleghi certi personaggi che prima s'erano presentati a me' (*Na* I, 817). Such thematization of plagiarism intersects somewhat uneasily with the repeated self-plagiarism of this *novella*, with its repeated citations from 'L'umorismo', which are both self-consciously highlighted and also casually inserted. There is also a kind of proleptic self-plagiarism, if that were possible, as the reader of the story, if he or she is familiar with Pirandello's complete oeuvre, will recognize passages which are later repeated word for word in *Sei personaggi* and *Uno, nessuno e centomila*. This forwards and backwards act of reading extends throughout all of Pirandello's texts and the contestation of the diachronic by the synchronic means that echo and anticipation almost become confused.

Venturing further into this labyrinth of Pirandellian self-quotation and intertextuality, we can uncover a source for 'La tragedia' in an article of journalism written by Pirandello two years earlier and published in the Roman journal *La preparazione*: entitled 'Da lontano', it features an identical protagonist, with merely a different name, Dr Paulo Post, who is also engaged in writing a book called *La filosofia del lontano*. With the transposition of Paulo Post into the later text, Pirandello violates the conventions which regulate the borders of fictional worlds, dissolving them at will. In 'Da lontano', Pirandello says that he is going to use the fictional character as a way of writing journalism: 'Io mi propongo di sottomettere di tanto in tanto al cannocchiale rivoltato del dottor Paulo Post i fatti più notevoli, le questioni più ardenti, gli uomini più celebri nell'arte, nella politica, nelle scienze dei giorni nostri', and in fact goes on to write two articles for *La preparazione* on contemporary issues such as feminism in the style of a dialogue between himself and Paulo Post.[57] This seemingly unproblematic historical 'Pirandello' conflicts with the confusion between 'Pirandello', Paulo Post and Dr Fileno (and Silvia Roncella). The multiple authors and narrators undermine the author-function (which Foucault points out is a 'certain functional principle by which, in our culture, one limits, excludes, and chooses').[58] The author's proper name, in this melee of hyper- and hypotexts, is not a guarantee of authenticity but a teasing question which, rather than yoking the name and the legal identity of the author together in a rigid bond, opens both the terms out to a series of potentially infinite authors. If Silvia in *Suo marito* is writing Pirandello texts, the classificatory role of the author-function is undermined; similarly, since Pirandello published two articles pseudonymously in *La critica* in 1896 (as well as a poem, 'Per la prossima estate') using the name Paulo Post, the confusion between real and fictional personae, as well as between fictional and non-fictional narratives, seems complete.[59] As a consequence of this, Pirandello's idea of the author as solitary

Romantic creator (emblematized by Silvia's epiphanic moments) is subverted by his own practice.[60]

Self-Quotation or Self-Plagiarism?

In this gallery or hall of mirrors of authorial masks and pseudonyms, the boundaries between the fictional and the explicitly factual are blurred, as Pirandello elides and crosses boundaries and thresholds between texts and paratexts, between proper name and pseudonym. In this intratextual and intertextual matrix of self-quotation and self-plagiarism, which extends between novels, *novelle* and essays, how should we read Pirandello's repetition: does his accretion of versions of texts on top of one another mean that the reader is forced to interpret each text, not individually, but in the broader context of its position as part of a network of texts and revisions of texts? The issue of self-plagiarism is a trickier one than Giovanni Macchia, for one, seems to imply in his description of Pirandello's borrowings from himself as '"plagi" da se stesso'.[61] For at the heart of the issue of plagiarism is the question of source and ownership of the literary work: plagiarism as theft or legal impropriety (its etymology is 'plagiarus', 'kidnapper') derives from a notion of ownership which is of course irretrievably author-centred. As Nick Groom comments, 'plagiarism [...] only has meaning in an artistic environment that emphasizes individual ownership by individual creation, that defines art as a commodity'.[62] It is interesting to consider this assertion in the light both of Giustino's attempt to assert his right of copyright over the imaginary island of *La nuova colonia* and also in the light of *umorismo* as a 'bricolage' of textual borrowings.[63]

In Antoine Compagnon's fascinating work on quotation, *La seconde main*, he points to quotation itself as a reading of other texts: 'toute citation est d'abord une lecture', and argues that the practice of quotation reasserts the material nature of the text, calling it an act of 'découpage' or 'collage': 'je fais un monde à mon image, un monde où je m'appartiens, et c'est un monde de papier'.[64] This idea of the recreation of the world as a paper world (we are reminded again of Pirandello's *novella* 'Mondo di carta') reminds us that the act of quotation implies a questing after authority from a prior text: Pirandello's texts seem to establish themselves as self-authorizing, self-justifying worlds, which negate the idea of priority. The intertextual relation between texts such as *Suo marito* and 'La tragedia d'un personaggio' reciprocally 'authorizes' each text, and runs them all together.[65] Renato Barilli's idea of the 'intercambiabilità' of much of Pirandello's work is relevant here—but can a chapter, paragraph or even character have the same significance when inserted into another work?[66] Is a text or character infinitely repeatable and always identical or does it take on a different meaning within each different context? Again, we return to the concept of the 'world' of fiction, and the continuity and identity which links all Pirandellian discourse. Is Pirandello, the historically existing author of the play *Se non così*, the same as the author of that play within *Suo marito*? And does the narrativization of that play automatically change its status? Are Dr Fileno and Paulo Post the same character?[67] Such a radical questioning of the commonplaces of literary production and interpretation can be discussed in the light of Pirandello's idea of the metaphorical status of character and text. Critical work on the concept of fictional worlds points to the interpretative conventions which hold these worlds together, as I mentioned in Chapter 1: according to Thomas Pavel, 'fictional worlds enjoy a certain discursive unity; for their readers the worlds they describe are not necessarily fractured along a fictive/actual line'.[68] The kinds of beliefs shared by readers about these worlds do not assume that they are real or that they refer to an extra-textual reality. Pavel points out that the convention of fictionality warns the reader that 'the usual referential mechanisms are for the most part suspended'.[69] Pirandello's movements in and out of fictional worlds, between the world of the text and the world of the book, and the insertion and transposition of portions of his own texts into other texts, seem provocative and parodic gestures aimed at highlighting the illusory nature of the fictional enterprise and function, like *umorismo*, as a mode of reading: both Pirandello and his reader construct his text and oeuvre out of readings of his other texts.

Before returning to *Suo marito* I would like to draw attention to the passage from 'La tragedia' which I mentioned earlier: it is Dr Fileno's speech which is later given to the Father in *Sei personaggi*, and it concerns the genesis of the literary character itself:

Noi siamo esseri vivi, più vivi di quelli che respirano e vestono panni, forse meno reali, ma più veri! Si nasce alla vita in tanti modi, caro signore; e lei sa bene che la natura si serve dello strumento della fantasia umana per proseguire la sua opera di creazione. E chi nasce mercé quest'attività creatrice che ha sede nello spirito dell'uomo, è ordinato da natura a una vita di gran lunga superiore a quella di chi nasce dal grembo mortale d'una donna. (*Na* I, 821)[70]

The debate on the analogies between artistic creation and pro-creation is dramatized in *Suo marito*, and it is necessary to return to that novel to examine such seemingly antithetical positions, and, in so doing, to provide Pirandello's narrative practice with a potentially new interpretative metaphor.

'Metafora dell'atto creativo'

Nino Borsellino refers to *Suo marito* as an extended 'metafora dell'atto creativo', as representative of 'l'arte come gestazione', pointing out how Silvia is not permitted to be both artist and mother:[71] she is absent from the premiere of *La nuova colonia* because she is giving birth to her son, and when she makes an appearance at the performance of *Se non così* in Turin at the novel's conclusion, her son dies.[72] It is also evident in *Suo marito* how form and content replicate each other, as the plots of *Se non così*, *La nuova colonia* and *Suo marito* all thematize maternity and childbirth and display Pirandello's anxiety with regard to procreation and legitimacy, as well as containing a series of images and metaphors which represent artistic creation in maieutic metaphors.[73] Plays such as *Tutto per bene*, *L'innesto*, *Pensaci, Giacomino!* and novels such as *L'esclusa* and *Il fu Mattia Pascal* testify to the problematic nature of paternity and maternity in Pirandello, and it is interesting, if we take Borsellino's definition of *Suo marito*, to note that the novel is structured around a series of birth images. Although, as I mentioned earlier, individual cases of metaphorization are much rarer in *Suo marito* than in *I vecchi*, there is one very significant example when Maurizio Gueli takes the Pirandellian trope of 'coscienza' and gives it a twist: referring to 'l'onesto tetto coniugale della nostra coscienza', he says 'è assai difficile che non si abbian poi tresche e trascorsi con le altre anime rejette da cui nascono atti e pensieri bastardi, che subito ci affrettiamo a legittimare' (*Tr* I, 794). Throughout the novel the narrator carries on a discussion of legitimacy and parentage, couched in images of creation: for example, Dora Barmis explains to Giustino that the 'poetessa Bertolè-Viazzi', who has been working on an epic poem for years, is unable to write it because of her pregnancy: 'Ebbene, a pensare che ella ha già nel capo una gestazione come quella, un poema vi dico, un poema! e poi a vederla contemporaneamente, povera donna, oppressa, deformata più giù, per un altro verso [...] O l'una cosa o l'altra, ecco!' (*Tr* I, 651–2). As well as images of pregnancy, there are other maieutic images: the critic Baldani, suggesting that Silvia adapt one of her *novelle* into a play, persuades her that it is as possible to write from life as it is to invent fantastic material: 'Credono gli sciocchi che sia più agevole creare fuori delle esperienze quotidiane, ponendo cose e persone in luoghi imaginari, in tempi indeterminati, quasi che l'arte abbia da impacciarsi della così detta realtà comune e non crei essa una realtà sua propria e superiore' (*Tr* I, 772). Baldani's flirting with Silvia is also laced with double entendres on artistic and physical conception, as when he says 'questo dramma ella lo ha scritto per me; ho insinuato io nella matrice della sua fantasia, per la fecondazione, questo nuovo germe vitale' (*Tr* I, 772). This image recurs in Pirandello's letter to the director of the *Corriere della Sera* in 1910, whilst writing *Suo marito*, when he objects that he is not able to write to order as he cannot control his creations:

Ma non dipende sempre da me. I *soggetti* nascono come i figliuoli, per un germe che la Vita lascia cadere nella matrice della fantasia. Talvolta il germe è irrimediabilmente triste, ed è allora una vera passione maturarlo e far che— venuto alla luce—sorrida anche mestamente e si faccia tollerare. Cure e carezze, da parte mia, non gliene mancano mai, nell'allevarlo. Ma capisco ch'io sono per lui come la mamma.[74]

To a certain extent, all of Pirandello's writing, his letters and essays, dramas and narrative, can be said to be permeated by this discussion on the maternity and paternity of the work of art. In *Suo marito* the image of the 'bruco' appears, in the chapter heading to chapter 5 of the novel, 'La crisalide e il bruco', to describe the metamorphosis of Silvia as a writer after Cargiore (when, let us not forget, she 'authors' Pirandello works) and the continuum between natural creation and natural generation of texts is evident in a review of Ugo Ojetti's *Il vecchio* in the journal *Ariel* as far back as 1898: 'siamo innanzi a un lavoro fatto, più o meno bene per quel che vuol essere, secondo le intenzioni dell'autore, non a un'opera d'arte *nata*. E noi vogliamo che l'opera d'arte nasca, nasca spontanea, crisalide dal bruco d'un pensiero.'[75] The idea of Silvia's two births, her 'two accouchements' (*Tr* I, 663), one of which dies, and the other of which becomes a Pirandello play, shows that the act of producing progeny in Pirandello, real or artistic, is also loaded with complications, because of the instability and fragility of the position of the author.[76] I have tried to show how the piecemeal, fragmented physical reality of Pirandello's texts undercuts the ideal metaphors of creation which he and his characters postulate. To that end, I feel that a more appropriate image for Pirandello's creative practice might be that indirectly suggested by Compagnon, who talks of the practice of quotation as a 'greffe', or grafting of one discourse onto another.[77] This immediately brings to mind Jacques Derrida's theory of the graft as expounded in *Dissemination*, where he talks of the 'analogy between the forms of textual grafting and vegetal grafting'.[78] Jonathan Culler, glossing this idea, comments that 'a treatise on textual grafting would [...] treat discourse as the product of various sorts of combinations or insertions. Exploring the iterability of language, its ability to function in new contexts with new force, a treatise on textual grafting would attempt to classify various ways of inserting one discourse in another.' Culler then asks: 'what are the points of juncture and stress where one scion or line of argument has been spliced with another?'[79]

Conclusion

Within a text such as *Suo marito*, therefore, we can argue that the presence of the quotation signals a grafting of two semiotic systems, as Compagnon says, and also that it foregrounds the idea of the paternity of the work of art—the source is immaterial, rather, it is the transformation of the material when it becomes absorbed into the new text which counts.[80] Pirandello's repeated metaphor in 'L'umorismo' of the text or discourse as plant authorizes this interpretation (and I pointed out in Chapter 1 his emphasis on 'L'umorismo' as a hybrid plant), just as the text of 'L'umorismo', itself a bastardization of other texts, 'authors' his thinking and stands as the 'origin' of his thought. Given such a poetics of bastardization, a more appropriate metaphor for Pirandello's creative practice, instead of the 'collage', 'bricolage', 'incastro' or 'puzzle' metaphors suggested by critics, might be that of the 'innesto', or graft.[81] Pirandello's 1921 play, 'L'innesto', will thematize the drama of procreation when a wife becomes pregnant following a violent rape, and attempts to force her husband to accept the child as his. The violent absorption of the foreign element is compared (rather heavy-handedly) to a plant graft as the discourse of the gardener to the wife makes clear:

c'è tanti modi d'innestare la buccia o la gemma, caccia dentro uno di questi talli qua, leghi bene; impiastri o impeci—a secondo—credi d'aver fatto l'innesto; aspetti... hai ucciso la pianta—ci vuol l'arte, ci vuole! [...] La pianta, bisogna che sia in succhio, signora... in amore, ecco! che voglia il frutto che per sé non può dare! (*Mn* II, 254)[82]

The 'art of the graft', the absorption of the extraneous element into a body which makes it its own, is a fascinating metaphor for Pirandello's artistic practice, as it retains the natural metaphor for creation, whilst also expressing the shock or trauma inherent in this process: it is a violation, an intrusion. As in the *novella* 'Il pipistrello', where the 'intrusione improvvisa e violenta di un elemento estraneo, casuale, che invece di mandare a gambe all'aria, come avrebbe dovuto, la finzione dell'arte, s'era miracolosamente inserito in essa, conferendole lì per lì, nell'illusione del pubblico, l'evidenza d'una prodigiosa verità', producing a new and unrepeatable artwork, Pirandello's fictions are grafts. In the graft, the main, dominant or historically grounded text accepts the foreign element and makes it stronger. Thus Pirandello's texts and different types of narratives may be of uncertain paternity, and I have demonstrated the difficulty of identifying their point of origin, but they are held together by sheer force of will, by a continuity of self-quotation which offsets the difference of quotation. The 'authenticity' of Silvia Roncella, which painstakingly establishes her as a naturally inspired writer, comes via a series of revelations recycled from other Pirandello texts; the fact that Silvia then 'gives birth to' Pirandello's own (patchwork) texts naturalizes and disguises the grafted nature of her own, and Pirandello's, texts, and deceptively rewrites authorship as organic and natural.

Notes to Chapter 4

1. Riccardo Scrivano, *Finzioni teatrali* (Messina: D'Anna, 1982), 253.
2. Cited in Elio Providenti, *Archeologie pirandelliane* (Catania: Maimone, 1990), 174.
3. In a letter to Ugo Ojetti in November 1909 Pirandello writes: 'Dopo tanti mesi di vacanza forzata [...] ho dovuto rimettermi *tutto* al romanzo, per poterlo consegnare al Treves alla fine del venturo marzo. Il romanzo è *Suo marito*: quello dedicato a te. Mi vien bene, sai. Ne son proprio contento.' Cited in *Carteggi inediti con Ojetti–Albertini–Orvieto–Novaro–De Gubernatis–De Filippo*, ed. Sarah Zappulla Muscarà (Rome: Bulzoni, 1980), 57.
4. Emilio Treves's playful letter to Pirandello is worth quoting here: writing to refuse the novel, he informs Pirandello that he is unable to accept it as he has just refused to publish a novel called *Sua moglie* (!), which alludes 'in modo evidente alla moglie di Lei, caro Pirandello [...] mettendola in ridicolo in modo tale che non si può [fare] a meno di riconoscerla'. Treves says that by refusing to publish this hypothetical novel he is saving Pirandello from the 'grave dispiacere di vedersi messo in burletta' and concludes, 'ella ha capito la parabola, e non ha bisogno di altre parole per spiegare l'impossibilità morale in cui mi trovo di pubblicare *Suo marito*'. Quoted in *Carteggi*, ed. Zappulla Muscarà, 60. Treves's response to Pirandello highlights not only the pressure exerted by Deledda to

prevent the publication of a fictionalized version of her life, but also *Suo marito*'s capacity to generate new texts, not all of them real, as we shall see.

5. See *Tr* I, 1048–9 for further details.

6. 'Si sa la sorte delle appendici: data in appendice, la parte rifatta sarebbero andati a leggerla ben pochi; i più la avrebbero saltata pari pari o degnata appena d'un'occhiata distratta, inconcludente.' Stefano Pirandello, 'Avvertenza' to *Giustino Roncella, nato Boggiòlo* (1941), reprinted in the Mondadori edition edited by C. Simioni and G. Griffini in 1980, pp. 3–5 at 4.

7. Genette links the paratext to the concept of narrative authority, calling it 'the conveyor of a commentary that is authorial or more or less legitimated by the author'; *Paratexts*, 2.

8. Lanfranco Caretti, 'Filologia e critica', in his *Antichi e moderni* (Turin: Einaudi, 1976), 471–88 at 477.

9. Enrico Malato, 'Filologia e critica', in AA.VV., *La critica del testo* (Rome: Salerno, 1985), 3–23 at 3.

10. Caretti, 'Filologia', 482. Interestingly, in their recent translation of the novel, Martha King and Mary Ann Frese Witt base their translation on the original version, claiming that 'the differences [between the two versions] are not on the whole significant'; 'Afterword', to *Her Husband*, trans. Martha King and Mary Ann Frese Witt (Durham and London: Duke University Press, 2000), 235–42 at 241. King and Witt's justification for using the earlier version seems based purely on convention: 'Italian publishers have in recent years preferred to reprint Pirandello's original novel, *Suo marito*, the text we have translated here' (p. 241).

11. 'Avvertenza', 5.

12. Malato, 'Filologia', 22.

13. 'Avvertenza', 3.

14. Riccardo Scrivano has made an interesting, if brief, examination of *Suo marito*'s textual complexity and the text's thematic replication of this complexity in 'Società e religione nel "teatro dei miti"', in Nicolosi and Moretti (eds.), *L'ultimo Pirandello: Pirandello e l'Abruzzo*, 87–107; see esp. 92–4. His comment that 'il testo esiste solo nel momento in cui è riusato, rivissuto, ripercorso' (p. 106 n. 2) leads him to contrast Pirandello's textual practice with a Romantic or idealist conception of the text. I will expand on this argument later in this chapter.

15. Lucio Lugnani writes of a 'scrittura pirandelliana caratterizzata da una formidabile memoria interna'; *L'infanzia felice e altri saggi su Pirandello* (Naples: Liguori, 1986), 15. However, Annamaria Andreoli corrects this idea of a Pirandellian textual 'memory', claiming it is part of Pirandello's own mythologizing of his creative practice, and pointing out that the systematic practice of self-plagiarism which he employs owes more to the copying out of set phrases kept in notebooks than to a 'prodigiosa memoria di Pirandello in Pirandello, quasi che egli appartenga a una remota civiltà orale'; 'Nel laboratorio di Pirandello', 215.

16. Guerra, 'Fragmentation in *Dubliners*', 44.

17. For more information on the status of women as both writers and heroines in this period see Giovanna Finocchiaro Chimirri, 'La donna scrittrice fra Capuana e Verga', in AA.VV., *Les femmes écrivains en Italie aux 19ᵉ et 20ᵉ siècles* (Aix-en-Provence: Université de Provence, 1993), 25–37; Lucienne Kroha, 'Pirandello and the woman writer', in *The Woman Writer in Late Nineteenth-Century Italy* (Lampeter: Mellen, 1992), 143–58; Marziano Guglielminetti, 'Le scrittrici, le

avanguardie, la letteratura di massa', in Sarah Zappulla Muscarà (ed.), *Letteratura siciliana al femminile* (Caltanissetta: Sciascia, 1984), 11–25. On the female *Künstlerroman* in general, see Susan Gubar, 'Birth of the artist as heroine', in C. Heilbrun and M. Hyonnet (eds.), *The Representation of Women in Fiction* (Baltimore: Johns Hopkins, 1983), 19–59.

18. For the revised version of this passage, see *Tr* I, 1069–70.

19. Rita Guerricchio, 'Il romanzo dell'*umorismo*', in *Suo marito*, ed. Guerricchio (Florence: Giunti, 1994), pp. ix–xxx at p. xv.

20. Giovanni Verga, *Mastro-Don Gesualdo* (Milan: Mondadori, 1993), 236.

21. Ibid. 237.

22. Carla Ricciardi talks of Verga's 'incapacità di superare il modello flaubertiano' in this sequence, and it is interesting that Verga's ecstatic moment derives from his heroine's reading of love poetry, while such moments in Pirandello come from the narrator's 'reading' of earlier Pirandello texts, as I will show. 'Introduzione' to *Mastro-don Gesualdo*, pp. v–xxxiii at p. xix.

23. See the following examples from *I vecchi*: 'La placida immobilità dei vecchi oggetti della stanza, impregnati tutti da un lezzo quasi ferino, i quali parevano in attesa ch'egli riprendesse tra loro la vita consueta, gli aveva suscitato una fierissima irritazione' (*Tr* II, 489) and 'sentendo nel silenzio cupo delle stanze, rimaste con tutti i mobili come in attesa, il vuoto, il vuoto in cui dal primo momento della sciagura si vedeva perduto' (*Tr* II, 414).

24. In Genette's terms, a hypertext is a 'text derived from another preexistent text [...] from which it originates through a process I shall provisionally call transformation, and which it consequently evokes more or less perceptibly without necessarily speaking of it or citing it'; Genette, *Palimpsests*, 5. The relation between 'L'umorismo' and Pirandello's other texts is slightly more complex in that Pirandello both evokes and cites 'L'umorismo', whilst not explicitly 'speaking of it', but I feel that these concepts of origin and transformation are relevant to Pirandello's narrative poetics and to the intricate relations between his texts.

25. Rino Caputo remarks on the diminution of Zio Ippolito's role here, saying that he has thus 'perso ogni nuance cosmico (e il riferimento vuol essere, esplicito, alla funzione anticipatrice nei confronti di don Cosmo)', but he does not link this episode to the others in the text, or note its intertextual function. 'La letteratura nel romanzo', in AA.VV., *Giornata di studi nel primo cinquantenario della morte di Luigi Pirandello* (Rome: La Nuova Copisteria, 1988), 75–90 at 82.

26. Again, these quotations come from the 'certi momenti di silenzio interiore' passage of 'L'umorismo': 'Lucidissimamente allora la compagine dell'esistenza quotidiana, quasi sospesa nel vuoto di quel nostro silenzio interiore, ci appare priva di senso, priva di scopo [...] tutte le nostre fittizie relazioni consuete di sentimenti e d'immagini si sono scisse e disgregate' (*Spsv* 152).

27. Rita Guerricchio comments that 'è stato spesso notato come *Suo marito* costituisca una sorta di contraprova "concreta" del saggio su "L'umorismo", non solo in relazione ai travasi testuali vistosamente operati, ma anche alla strategia compositiva del romanzo'; 'Il romanzo dell'*umorismo*', p. xiii. Claudia Micocci merely comments that in these pages just quoted 'sono inserite parti centrali del saggio sull'*umorismo*'; 'Silvia Roncella e/o Giustino Boggiòlo', in Enzo Lauretta (ed.), *Il 'romanzo' di Pirandello* (Palermo: Palumbo, 1976), 125–41 at 127.

28. Other borrowings in this passage include the 'arresto del tempo e della vita' (*Tr* I, 647), a direct lift from 'L'umorismo' ('come un arresto del tempo e della vita', *Spsv* 153); 'Oh perché proprio doveva essere così, lei, con quella faccia? con quel corpo? Alzava una mano, nell'incoscienza; e il gesto le restava sospeso. Le pareva strano che l'avesse fatto lei. *Si vedeva vivere*' (*Tr* I, 646); cf. *Spsv* 152: 'Alziamo una mano, nell'incoscienza; e il gesto ci resta sospeso. Ci pare strano che l'abbiamo fatto noi. *Ci vediamo vivere*.'

29. Claudia Micocci says that Silvia 'dimostra la possibilità di legare in modo strettissimo il processo che dà luogo all'opera umoristica, al processo generale della creazione artistica'; 'Silvia Roncella e/o Giustino Boggiòlo', 130, and Luciana Martinelli points out perceptively that 'Silvia è dunque il personaggio umoristico, ancor prima di essere, come è stato detto, scrittrice umoristica. Si può anzi affermare che diviene scrittrice umoristica perché è personaggio umoristico'; 'Silvia Roncella (una lettura di *Suo marito* di Luigi Pirandello)', in Zappulla Muscarà (ed.), *Letteratura siciliana al femminile*, 103–23 at 112–13.

30. Martinelli says that 'la creatività di Silvia è, certo, la creatività dell'artista, ma di un'artista che diviene tale perché ha recuperato il nucleo, profondo e originale, del suo universo femminile'; *Lo specchio magico: immagini del femminile in Luigi Pirandello* (Bari: Dedalo, 1992), 60.

31. Martinelli, *Lo specchio magico*, 101.

32. There is a relatively large body of criticism on this topic, of which the most relevant works are probably Roberto Alonge's 'Madri, puttane, schiave sessuali e uomini soli', in id. et al. (eds.), *Studi pirandelliani: Dal testo al sottotesto* (Bologna: Pitagora, 1986), 91–110; Laura Granatella, 'Proposta per una lettura del mito maternocentrico come metafora dell'atto creativo', in Milioto (ed.), *La donna in Pirandello*, 11–21; Daniela Bini, 'La creazione artistica come sconfitta della morte', in Lauretta (ed.), *Pirandello e l'oltre*, 233–43; Maria Antonietta Grignani, 'Incursioni al femminile nei romanzi di Pirandello', in Milioto (ed.), *La donna in Pirandello*, 23–35; Lucienne Kroha, 'Scrittori, scrittrici e industria culturale: *Suo marito* di Pirandello', *Otto/Novecento* 19/5 (1995), 167–82.

33. Rita Guerricchio notes that Silvia is an 'esercizio del "doppio" da parte dell'autore di così trasparente evidenza da farne un portavoce fin troppo riconoscibile'; 'Il romanzo dell'*umorismo*', p. xx.

34. Guglielminetti limits himself to describing how Pirandello 'sia giunto in *Suo marito* a cogliere dei "momenti" di "silenzio interiore" utilizzando la sintassi frammentaria del diario, della novella e della lirica'; *Il romanzo del Novecento*, 86 n. 45.

35. 'Cargiore', published in *La Riviera Ligure*, np. 46, February 1903, reprinted in *Spsv* 826.

36. 'Laòmache', published in *La Rivista di Roma*, February 1906, and reprinted in *Spsv* 722. 'Grilli' are a constant presence in the immobile Pirandellian landscape, one of his signature elements, almost a guarantee of his authorship.

37. 'Ah che incanto! che pace! Pareva che la Luna inondasse di luminoso silenzio quei prati: d'un silenzio attonito e pur tutto pieno di fremiti [...] Alla vecchina, guardando assorta, pareva che quel silenzio sprofondasse nel tempo, e altre notti pensava, remote, simili a questa, vegliate dalla Luna; e tutta quella pace fascinosa assumeva a gli occhi di lei quasi un senso arcano' (*Na* I, 256–7).

38. To cite merely a few examples, 'Ah, che profonda, arcana/malinconia, che

nostalgia m'assal'; 'Torna, Gesù', in *Spsv* 807; 'Trema ne l'aria un lieve/canto lontano, e arcana/spande mestizia intorno'; 'Pasqua di Gea', *Spsv* 532; 'non sei tu forse arcana/de la terra preghiera?'; 'Pasqua di Gea', *Spsv* 513; 'quante al sovrano incanto/cessero ed a l'arcano/legamento del loco?'; 'Pasqua di Gea', *Spsv* 515.

39. This passage is also taken from the 'Taccuino di Coazze': 'Gran parte delle acque corre incanalata nei lavori di presa – Lì, rumorosa, libera, vorticosa, spumante, tra i massi del letto; qui, placida, pel canale, assoggettata all'uomo, all'industria'; *Spsv* 1241.

40. Nino Borsellino, *Ritratto di Pirandello* (Bari: Laterza, 1983), 33.

41. Michel Foucault's designation of the author as 'a certain functional principle by which, in our culture, one limits, excludes, and chooses' posits the author's proper name as a unifying principle: 'The author's name serves to characterize a certain mode of being of discourse: the fact that the discourse has an author's name, that one can say "this was written by so-and-so" or "so-and-so is its author", shows that this discourse is not ordinary everyday speech that merely comes and goes, not something that is immediately consumable'; 'What is an author?', in J. V. Harari (ed.), *Textual Strategies* (Ithaca: Cornell University Press, 1979), 141–60 at 159 and 147.

42. Pirandello wrote to Ugo Ojetti in December 1908: 'Manderò pure al Treves, spero in aprile, il romanzo *Suo marito*. Son partito dal marito di Grazia Deledda. Lo conosci? Che capolavoro, Ugo mio! Dico, il marito di Grazia Deledda – intendiamoci...'; following Treves's refusal to publish the novel he wrote to Ojetti admitting that Silvia was based on Deledda, but denying any simple equation between the two: 'Evidentemente la Ddda [*sic*], la quale ha saputo dell'invio da un giornale di Roma che mi ha "intervistato" è corsa al riparo dal Treves [...] Ti assicuro, mio caro Ugo, che è una persecuzione ingiustissima! Io non ho preso dalla realtà che un semplice *spunto*, il che è perfettamente legittimo; poi ho lavorato liberamente con la fantasia, ho creato *personaggi* azioni e tutto.' Cited in *Carteggi inediti*, ed. Zappulla Muscarà, 28 and 60 (italics in original).

43. Beatrice Alfonzetti, 'La scrittura selvaggia: l'immagine di Grazia Deledda in *Suo marito*', in Ugo Collu (ed.), *Grazia Deledda nella cultura contemporanea*, 2 vols. (Nuoro: Satta, 1992), ii. 285–303. See also Gigliola De Donato, 'Un "personaggio da romanzo": Grazia Deledda in *Suo marito* di Pirandello', *Rivista di studi pirandelliani* 6/7 (1991), 21–41. De Donato notes the differences and affinities between Silvia and Deledda's fictional characters, saying that Deledda's female protagonists 'coagulano [...] una fissità potenzialmente tragica, arrestata bruscamente dalla paura del nuovo', whereas 'giusto da quel punto di esitazione e di ristagno dell'anima, Pirandello fa iniziare la storia dei suoi personaggi: storia di sentimenti dissimulati, di disgregazione interiore, di improvvisi sussulti' (p. 32).

44. Franca Angelini also plausibly suggests Sibilla Aleramo as a model for Silvia (Pirandello reviewed *Una donna* favourably in 1906) and says 'Non so se la vicenda personale e il romanzo della Aleramo abbiano influenzato la trama di *Suo marito*.' 'Un nome e una donna', in A. Buttafuoco and M. Zancan (eds.), *Svelamento: Sibilla Aleramo: una biografia intellettuale* (Milan: Feltrinelli, 1988), 64–72 at 69. The conjunction of Silvia Roncella as a 'pseudonym' for Sibilla Aleramo (itself a pseudonym), and the similarity in subject matter, the protagonists' inability to be both mother and writer, are suggestive, yet it should

be remembered that at the turn of the century the use of (frequently male) pseudonyms by women was a widespread practice among female writers. See Kroha, *The Woman Writer in Late Nineteenth-Century Italy*, 143–58, for details. Emma Grimaldi, in her excellent recent monograph, suggests *L'esclusa's* Marta Ajala as a model for Silvia; *Come un quadro sottosopra: aspetti e problematiche del femminile in alcune opere di Pirandello* (Cava de' Tirreni: Avagliano, 2001), 105–8.

45. On the relationship between *Suo marito* and the Pirandello texts represented within it, particularly in relation to the theme of maternity, see Grimaldi, *Come un quadro sottosopra*, *passim*.

46. 'Quando leggiamo un romanzo o una novella, c'ingegniamo di raffigurarci i personaggi e le scene come a mano a mano ce li descrive e ce li rappresenta l'autore. Ora supponiamo per un momento che questi personaggi, a un tratto, per un prodigio, balzino dal libro vivo innanzi a noi, nella nostra stanza, e si mettono a parlare con la loro voce e a muoversi e a compiere la loro azione senza più il sostegno descrittivo o narrativo del libro. Nessun stupore! Questo prodigio appunto compie l'arte drammatica. [...] Ma perché dalle pagine scritte i personaggi balzino vivi e semoventi bisogna che il drammaturgo trovi la parola che sia l'azione stessa parlata, la parola viva che nuova'; 'Illustratori, attori e traduttori' (1908), *Spsv* 213–14. The anxiety surrounding the passage from printed page to three-dimensional reality anticipates 'La tragedia d'un personaggio', which I will discuss later.

47. 'Il pipistrello' is an intriguing commentary on theatrical practice: the lead actress's 'grido' is caused by the irruption into the scene of a real bat and she declares that she cannot repeat the same cry the next night; the director closes the play, unable to repeat the 'intrusione improvvisa e violenta di un elemento estraneo, casuale, che invece di mandare a gambe all'aria, come avrebbe dovuto, la finzione dell'arte, s'era miracolosamente inserita in essa, conferendole lì per lì, nell'illusione del pubblico, l'evidenza d'una prodigiosa verità'; *Na* I, 233.

48. For further details on the composition and production history of this play, see Alessandro d'Amico, 'Notizia', to *La ragione degli altri*, in *Mn* I, 139–58.

49. See Providenti, *Archeologie pirandelliane*, 200, on the discovery of 'Il nido'.

50. Malato, 'Filologia e critica', 21–2.

51. Pirandello's use of Séailles's terminology is traced by Gösta Andersson, who examines Pirandello's appropriation of Séailles's language from *Essai sur la génie dans l'art*: Séailles's 'mais dans l'art, oeuvre de désintéressement et de loisir, l'image doit être voulue, aimée pour elle-même' reappears in 'L'umorismo' as 'la finzione dell'arte è voluta [...] voluta per sé, e per sé amata, disinteressatamente'. 'Pirandello saggista, lettore di Gabriel Séailles', in Paola Giovanelli (ed.), *Pirandello saggista* (Palermo: Palumbo, 1982), 303–19 at 306.

52. Luciana Martinelli characterizes *Suo marito* as 'la contrapposizione tra la concezione dell'arte come valore puro, disinteressato, propria di Silvia, scrittrice famosa, e la riduzione del prodotto di lei a merce, a strumento di escalation economico e sociale, operata da Giustino'; *Lo specchio magico*, 8, a hypothesis backed up by Gigliola De Donato in 'Un "personaggio da romanzo"', 36–7 and by Mario Ricciardi in *La rivincita della letteratura* (Turin: Stampatori, 1979), see esp. 70–5; see also Fabio Todero, 'Pirandello e la fabbrica del successo: l'autore e il pubblico in *Suo marito*', in G. Petronio (ed.), *Scrittore e lettore nella società di massa* (Trieste: LINT, 1991), 531–53.

53. Foucault emphasizes the relation between the development of eighteenth-century copyright laws and the principle of the author's ownership of his texts by virtue of the establishment of his individuality as a creating power, saying 'since the eighteenth century, the author has played the role of the regulator of the fictive, a role quite characteristic of our era of industrial and bourgeois society, of individualism and private property'; 'What is an author?', 159. Thus the question of authorship is also one of ownership, of who has the right to profit materially from the text, and plagiarism constitutes a legal, not a moral impropriety.

54. On the relation between the development of copyright law and the individuality of the author as sole originator of a text see Mark Rose, 'The author as proprietor', *Representations*, 23 (1988), 51–85; Martha Woodmansee, 'The genius and the copyright: economic and legal conditions of the emergence of the author', *Eighteenth-Century Studies* 17 (1984), 425–48; Francoise Meltzer, *Hot Property: The Stakes and Claims of Literary Originality* (Chicago: University of Chicago Press, 1994), esp. 1–7; Susan Stewart, *Crimes of Writing: Problems in the Containment of Representation* (Oxford: Oxford University Press, 1991), esp. 3–30. On the slightly later emergence of Italian copyright law, see *Manuale enciclopedico della bibliofilia*, ed. V. Di Giuro (Milan: Bonnard, 1997), 70–2.

55. Interestingly, Ruthven points out that behind the use of the economic metaphor for writing often lurks an anxiety about the origin of writing and the possibility of counterfeiting it, *Faking Literature*, 49.

56. 'La tragedia' is also an apposite text to examine in relation to *Suo marito* because of its various sources and anticipations: it was preceded by the 1906 *novella* 'Personaggi' and was followed by a similar metafictional *novella*, 'Colloquio coi personaggi' (1915). It also famously anticipates the metafictional device of the paratextual 'Prefazione' to *Sei personaggi* (added in 1925). Daniela Bini also examines 'La tragedia' in conjunction with *Suo marito* , but as part of a discussion on artistic creation, which I shall address later: see 'La creazione artistica come sconfitta della morte', 239–40. See also 'Illustratori, attori e traduttori', where Pirandello writes of the characters who leap from the pages of a book 'vivi innanzi a noi, nella nostra stanza' (*Spsv* 214).

57. 'Da lontano', in *Spsv* 1067–8; for the dialogues with Paulo Post, see 'Feminismo' [*sic*] (1909) and 'Ricomincio a vedere l'Europa' (1909), in *Spsv* 1068–75.

58. 'What is an author?', 159.

59. See 'Una spazzola' and 'I filatori', in *Spsv* 1060–1. 'Per la prossima estate' (*Spsv* 808) is a polemic against literary imitation of French trends and takes aim at D'Annunzio amongst others; it anticipates the later essays 'Un critico fantastico' (1905) and 'Teatro nuovo e teatro vecchio' (1922), which repeat some of it verbatim.

60. On the Romantic myth of the original genius see N. Fruman, 'Originality, plagiarism, forgery and romanticism', *Centrum* 4/1 (1976), 44–9; Thomas McFarland, *Originality and Imagination* (Baltimore: Johns Hopkins University Press, 1985); Jack Stillinger, *Multiple Authorship and the Myth of Solitary Genius* (Oxford: Oxford University Press, 1991), esp. 3–24.

61. Macchia, 'Introduzione' to *Tutti i romanzi*, *Tr* I, p. xlviiii.

62. Nick Groom, 'Forgery or plagiarism?', *Angelaki* 1–2 (1993–4), 41–51 at 51. Linda Hutcheon makes a similar point when she charges that 'perhaps only in a

Romantic (and capitalist?) context where individuality and originality define art can the "borrowing" from other texts be considered plagiarism—or "stealing"; 'Literary borrowing... and stealing: plagiarism, sources, influences, and intertexts', *English Studies in Canada* 12/2 (1986), 229–39 at 234. Croce, however, rejects the idea of plagiarism on the grounds that the content of a book is purely ideal: 'il plagio non esiste [...] chi si appropria un'opera letteraria altrui, non muta in nulla l'essenza di quell'opera, che resta quella che è, di qualunque autore sia segnato'; *Problemi di estetica* (Bari: Laterza, 1910), 68. What price then Pirandello's oft-repeated 'signature' passages from 'L'umorismo' in this context?

63. 'Bricolage' is Macchia's term for the construction of 'L'umorismo': cf. 'Introduzione', p. xiv.

64. Antoine Compagnon, *La seconde main ou le travail de la citation* (Paris: Seuil, 1979), 19 and 16. This definition of course reminds us of Julia Kristeva's work on intertextuality, in which the concept of 'écriture' as 'lecture' produces a text which is a 'mosaic of quotations; any text is the absorption and transformation of another'; *Desire in Language*, trans. Thomas Gora, Alice Jardine and Leon S. Roudiez (Oxford: Blackwell, 1993), 54. Kristeva remarks of quotations that 'they are carried intact from their own space into the space of the novel being written; they are transcribed within quotation marks or they are plagiarised', which again raises the question of what is in between quotation and plagiarism.

65. On questions of textual authority and priority raised by quotation, see Mary Orr, *Intertextuality: Debates and Contexts* (Oxford: Polity, 2003), 130–7.

66. Barilli, *La linea Svevo-Pirandello*, 159. Macchia calls the phenomenon 'una sorta d'intercomunicabilità a lungo raggio tra un genere e un altro'; *Pirandello o la stanza della tortura*, 24.

67. The slippage between the names Dr Fileno and Paulo Post reflects a more generalized Pirandellian ambiguity with regard to the proper name and their relation to fictional characters and forms part of a broader critical discussion on the ability of proper names in fiction to refer; Annie Thomasson asks if Sherlock Holmes is always the same character in each Conan Doyle novel or if we must 'speak of many different Holmeses, each the Holmes of a particular work'; *Fiction and Metaphysics* (Cambridge: Cambridge University Press, 1997), 61. Similarly, Gérard Genette refers to what he calls the 'pseudoreference' of the fictional text which pretends to assert something—the fictional name would thus be a pseudoreferential one, as Genette says: 'If Napoleon designates an actual member of the human race, "Sherlock Holmes" and "Gilberte Swann" designate no-one outside Doyle's text or Proust's'; *Fiction and Diction*, trans. C. Porter (Ithaca: Cornell University Press, 1993), 25–6.

68. Pavel, *Fictional Worlds*, 16.

69. Ibid. 123. Annie Thomasson suggests that 'describing fictional characters as "here" in a work of literature is at best metaphorical. It is to mistake the abstract literary work, which has no spatiotemporal location, with its concrete copies, which do'; *Fiction and Metaphysics*, 37.

70. Daniela Bini also quotes this passage as an example of Pirandello's affirmation of the 'superiority of art over nature'; 'La creazione artistica', 52. On birth imagery in Pirandello, see M. Jean Lacroix, 'La *novella* pirandelliana come maieutica della personalità', in E. Lauretta (ed.), *La 'persona' nell'opera di Pirandello* (Milan: Mursia, 1990), 205–20.

71. Borsellino, *Ritratto*, 54–5.
72. See also Granatella, 'Proposta per una lettura del mito maternocentrico'.
73. This point has been widely discussed by critics: see, in particular, Daniela Bini on 'l'incompatibilità tra maternità e arte' in Pirandello in 'La creazione artistica', 237; also Giovanna Tomasello, 'La donna ne *La nuova colonia*', in *La donna in Pirandello*, 57–63, on Pirandello's ambivalent representations of maternity.
74. Cited in *Carteggi inediti*, ed. Zappulla Muscarà, 148.
75. Ibid. 17.
76. Gösta Andersson has succinctly demonstrated the influence of Séailles on Pirandello's ideas of art as conception and organic growth; see *Arte e teoria*, 180–2.
77. Compagnon, *La seconde main*, 29.
78. Jacques Derrida, 'The double séance', in *Dissemination*, trans. B. Johnson (London: Athlone, 1997), 202.
79. Jonathan Culler, *On Deconstruction* (London: Routledge, 1983), 135. Derrida quotes Gaston Bachelard to the effect that 'It is the graft that can transmit the variety and density of matter to the formal imagination. It forces the seedling to flower and gives matter to the flower. In a completely nonmetaphorical sense, the production of a poetic work requires that there be a union between a dreaming activity and an ideating activity. Art is grafted nature'; 'The double séance', 203. On the contradiction in Pirandello between the 'organic' ideal of art and the textual practice of self-quotation, see Vicentini, 'I "furti" di Pirandello', 46.
80. Compagnon notes that 'la citation met en correspondance deux systèmes sémiotiques'; *La seconde main*, 359.
81. 'Bricolage', as I mentioned, is Giovanni Macchia's term for Pirandello's oeuvre; Sarah Zappulla Muscarà talks of how 'tutta l'opera pirandelliana può paragonarsi ad un complessivo lavoro d'incastro, quasi la composizione e la scomposizione di un singolarmente fantasioso *puzzle*'; *Carteggi inediti*, 131. Several critics casually use the word 'innesto' to describe Pirandello's practice of quotation, but they do not follow it up: Antonio Illiano talks of Pirandello's use of 'l'arte e la tecnica (o "retorica") della citazione come innesto vivo nel vivo tessuto della narrazione'; *Metapsichica e letteratura in Pirandello*, 61.
82. On *L'innesto*, see particularly Daniela Bini, 'Woman as creator: Pirandello's *L'innesto*', *Pirandello Studies* 17 (1997), 34–45 and Roberto Alonge, 'Madri, puttane, schiave sessuali e uomini soli', esp. 100–5.

CHAPTER 5

'Non Conclude'?:
Uno, nessuno e centomila and the
Dangers of Overinterpretation

In Chapter 4 I highlighted the importance of studying the text's composition and production, identifying these as central to any discussion of its formal and thematic concerns, and pointed out the need to unite an examination of the editorial practice and publishing history of Pirandello's novel with a critical discussion of it. Examining the text as both an ideal and a material creation inevitably brings into question the status of the author as producer of the text, and interrogates the links between publication, the manipulation of the text after publication, and the spontaneity of the writing act. I would like to extend this type of dual focus to Pirandello's last novel, *Uno, nessuno e centomila*, the third in his 'trilogy' of first-person narrator novels, after *Il fu Mattia Pascal* in 1904 and *Si gira!* (1915–16) (published in 1925 as *Quaderni di Serafino Gubbio*).

Uno, nessuno e centomila is a text which has, paradoxically, been both over- and underinterpreted: it has been overinterpreted in the sense that critics have devoted much attention to it and to its status as a *summa* of Pirandellian thought, and underinterpreted in the sense that there has not yet been a reading of it which satisfactorily considers the textual issues I will raise as crucial to the novel's form and meaning. If the problems of textuality regarding *Suo marito* (and, to a lesser extent, *I vecchi e i giovani*) concerned textual revisions post-publication, at issue in *Uno, nessuno e centomila*'s tortuous journey towards publication are three related ideas: the first is the question of authorship, with Pirandello as not only the producer of the written text, but also the privileged pronouncer on the status and meaning of that text, who (over)determines its critical reception and attempts to fix its meaning. These ideas of authorship are intriguingly interrogated and undercut within the novel by the novel's own processes, as the problematic 'authorship' of Moscarda, narrator and producer of his material text, takes centre stage. Moscarda also seems, at times, uncertain what kind of text he is writing: confessional autobiography, *giallo*, or hagiographical conversion narrative, and this generic uncertainty is mirrored by the text's material instability, composed as it is of discrete fragments of other texts.

The second idea is the related one of readership, and principally that of the 'real' reader, in Wolfgang Iser's terminology, represented in the critical reception of Pirandello's novel by professional (and amateur) critics. I will examine the extent to which these 'public' responses are guided by Pirandello's paratextual authorial pronouncements (both public and private); I will argue that such responses have produced, virtually since the novel's first publication, a series of autobiographical and teleological readings, seemingly authorized by Pirandello himself, and will address these filiations between authorial paratexts and critical descriptions of the work. The responses of these 'real' readers merge intriguingly with the 'intradiegetic' reader, the figure of the reader inscribed within the novel and addressed by Moscarda.[1]

Thirdly, there is the problem of the text itself, and its relationship to the texts which precede it: before the novel's 'definitive' publication in serial form in *La fiera letteraria* in 1925–6, and in volume by Bemporad in 1926, Pirandello had already published several articles and *novelle* in which sections of text appear which are later repeated in the novel. This replication of material accords with Pirandello's sustained practice of 'self-plagiarism', and I will discuss the need for an interpretative strategy capable of coming to terms with the movement of material between *Uno, nessuno* and other texts.

I will also examine the problematic finale of *Uno, nessuno e centomila*, the chapter entitled 'Non conclude', which has puzzled critics since its publication: my reading of this chapter will be filtered through the framework of my earlier discussions of epiphany and metaphor, and intends to resituate this complex passage as central to both of those themes.

The Gestation of *Uno, nessuno e centomila*

As was the case with *Suo marito* (and as is the case with all of Pirandello's works), identifying a moment of definitive origin or inception of the composition of *Uno, nessuno e centomila* is difficult, primarily because there is no surviving complete manuscript, but rather a series of undated handwritten 'foglietti', which represent different stages of the novel's elaboration.[2] These fragmentary 'foglietti' do not themselves throw up new insights into the completed novel, but, as Mario Costanzo has noted, their very paucity has encouraged critics to focus attention instead on Pirandello's own pronouncements about the text, creating an imbalance between the critical attention devoted to the composition of the text and that devoted to unthinkingly reproducing *loci communes* about the novel.[3] The projected composition of *Uno, nessuno e centomila* is narrated by Pirandello in a series of declarations, both public and private, of his intentions. This narration of the novel's gestation (and that suggested by the various *novelle* which also seem to 'narrate' its composition) should be read with extreme care, in order to avoid the highly problematic series of critical assumptions which have dominated critical responses to the novel, assumptions based on questionable ideas of authorial intention, autobiography and chronology.

The first recorded mention by Pirandello of his projected novel was in 1910, in a letter to Massimo Bontempelli: 'Se sapesse in quale tetraggine io mi sento avviluppato senza più speranza di scampo! Lo vedrà dal mio prossimo romanzo: *Monarda* [*sic*] – *Uno, nessuno e centomila*.'[4] Already the novel is talked of by its author as constituting a literary reflection of Pirandello's difficult autobiographical situation of those years. This impression of the exemplary status of *Uno, nessuno e centomila* within Pirandello's oeuvre gains momentum when Pirandello writes in his 'Lettera autobiografica', which was published in 1924 in *Le lettere*, although written around 1911 or 1912: 'E un altro romanzo ho anche per le mani, il più amaro di tutti, profondamente umoristico, di scomposizone della vita: *Moscarda, uno, nessuno e centomila* uscirà su la fine di quest'anno nella *Nuova antologia*.'[5] The novel has thus already undergone its first pre-publication title change. As Pirandello indicates in this letter, which is, after all, a public manifestation of a private genre, the composition of some parts of *Uno, nessuno* is thus roughly contemporaneous with that of *I vecchi e i giovani* ('ora attendo a compiere il vasto romanzo *I vecchi e i giovani*').[6]

The laborious gestation of *Uno, nessuno e centomila*, accompanying as it does the most significant period of Pirandello's literary career, when he achieved widespread theatrical recognition, means that the text has been accorded the status of 'bilancio teorico' of Pirandello's work (in the words of Claudio Vicentini):[7] thus critical opinion has tended to assume that the novel is an elaboration of 'L'umorismo'. This is the central point of Marziano Guglielminetti's argument when he states that the novel was 'deputato a soddisfare il programma dell'arte umoristica'.[8] Pirandello encouraged such an interpretation in 1919, when he assigned a paradigmatic or exemplary value to the novel, describing it as a 'specie di formula filosofica': 'Sto ora ultimando un romanzo che avrebbe dovuto uscire prima di tutte le mie commedie. Si sarebbe forse avuta una visione più esatta del mio teatro. In questo romanzo c'è la sintesi più completa di tutto ciò che ho fatto e la sorgente di quello che farò.'[9] This 'monumental' aspect of *Uno, nessuno e centomila* is highlighted by Pirandello in a letter to Nino Martoglio in the same year: 'son tornato a scriver novelle e a dar fine al mio romanzo *testamentario*'.[10] The etymology of 'testament', from the Latin 'testari', interestingly includes both the meaning of 'to bear witness' and to 'register', containing both the sense of subjective, personal expression and objective affirmation that something happened. The idea of the novel as epitaph or summation for posterity of his work was obviously one which attracted Pirandello: he himself places the author figure firmly at the centre of the debate surrounding the novel, and also introduces the problem of intentionalism into the critical debates on *Uno, nessuno*, producing an interpretation of the novel in which authorship and autobiography are difficult to separate.

In a 1924 interview Pirandello refers to the novel as the last word on (or of) his narrative production : 'ho scritto, inoltre, un romanzo: *Uno, nessuno e centomila*. Esso comprende il significato e l'essenza di tutta l'opera mia. Sarà come il mio testamento letterario, dopo la sua pubblicazione dovrei tacere per sempre.'[11] It is worth examining the dual aspects of such self-positioning and explication of this text: on the one hand, the novel is presented as being the last word pronounced on Pirandello's novelistic production and, on the other, as a seemingly paradoxical mixture of 'sintesi' and 'sorgente', of synthesis and source: this position, which would point both backwards and forwards, inscribes the roots of Pirandello's narrative trajectory within its would-be conclusion, and presents *Uno, nessuno* as both a paraphrase of Pirandello's previous work and as containing within it the seeds of a putative palingenesis. The conflation of 'sintesi' and 'sorgente' also suggests (as well as a tension between synchrony and diachrony) the problem of identifying origins in Pirandello's narrative, a problem which will be mirrored within the text. The confusion of origin and *telos* is a remarkably Pirandellian characteristic, as each work (or passage, or character) hints at its buried predecessors and successors.

The importance of the position occupied by *Uno, nessuno e centomila* within Pirandello's oeuvre is confirmed by what the author had said in the interview 'Conversando con Pirandello' two years earlier in 1922: 'Avrebbe dovuto essere il proemio della mia produzione teatrale e ne sarà, invece, un epilogo. È il romanzo della scomposizione della personalità. Esso giunge alle conclusioni più lontane, alle conseguenze più estreme.'[12] Pirandello reiterates this view in 1925, substituting for the purely chronological view of *Uno, nessuno e centomila*'s delayed appearance a more profound reflection on the novel's belatedness, saying of Moscarda, 'questo personaggio doveva annunziare i grandi personaggi del mio teatro e ne è oggi, di essi, soltanto l'eco', again confusing origin and echo.[13] The evolution and metamorphosis of *Uno, nessuno e centomila* from *Monarda* to the version published 'a puntate' in the *Fiera letteraria* in 1925–6 with the Sternian title *Considerazioni di Vitangelo Moscarda, generali sulla vita degli uomini e particolari sulla propria, in otto libri*, is thus accompanied by Pirandello's auto-commentary and autointerpretation. This latter seems to exclude any interpretation of the novel other than a purely intentionalist one, since Pirandello's paratextual comments exhibit a desire for the novel to be read as closure to a narrative programme, viewed teleologically as having an inevitable endpoint in this novel.

The autobiographical reading of this work, while encouraged by Pirandello's statements, seems to have been authorized first by Stefano Pirandello in his 1925 Preface to his father's novel in the *Fiera letteraria*, where he figures it as a personal and spiritual testimony:

Non hai scritto. Hai esercitato il tuo spirito, come in atti di vita. *Uno, nessuno e centomila* [...] è la storia della tua vittoriosa tragedia di uomo-fanciullo, schietto e sano, posto a contatto con la forma più perfetta [...] della vita, con il caos perpetuo veloce creatore e distruttore di realtà momentanee: mia madre pazza. È tutto sperimentato e sofferto. È tutto saggiato.[14]

In the last chapter, I discussed Stefano Pirandello's editorial intervention in the 1941 edition of *Suo marito*; in this preface (written under the pseudonym Stefano Landi, with which he signed his journalistic and fictional output), Stefano composes a strikingly intimate address to his father, detailing the anguished composition of *Uno, nessuno e centomila*, an address which is all the more striking

because of the public situation of prefatorial communication in which
it is presented. Stefano's reading of the novel implicitly unites life and
work: 'Quando ti mancò la stima di chi tu ami, e il suo amore, e
l'amicizia degli uomini, la comprensione dei tuoi atti, quando ti
sentisti [...] povero, nudo, solo e non sapevi più bene chi eri perché ti
sentivi uno spirito senza volto, con mille volti, allora possedesti te
stesso come un pazzo, come un eroe, come un santo' (*Tr* II, 1060).
This interpretation, in which Pirandello's situation is seen to mirror
Moscarda's, has proved influential in conditioning critical reception to
the novel. Stefano also attributes to the novel an exemplary (and
rather vague) ethical significance: 'Chi creda a questo libriccino potrà
seguire una delle tante vie d'attività ch'esso apre allo spirito, e sarà
sempre un uomo. È un buon libro per noi italiani d'oggi' (*Tr*
II,1060).[15] The other significant critical response to the novel, which
can be read alongside both Stefano's and his father's pronouncements
on it, is that of Adriano Tilgher, the theatrical critic whose tangled
relationship with Pirandello provides a fascinating insight into the
nexus of relations between Pirandello and his critics. Tilgher's
'construction' of Pirandello in his 1922 essay 'Il teatro di Pirandello'
presented an idea of 'pirandellismo' centred on the relation between
'Vita' and 'Forma'.[16] What interests me here, however, is the
intriguing possibility that Tilgher's essay was inspired by a reading of
Uno, nessuno e centomila: Tilgher charts the progress of Pirandello's
works, ascribing to them a 'magnifico movimento ascensionale'.[17]
This 'ascensional' movement manifests itself, according to the critic,
in a desire for a climactic work: 'Come tutta l'opera di Pirandello
aspira al teatro, così tutto il teatro di lui aspira a un'opera perfetta che
totalmente esprima l'intuizione pirandelliana della vita: piramide
aspirante a una punta che risolva e comprenda in sé tutto ciò che è al
di sotto di lei.'[18] The hypothesis that Tilgher's essay (which,
intriguingly, is full of quotations from 'L'umorismo') was written after
he saw a draft of *Uno, nessuno* is provided by Pirandello: in 1927
Pirandello wrote in a letter to Silvio D'Amico: 'Vi basti sapere che
Tilgher lesse nel MS *Uno, nessuno e centomila* prima di scrivere il suo
saggio; e che tutto quello che in questo saggio è scritto era stato
scritto prima da me, con le stesse stessissime parole nei miei romanzi
e in tante e tante novelle.'[19] This competition over ownership and
genesis of Pirandello's ideas (reminiscent of *Suo marito*), alludes to the
possibility that Tilgher's immensely influential, teleological reading of
Pirandello, which sets the stage for *Uno, nessuno* as Pirandello's

'climactic'work, is produced by a reading of the novel, or may even have contributed to its creation.

To a large extent then, critical consensus on *Uno, nessuno e centomila* has reflected the self-image projected by Pirandello of his novel as a summary of his humoristic and novelistic technique.[20] Such critical opinion also reads Pirandello's oeuvre from its endpoint and implicitly ascribes to his narrative output a retrospective trajectory of evolution or maturation, ending in a conclusive closure, a movement belied by the process of revision, self-quotation and copy which I have described, and by the problematic and fragmentary nature of *Uno, nessuno e centomila* itself as a text which, by 1926, had already appeared in various other contexts. The most interesting of these appearances was the publication of Book 2, chapters 6–11 as the article 'Ricostruire' in 1915 in the journal *Sapientia*.[21] There are also borrowings from *novelle* including 'Quand'ero matto' and 'Canta l'epistola', the earliest of which dates back to 1900. My own critical approach aims to examine the publishing and editorial history of the novel and its 'precursors' in a way which does not attempt to give priority to earlier or later versions of the text, and which aims instead, by taking into consideration all drafts and variants of a text, to illuminate its prehistory, its journey from conception to execution. The concomitant idea of restoring the concept of the text as openness, of conceptualizing it as a process of becoming and progression, interlinks with the fragmentary status of writing in *Uno, nessuno* and explodes the idealist conception of the work of art as intuition (an interpretation which lingers in some mainstream criticism). As Vittore Branca remarks apropos Italy's 'nuova filologia': 'la così detta "poesia" è un continuo divenire, una lenta e faticata conquista, e non un essere opposto assolutamente a un non essere, non una folgorante rivelazione che scoppia in un buio assoluto.'[22]

The 'Scomposizione' of Narrator, Author and Character

There are various ways in which these critical questions regarding the text's fragmentary nature, its position as 'exemplary' endpoint towards which all of Pirandello's narrative inevitably tends, are enacted within the text itself. I will begin by citing Guglielminetti's observation on what he considers the specificity and uniqueness of *Uno, nessuno*'s project of 'scomposizione', when he claims that the evidence of the textual borrowings from 'L'umorismo' present in the novel 'esclude però che un altro romanzo potesse sin da allora essere deputato a soddisfare il programma dell'arte umoristica'.[23] This insistence on *Uno, nessuno*'s project of 'scomposizione' itself draws upon the vocabulary of *umorismo*, and, specifically, Pirandello's closing prescription regarding the characteristics of the truly 'humoristic' work of art:

Di qui, nell'umorismo, tutta quella ricerca dei particolari più intimi e minuti, che possono anche parer volgari e triviali se si raffrontano con le sintesi idealizzatrici dell'arte in genere, e quella ricerca dei contrasti e delle contradizioni, su cui l'opera sua si fonda, in opposizione alla coerenza cercata dagli altri; di qui quel che di scomposto, di slegato, di capriccioso, tutte quelle digressioni che si notano nell'opera umoristica, in opposizione al congegno ordinato, alla *composizione* dell'opera d'arte in genere. (*Spsv* 159)

In Guglielminetti's view, the project of humoristic digression and disruption translates into *Uno, nessuno*'s narrative 'scomposizione'. The novel's structure certainly mirrors that of the discourse of its protagonist Moscarda, as he embarks upon his project of auto-destruction ('esperimento della distruzione d'un Moscarda'; *Tr* II, 97), which leads ultimately to his aphasia and marginalization at the end of the novel, alone and nameless.[24]

Moscarda aims to 'destroy' himself as narrator, as author, and as literary character. As narrator, he exposes the unreliability of his own narrative processes, and the novel dramatizes, through its narrative techniques, the arduous production of literary meaning.

The dramatization of the production of literary meaning as frequently unsuccessful toil (antithetical to the idea of the creative act as an act of spontaneous inspiration) occurs primarily in Book 2: here, the themes of linguistic incomprehension, digression and narrative breakdown come together in the chapter entitled 'Con permesso?', which is structured as a digression from the main body of the text. The chapter playfully parodies through literalizing it the nineteenth-century device of authorial intrusion into the text as the self-consciously faithless narrator ('non dico che possiate fidarvi molto di me'; *Tr* II, 772) crosses over into the space of the reader and stands on the threshold of the reader's 'room': 'Picchio all'uscio della vostra stanza' (*Tr* II, 767). He then leads the reader by the hand into the time and space of the novel: 'via, via, aspettate che vi dia una mano per tirarvi sù. Siete grasso, voi. Aspettate: su la schiena v'è rimasto qualche filo d'erba' (*Tr* II, 776) and dispenses kindly warnings: 'Strada brecciata; e attenti alle scaglie. E quelle sono fanali.' This figuring of the 'world' of the narrative as one into which the reader can literally enter occurs as a parody of the trope of authorial intrusion, and indeed the entire chapter is a concentrated parody of the tropes of the realist novel. The episode also enacts the negotiation of the production of a mutually agreed meaning between narrator and 'narratee' as an agreement which could be compromised at any time, and as an obvious parallel with the relation between narrator and extradiegetic reader.[25]

It is in such episodes that Moscarda's inability to be a narrator is emphasized, as the character thematizes the failure of language to be understood, enacting in his dialogue with the reader the problems inherent in the act of reading itself. Moscarda's discourse is fragile, as we see when he echoes the words of the Padre in *Sei personaggi*: 'Abbiamo usato, io e voi, la stessa lingua, le stesse parole. Ma che colpa abbiamo, io e voi, se le parole per sé sono vuote? Vuote, caro mio. E voi le riempite del senso vostro' (*Tr* II, 769).[26] Moscarda's conscientious attempts to establish a bilateral understanding between himself and his listener only serve to underline the fragility of any such understanding, and foreground the difficulty of the reader's task: 'Ah, quei monti azzurri lontani! Dico "azzurri"; anche voi dite "azzurri", non è vero? D'accordo. E questo qua vicino, col bosco di castagni: castagni, no? vedete, vedete come c'intendiamo? della famiglia delle cupulifere, d'alto fusto. Castagno marrone. Che vasto pianura davanti ("verde", eh? per voi e per me "verde": diciamo così, che c'intendiamo a maraviglia)' (*Tr* II, 773).

Moscarda's role as reliable narrator is undermined by his narrative itself: he is constantly declaring that his discourse is a repeated one, a 'storia vecchia' as he says twice (*Tr* II, 768 and 769). He is continually recapitulating what he said earlier, for example: 'Non m'ero visto io stesso sulla strada maestra della pazzia incamminato a compiere un atto che agli occhi di tutti doveva apparire appunto contrario a me stesso e incoerente, ponendo fuori di me la mia volontà, come un fazzoletto che mi cavassi di tasca?' (*Tr* II, 858). This is a recap of what Moscarda had earlier declared, before the beginning of his 'esperimento' (and a conflation of two earlier passages): 'Seguitavo a camminare, come vedete, con perfetta coscienza su la strada maestra della pazzia, ch'era la strada appunto della mia realtà' (*Tr* II, 820) and 'andavo a porre graziosamente la mia volontà fuori di me, come un fazzoletto che mi cavassi di tasca' (*Tr* II, 813). In fact, Moscarda is a very bad storyteller, despite his frequent attempts to control his narrative, giving away either too much or too little information: 'Ma non anticipiamo'

(*Tr* II, 814) or 'come vedrete' (*Tr* II,785) or 'andiamo avanti' (*Tr* II, 806). It is thus ironic that a novel featuring such an inept narrator (and an author who implicitly rejects his right to authorship) should be read as a *summa* of Pirandellian thought.

Moscarda, significantly, is not merely the narrator of his text, but is also presented as its (self-deprecating) author: 'mentre stavate a leggere questo mio libretto col sorriso un po' canzonatorio che fin da principio ha accompagnato la vostra lettura' (*Tr* II, 804), 'Sù, sù, tornate a leggere questo mio libretto, senza più sorridere come avete fatto finora' (*Tr* II, 806). The confusion between authorial and narrative roles demonstrates Pirandello's dismantling of the authorial role within the text. Moscarda the unreliable narrator confuses himself further with the authorial voice by appropriating the novel's paratextual indices as part of his own discourse: these paratextual indices include the 'intertitoli', which are both inside and outside the text, both previewing and reviewing it, for example the proleptic 'oggi vi fissate in un modo e domani in un altro. Vi dirò poi come e perché', immediately followed by the chapter heading '*Anzi, ve lo dico adesso*' (*Tr* II, 770).[27] Similarly, the narrator's interior monologue is confused with the traditional authorial function of the intertitle, as in Moscarda's title to Book 4, chapter 7, '*Ma io intanto dicevo tra me:*', in which the entire chapter is rendered in brackets (*Tr* II, 848). On another occasion the intertitles announce and enact the parenthesis, in Book 3, chapter 7, '*Parentesi necessaria, una per tutti*', which is followed by '*Chiudiamo la parentesi*'. Gérard Genette says of intertitles that they 'establish the narrator-hero as someone with not only narrative authority but also literary authority, as an author responsible for putting together, managing and presenting the text and aware of his relation to the public'.[28] Ironically, the authority with which Moscarda invests himself is used by him in order to undo his narrative authority: the recurring lists, intertitles and even the appearance of a footnote at one point, all challenge the textual hierarchy which assigns certain spaces to the narrative voice.[29] At the end of the novel (which is, after all, his fictional autobiography), Moscarda renounces his name (or rather names, as he is both Vitangelo and Gengè, his wife's pet name for him) with the words 'nessun nome' (*Tr* II, 901), in an act of renunciation and revolt against the name as totalizing emblem of identity and individuality.[30] The play with the power of the proper name as a token of referential stability is a constant in Pirandello's work,[31] from Mattia Pascal's self-baptism as Adriano Meis to the

pseudonymic game of Dr Fileno and Paulo Post and it becomes
central to the discourse of Moscarda, as he oscillates between
character, narrator and author of his text, which both depends upon
and subverts the conventions of autobiography as testimony.[32]
Moscarda also describes himself as 'stipulante', the agreeing party to a
contract, a contract which is, above all, a narrative one: yet his
narrating contract with the reader is the antithesis of that famously
proposed by Philippe Lejeune where the 'autobiographical pact' is
predicated on the stability of the proper name.[33] Moscarda instead
parodies such an idea of an unproblematic factual continuity between
narrator and character. Moscarda's rejection of his name is thus also a
refusal to be a literary 'character'; it contests the unproblematic
equivalence of name and essence which fiction habitually posits.
Moscarda had already done this in the novel: 'Io infine non ero quel
nome, che quel nome era per gli altri un modo di chiamarmi, non
bello ma che avrebbe potuto tuttavia essere anche più brutto. Non
c'era forse un Sardo a Richieri che si chiamava Porcu? Sì. – Signor
Porcu... E non rispondeva mica con un grugnito. – Eccomi, a
servirla...' (*Tr* II, 788). The proper name is also a guarantor of the
'author-function', central to Michel Foucault's argument which
asserts the role of the author as proprietor and possessor of his texts:
'an author's name is not simply an element in a discourse (capable of
being either subject or object, of being replaced by a pronoun, and
the like); it performs a certain role with regard to narrative discourse,
assuring a classificatory function. Such a name permits one to group
together a certain number of texts, define them, differentiate them
from and contrast them to others.'[34]

Moscarda is the narrator and 'author' of his text, but is also, of
course, a character in it. Consonant with the text's dismantling of the
authorial and narrative apparatus, there is a progressive undoing of the
idea of literary 'character'. Moscarda 'creates' himself as a character:
just as the crucial scene in *Il fu Mattia Pascal* has Mattia rebaptize
himself as Adriano Meis, so in *Uno, nessuno e centomila* there is a pivotal
moment when Moscarda baptizes his specular image, when he first
sees it as distinct from himself, as a symbol of his own alterity:
'"Moscarda", mormorai, dopo un lungo silenzio. Era là, come un
cane sperduto, senza padrone e senza nome, che uno poteva chiamare
Flik, e un altro *Flok*, a piacere [...] non conosceva nulla, né si
conosceva [...] E in quella testa lì, immobile e dura, potevo mettere
tutti i pensieri che volevo' (*Tr* II, 756). Moscarda here, as an author-

narrator and hero, is represented as a tabula rasa, without history, ideas or language and without any existence before the novel, waiting to be inscribed with knowledge by his 'creator'. This act of naming parodies the concept of novelistic character itself, as a creation *ex nihilo*: hence Marchesini's idea of the self as purely metaphorical, extended by Pirandello in the metaliterary poetics of *Suo marito* and 'La tragedia d'un personaggio', is here brought to completion as we see firstly the moment of parodic 'creation' of the character and later its willed dissolution, in Moscarda's 'nessun nome' as he escapes to the margins of his own discourse, into aphasia, renouncing the name which marks out and individuates his character.

The role of the author here is that of originator and creator, one who initiates or invents: Pirandello's paradoxical conception of authorship, in which a preoccupation with originality and beginnings is undercut by processes of revision, plagiarism and repetition, will be exemplified in the repetitive prose of Moscarda, the 'new' character and author. Edward Said has discussed the concept of authorship and originality, arguing that the 'author' is:

the person who originates or gives existence to something, a begetter, beginner, father or ancestor, a person who also sets forth written statements. There is still another cluster of meanings: *author* is tied to the past participle *auctus* of the verb *augere*, therefore *auctor* [...] is literally an increaser and thus a founder. *Auctoritas* is production, invention, cause, in addition to meaning a right of possession.[35]

These twin concepts are crucial to my reading of *Uno, nessuno e centomila*: Moscarda the founder of his text, of himself (within a text founded by Pirandello) at the end renounces his right to own possessions ('facendo dono di tutto, anche della casa e d'ogni altro mio avere, per fondare con quanto mi sarebbe toccato dalla liquidazione della banca un ospizio di mendicità'; *Tr* II, 899) and also his right to authorship and to the status of character. Incapable of asserting his authorial authority, aware of the repetitive nature of all that he says ('io non ho la pretesa di dirvi niente di nuovo'; *Tr* II, 768, and 'Io non pretendo dir niente di nuovo'; *Tr* II, 769), in renouncing material possessions and capital he is also renouncing the right to be identified as the author of his discourse—as I will discuss in the final section, he ultimately loses the 'rights' to his tale, in accordance with the idea of the author-function in which the author's name is inseparable from its economic and juridical status:

Se il nome è la cosa; se un nome è in noi il concetto d'ogni cosa posta fuori di noi; e senza nome non si ha il concetto, e la cosa resta in noi come cieca, non distinta e non definita; ebbene, questo che portai tra gli uomini ciascuno lo incida, epigrafe funeraria, sulla fronte di quella immagine con cui gli apparvi, e la lasci in pace e non ne parli più. (*Tr* II, 901)

As well as asserting the semantic fragility of his spoken discourse, Moscarda's narrative ultimately insists that written language is inadequate to convey his experiences. The printed word as chronicle of history or biography, the founding *logos* of history and narrative, is revealed to be unstable, as Moscarda deliberately undoes his narrative:

Ah, il piacere della storia, signori! Nulla più riposante della storia. Tutto nella vita vi cangia continuamente sotto gli occhi; nulla di certo [...] Tutto determinato, tutto stabilito, all'incontro, nella storia: per quanto dolorose le vicende e tristi i casi, eccolì lì, ordinati, almeno, fissati in 30, 40 paginette di libro: quelli e lì, che non cangeranno mai più almeno fino a tanto che un malvagio spirito critico non avrà la mala contentezza di buttare all'aria quella costruzione ideale, ove tutti gli elementi si tenevano a vicenda [...] e ogni avvenimento si svolgeva preciso e coerente in ogni suo particolare, col signor duca di Nevers, che il giorno tale, anno tale ecc ecc. (*Tr* II, 817–18)

This is precisely what Moscarda will do in the bank in the next chapter, when he upsets and disorders all the legal papers documenting his life: 'tutto ormai ingombro di carte ammonticchiate e con un'altra pila di carte io stesso qua sulle ginocchie' (*Tr* II, 830). This humoristic plea for the disruption of narrative chronology and the disordering of narrative order is emphasized by its anticipation of the events of the next scene. The 'piacere della storia' is also the pleasure of the linear plot, disordered in the narration of it given by Moscarda, the 'malvagio spirito critico'. It represents the pleasure of a complete symbolic reading, a pleasure which will be denied to readers of Moscarda's text. Such metaliterary concerns also identify Moscarda's upheaval of the papers purporting to narrate his life as a metaphor for *Uno, nessuno e centomila* itself, the unitary text which proves itself to be, on closer examination, a jumble of papers of differing dates and provenance, a series of incomplete fragments.

Moscarda is also uncertain what kind of text he is writing or narrating, this generic confusion matching the text's material instability: in Book 4 as well as Book 7, the 'piacere della storia' becomes problematic as the narrative experiments even more with the pleasure of the (linear) plot. Moscarda sets his narrative up as two

conflicting types of narrative, incorporating other generic conventions, firstly those of the conversion narrative. This is evidenced by
the fact that the narrative is 'written' from its endpoint, from a present
of 'guarigione', so that it is retrospectively presented as a salvific
journey: Moscarda's 'via della salute' (*Tr* II, 814), his madness and his
search for 'il rimedio che doveva guarirmene' (*Tr* II, 742), institute a
teleological reading of the text as inevitable progression towards the
ecstatic mysticism of the conclusion. This is intensified in the
description of events in Books 4 and 7: Moscarda proclaims that he
has come to speak 'parole nuove!' (*Tr* II, 826) and visits the notary to
divest himself of his possessions in Via del Crocefisso (*Tr* II, 831),
before visiting Marco di Dio's house in Via dei Santi (*Tr* II, 834).
Moscarda's explanation that he is 'in attesa del miracolo: la mia
trasfigurazione' (*Tr* II, 833) completes the impression of this as an
Augustinian conversion narrative, centred around a revelation which
provokes a crisis and turning point in the protagonist. Moscarda's
'confessione' (*Tr* II, 898) to one of the two authority figures in Book
7, Don Antonio Sclepsis, is figured as an 'eroico ravvedimento' (*Tr* II,
899), a turning point which marks Moscarda's conversion and
'salvazione' (*Tr* II, 898). This revelation will be, as always in Pirandello,
frustratingly elliptical.

However, the same events are also and equally represented by
Moscarda as forming part of a *giallo*: in the mysterious sequence with
Anna Rosa in Book 7 in the gloomy crime scene of the Badia, and
during the two shootings which are explained in the vaguest terms,
Moscarda performs the dual roles of suspect and detective, seeking
(and giving) answers which are always insufficient. Anna Rosa's
'spiegazioni' of her attempt to kill Moscarda ('devono essere vere le
ragioni ch'ella poi disse in sua discolpa'; *Tr* II, 893) does nothing to
reveal what really happened: 'Non so precisamente come avvenne' (*Tr*
II 893). The 'official' explanation, propagated through the unreliable
source of local gossip in the free indirect style, attributes it to a 'crime
passionel': 'Io la tradivo; e solo per farmi bello agli occhi di quella
ragazza esaltata avevo protestato di non volere più che in paese mi si
chiamasse usuraio!' (*Tr* II, 898).[36] Moscarda's version of what happens
is contested by the official statements given to the judge, the other
representative of institutional discourses, by Anna Rosa ('se non avesse
assicurato con giuramento il giudice'; *Tr* II, 895) and Dida ('la
giustizia doveva già anche trovarsi in possesso d'una prima deposizione
di mia moglie'; *Tr* II, 895).

The judge attempts to prise a definitive statement from Moscarda to resolve this enigma: Anna Rosa has claimed that it was Moscarda's 'dangerous' discourse which led her to shoot him: 'non c'era stata veramente nessuna aggressione da parte mia, ma solo quel tale fascino involontariamente esercitato su lei con le mie curiosissime considerazioni della vita' (*Tr* II, 895). Moscarda refuses to repeat these 'considerazioni', which he claims not to remember ('parole che più non ricordo'; *Tr* II, 895) and offers the judge an alternative, transcendent explanation: 'Le mie considerazioni sulla vita? – Ah, signor giudice, – gli dissi – non è possibile, creda, ch'io gliele ripeta. Guardi qua! Guardi qua! E gli mostrai la coperta di lana verde, passandoci sopra delicatamente la mano' (*Tr* II, 897). The 'considerazioni' of Moscarda form the narrative itself (the original subtitle of the novel being, as is known, *Considerazioni di Vitangelo Moscarda, generali sulla vita degli uomini e particolari sulla propria, in otto libri*); the entire narrative is thus figured as bearing an inexpressible 'truth' whose revelation is impossible. The 'explanation' offered by Moscarda is not an explication, but rather the 'epiphanic' bedcover itself, a silent moment of simultaneity, which denies sequential narration, and anticipates the novel's final failure to narrate.

'La Rovina d'un romanzo': The 'Scomposizione' of the Text

Pirandello's statement that *Uno, nessuno e centomila* should have been the prologue to his theatrical production but is, rather, its 'echo', raises interesting questions about copy, quotation, influence and precedence: influence and quotation imply precedence, the priority of the early over the late. The *novelle* which are regarded as echoed or quoted in the text will raise some crucial questions about the relation of part to whole in Pirandello's narrative oeuvre: these *novelle* are either directly cited within the text or there are allusions to their themes and motifs. Although these lifts have been noted by the editors of the Mondadori critical edition of Pirandello's novels, there has been little attempt to analyse the effect which such a 'citationary' practice has had on the later text.

The first *novella* to be directly cited in the novel is 'Alberi cittadini' of 1900, which is repeated more or less verbatim in Book 2, chapter 2 ('Rientrando in città'). The presence of two later *novelle*, 'Quand'ero matto' (1902) and 'Stefano Giogli, uno e due' (1909), is more allusive: the saintly Franciscan protagonist of the former who loses his possessions, including the bank owned by his father, is an obvious analogue of Moscarda, while 'Stefano Giogli, uno e due' describes the case of a man who realizes that his wife has constructed an idea of him which does not correspond to his own, and anticipates Book 2, chapter 12 of *Uno, nessuno*, where Moscarda's wife does exactly the same. 'Stefano Giogli, uno e due', called by Mario Costanzo 'la prima traccia del romanzo *Uno, nessuno e centomila*',[37] is particularly interesting, because it is here that Pirandello uses Marchesini's terminology from *Le finzioni dell'anima*, of which he had also made use in 'L'umorismo', regarding the self as a metaphorical locus, and characters' awareness of their own fictionality: 'quando Lucietta lo abbracciava, non abbracciava lui, ma quell'odiosa metafora di lui ch'ella s'era creata' (*Na* III, 1121). This idea of the metaphorical status of the fictional character, made literal in 'Stefano Giogli', is implicitly restated throughout *Uno, nessuno*, through the novel's metaliterary and metatextual concerns, and through Moscarda's awareness of himself as a literary character.

Large chunks of text are also lifted from 'Il dovere del medico' (1910) and also from *I vecchi e i giovani*: in Moscarda's encounter with the bishop (in Book 7, chapters 5–7) the physical description of the palace is almost entirely lifted from *I vecchi*. As I mentioned earlier, Book 2, chapters 6–11, a meditation on the destruction of the environment, had been published in essay form, entitled 'Ricostruire', in the journal *Sapientia* in 1915. This easy transposition of material from one locus to another, and from genre to genre, is an index of the patchwork nature of *Uno, nessuno* and contradicts any unitary view of the text.

The imposing presence of much of 'Ritorno' (1923), which forms the cornerstone of Book 2, chapter 2, 'E allora?', is worth studying. Here, the exactitude of the linguistic copy intersects with the thematic similarity, as themes of regression, memory and loss are foregrounded. To a textual return to (or recollection of) earlier texts is added a metaphorical significance: the father's abandoned and unfinished house constitutes a space of primal, childhood memory and is also an obvious metaphor for the threatened space of selfhood: 'Finché visse mio padre, nessuno s'attentò a entrare in quella corte. Erano rimaste per terra tante pietre intagliate; e chi passava, vedendole, poté dapprima pensare che la fabbrica, per poco interrotta, sarebbe stata presto ripresa' (*Tr* II, 763). The metaphor of the self as literal construction or edifice is repeated throughout *Uno, nessuno e centomila*:

('l'uomo piglia a materia anche se stesso, e si costruisce, sissignori, come una casa'; *Tr* II, 778), and in 'Quand'ero matto', 'non stavo di casa in me. Ero infatti divenuto un albergo aperto a tutti' (*Na* II, 785). The metaphor reveals a homology between self and text: the atomization or destruction of Moscarda is reflected in the atomization of his narrative. The threshold of the text itself is crossed and recrossed, as its construction is interrupted.

There is also, in 'Ritorno', a literal return to or revisiting of his past by Pirandello, as the *novella* includes an incident in which the protagonist goes to surprise his father and his father's mistress together, a scene which is identical to one reported by Gaspare Giudice in his biography of Pirandello—Giudice, incidentally, read the novella as pure autobiography.[38] This return of the repressed text has thus become inextricably intertwined with Giudice's reading of the novel as autobiography, as the fictional and biographical have become layered over each other, as was the case with Stefano Pirandello's reading.

I noted at the beginning of the chapter that the problems of dating the various stages of the novel's composition, allied to the lack of an authoritative manuscript, problematize the idea of a simple transfer of material in one direction only. Macchia and Guglielminetti both contest this idea of *Uno, nessuno e centomila* as mere echo of the *novelle*, with Macchia saying 'non le pagine di *Uno, nessuno e centomila* siano state riprese da novelle già pubblicate. Ma più d'una volta quelle stesse pagine hanno dato lo spunto o hanno offerto citazioni ad alcune novelle e a momenti dei suoi drammi.'[39] Guglielminetti concurs, saying that 'occorre evitare di ritenere [...] verificata un'operazione di autoplagio, o dal romanzo ai danni della novella, o [...] viceversa'.[40] I have quoted Guglielminetti's call for a 'genetic' criticism of *Uno, nessuno* and I would like to supplement that by adding that genetic criticism concerns itself with reconstructing the genesis of a particular text, through the use of what is called the 'pre-text', or the variety of documents which chart the process of composition.[41] To regard Pirandello's *novelle* as 'pre-texts' is to assign them chronological priority: they are obviously not mere drafts, as each is complete in itself but part of the entire corpus of *Uno, nessuno e centomila* and it is useful to bear in mind Genette's maxim that 'the recovery of origins must not end up assigning any kind of hermeneutic privilege to what is earliest'.[42] Pirandello's text is composed by continual re-elaboration and revision, borrowing and adding, and thus it is almost impossible to distinguish origin from *telos*. It is instructive at this point to quote Giovanna Rigobello's view that '*Uno, nessuno e centomila* raccoglie, rappresa in alcune formule, che ritroviamo sparse e pressoché invariate in novelle, romanzi, drammi e saggi, la visione della vita [...] porta a maturazione, applicandone in pieno i requisiti, la poetica, enunciata nel trattatello su "L'umorismo".'[43] Rigobello's opinion, which reads Pirandello's narrative as moving towards its inexorable climax in *Uno, nessuno e centomila*, is emblematic of much Pirandello criticism which has confused origin with source, unsure as to whether *Uno, nessuno* is absorbing earlier works or is, in fact, generating them, thus raising the problem of completion, of text as 'continuo divenire'. Hay's opposition of writing and the written work takes on a wider significance here: the (in)complete form of the written text challenges the reader to reassess the conventional idea of *Uno, nessuno* as endpoint or monument to Pirandello's work.

Against the reductive readings of the text as either purely autobiographical (carried out by Stefano Pirandello and Giudice), or as unproblematic epitaph to Pirandello's narrative career (the view of most Pirandello criticism), I would like to suggest two possible metaphors for a reading practice of *Uno, nessuno*, both taken from critical discourse on the novel, which point to the need for a more complex way of reading the text. The first is that of Giovanni Cappello, who suggests that, because of its plagiarized passages, 'il testo non è più un romanzo, ma la rovina d'un romanzo'.[44] This view of the novel is one that I like very much as it recognizes the fractures which Pirandello's practice of self-quotation effects upon the structure of the text, as well as picking up on the narrative's building imagery. Such exactly repeated moments interrupt the text and they also, significantly, involve the reader in a process of intertextual 'plotting'— as only the competent reader, the 'lettore accorto' as Corrado Donati says, who is familiar with most or a large part of Pirandello's oeuvre, will receive the full revelation of the identical (and intertextual) nature of these discrete segments.[45] The other metaphor for the text is the one suggested by Giancarlo Mazzacurati, who says that the final version of the novel 'ha per molti aspetti l'aria di una dispensa donde siano state sottratte nel tempo e poi riportate, con diverse etichette e funzioni, vivande che lettori e spettatori di Pirandello avevano avuto modo di assaggiare prima'.[46] This utilitarian image of the text as a pantry to be raided when the occasion demands postulates a competing view of the movement from text to *novelle*. Critical readings of

the novel from a position of posterity, founded on the completion
necessary to get the whole picture of Pirandello's output, ignore the
challenge with which *Uno, nessuno e centomila* provides the reader: the
challenge to relinquish the 'piacere della storia', the pleasure of linear
plot and of a linear progression through Pirandello's works to a perfect
final synthesis, the challenge to disorder our ideas of completion and
sequence for the uncertainty of variants.

'Non conclude'

The final chapter of *Uno, nessuno e centomila*, 'Non conclude', parts of
which are copied from his 1909 article of the same title, has presented
itself to Pirandello critics as an interpretative challenge since the
novel's publication.[47] The chapter is negatively distanced from the
body of the novel, almost as an epilogue, is narrated in the present
tense and is characterized by a proliferation of negatives ('nessun
nome', 'nessun ricordo'; *Tr* II, 901), which set the ending apart as an
autonomous fragment. Moscarda, the writing 'I', stripped of his
possessions and exiled to the countryside, seems to dissolve into
nature, in an act of narration which is potentially open-ended: 'Io
sono vivo e non concludo. La vita non conclude. E non sa di nomi,
la vita. Quest'albero, respiro tremulo di foglie nuove. Sono
quest'albero. Albero, nuvola; domani libro o vento; il libro che leggo,
il vento che bevo. Tutto fuori, vagabondo' (*Tr* II, 901). As I
mentioned earlier, critical response has been almost unanimous in
asserting what it perceives to be the pantheistic nature of this
chapter.[48] While there is undoubtedly such a pantheistic impulse
present in all of the moments of Pirandellian epiphany which, to a
certain extent, involve the dissolution of the subject in the external, I
would like to propose an alternative reading, one which I feel does
justice to the overall textual and philological issues which I have
raised, and which aims to link these issues with the concept of
epiphany. In the penultimate chapter, 'La coperta di lana verde', the
convalescent Moscarda anticipated his final ecstatic disintegration and
reconstitution by gazing at his bedspread, which he had earlier offered
as a mute 'explanation' to the judge:

me ne stavo in quei giorni adagiato beatamente su una poltrona vicino alla
finestra, con una coperta di lana verde sulle gambe [...] con le punta delle dita
carezzavo lievemente la peluria verde di quella coperta di lana. *Ci vedevo la
campagna*, come se fosse tutta una sterminata distesa di grano: e, carezzandola,

me ne beavo, sentendomici davvero, in mezzo a tutto quel grano, con un senso di così smemorata lontananza, che quasi ne avevo angoscia. Ah, perdersi là, distendersi e abbandonarsi, così, tra l'erba, al silenzio dei cieli; empirsi l'anima di tutta quella vana azzurrità, facendovi naufragare ogni pensiero, ogni memoria. (*Tr* II, 896; my italics)[49]

This is, of course, what Moscarda does in the next chapter. The 'epifania della coperta', as Barilli calls it, comes not from a visual or sensory experience of the landscape, as is usual in Pirandello, but from a simulacrum of it, an imaginative reproduction of it.[50] The 'coperta' seems to function as a kind of anti-madeleine, as it plunges the character into an imaginative recall, which is both memory and anticipation: Moscarda's vision of this figurative 'landscape' is the kind of humoristic 'second sight' described in Chapter 2, embedding one narrative within another, fantastic, one. Moscarda's 'vision' both anticipates the next diegetic moment and recalls previous (textual) experiences.

It signals the movement of Moscarda to a new kind of epiphany, one in which temporality seems not to exist, or is rather consumed in a simultaneity, a series of ecstatic present tenses which render conventional narration impossible. Thus Moscarda's narrating epiphanies bring him closer to characters such as the protagonist of 'La carriola', described in Chapter 2, for whom ending and beginning are the same.

Significantly, in the imaginary world of *Uno, nessuno*'s final chapter, the priority of the literal over the metaphorical is finally dissolved, and meaning is new and has not had a chance to become codified. Pirandello's 'albero', mentioned in 'L'umorismo' as the organic metaphor for the creative work, reappears, and there is now an equivalence between the two terms, articulated in the radical copular metaphor of Moscarda's 'sono quest'albero'.

Moscarda's modernist dissolution of the self into the book ('sono quest'albero. Albero, nuvola; domani libro o vento: il libro che leggo') brings us back to his position as narrator, still narrating, *in medias res*, in a narration which is potentially endless. I mentioned earlier Moscarda's right to recognition as an author which he ceded with the loss of his name; the (in)conclusion of the text shows us that Moscarda, reborn as narrator, is engaged in an endless and ahistorical act of storytelling which counters the published written form of the text, a form which denies simultaneity and discourages the provisional and the open-ended. This opposition of the writing moment to the completed text (whose conclusion is resisted in Moscarda's 'io sono vivo e non concludo', in which origin and *telos* finally and ecstatically collide), shows us how the Pirandellian epiphany emblematizes the incomplete creative process within the completed form of the work.[51] The potential embodied in the series of infinitives at the novel's ending ('Rinascere attimo per attimo. Impedire che il pensiero si metta in me di nuovo a lavorare [...] Pensare alla morte, pregare'; *Tr* II, 902) combines with the narrator's attempt to erase his memory ('nessun ricordo oggi del nome di ieri') and signals the Pirandellian epiphany as both memory and the simultaneous erasure of memory, in the blankness of the anti-descriptive wordless moment. The novel's ending, with its paradoxical repetition of infinitives which describe Moscarda's desire to avoid or transcend repetition, exemplifies the practice of epiphany in Pirandello (the sameness which produces difference); it is also a metaphor for the text's attempt to subsume its previous existence and 'make it new', with no loss of origins and no priority, chronological or otherwise—it is a text which, as Marziano Guglielminetti has aptly expressed it, 'non è mai stato se stesso'.[52] The attempt to avoid repetition is also an attempt by Moscarda to avoid self-quotation, yet the text is quoting from 'L'umorismo', 'Non conclude' and 'Il dovere del medico' in this chapter alone. Edward Said points out that quotation is always a 'reminder that other writing serves to displace present writing, to a greater or lesser extent, from its absolute, central, proper place'.[53] If quotation itself is a figure of the tension between past and present writing, the ending of *Uno, nessuno e centomila* signals this process of material displacement from authorizing past to consuming present as the *modus operandi* of Pirandello's writing, which, rather than ending in Moscarda's 'climactic' epiphany, announces its intention to begin again and again.

Notes to Chapter 5

1. Iser claims that 'the real reader is invoked mainly in the studies of the history of responses, i.e., when attention is focused on the way in which a literary work has been received by a specific literary public'. These responses are obviously institutionalized and documented in the practice of literary criticism. Wolfgang Iser, *The Act of Reading: A Theory of Literary Response* (Baltimore: Johns Hopkins University Press, 1991), 28.

2. See Mario Costanzo's bibliographical notes to the Mondadori edition of *Tutti i romanzi*, edited by him, for a description of the contents of these 'foglietti', in which he states that 'quanto alla datazione del testo manoscritto con quello pubblicato nella *Fiera letteraria*, cit., sembra confermare l'ipotesi che il ms. documenti una fase di elaborazione precedente a quella della stesura precedente'; 'Note ai testi e varianti', in *Tr* II, 1061–3. See also the extended version of this

explanatory article, 'Per un'edizione critica di *Uno, nessuno e centomila*', *Quaderni dell'Istituto di Studi Pirandelliani* 1 (1973), 109–19. In this article Costanzo notes the lack of extant documentation pertaining to the drafting of the novel. There are two comprehensive overviews of the editorial status of the novel: the first is Marziano Guglielminetti's 'Le vicende e i significati di *Uno, nessuno e centomila*', in Lauretta (ed.), *Il 'romanzo' di Pirandello*, 183–207 (esp. 183–6) (this essay was later republished as '*Uno, nessuno e centomila*: genesi e significato' in Guglielminetti's *Il romanzo del Novecento*, 161–95). Guglielminetti refuses to accept the 'foglietti' (which cover the first four 'books' of the novel) as constituting a manuscript, which he considers as 'finora latitante' ('Le vicende', 183). The second is Paola Pestarino's article 'Ipotesi sulle redazioni manoscritte di *Uno, nessuno e centomila*', *Rassegna della letteratura italiana* 7 (1978), 442–65: she says that 'i primi foglietti risalgono al 1912 circa' (p. 454) and 'i vari indizi notati convergono tutti concordemente nel determinare le date della maggior parte dei fogli del MS fra il 1915–16 e il 1920–21' (p. 464). Giancarlo Mazzacurati calls for a critical edition of the novel which, unlike the Costanzo-edited Mondadori critical edition, would display all the stages of the novel's composition. See 'Ombre e nasi: da Tristram Shandy a Vitangelo Moscarda' in his *Pirandello nel romanzo europeo*, 269–303 at 291.

3. On the disparity between the relative critical attention devoted to Pirandello's composition process and to the interviews and letters in which he discusses the text, see Costanzo, 'Per una edizione critica di *Uno, nessuno e centomila*', 117.

4. Cited in Vicentini, *L'estetica di Pirandello*, 220.

5. 'Lettera autobiografica', reprinted in *Spsv* 1288. In this letter, Pirandello mentions that his poetry collection *Fuori di chiave* (1912) has recently been published, thus establishing an approximate date for the letter.

6. Gérard Genette comments on the paratextual function of authorial correspondence and remarks that 'we can use the correspondence of an author as a certain kind of statement about the history of each of his works: about its creation, publication and reception by the public and critics, and about his view of the work at all stages of this history'. More interestingly, perhaps, he suggests that on a later audience such paratextual statement has a paratextual *effect* which conditions critical response: 'To the extent that a letter from a writer bears on his work [...] we may say that it exerts on its first addressee a paratextual function, and, more remotely, on the ultimate public simply a paratextual effect'. Genette, *Paratexts*, 373–4. I will be responding to this by addressing the filiations between authorial paratexts and critical descriptions of the work.

7. Vicentini, *L'estetica*, 220.

8. Guglielminetti, 'Le vicende e i significati di *Uno, nessuno e centomila*', 185.

9. Interview in *Il Messaggero della Domenica*, 23 February 1919, cited in Guglielminetti, *Il romanzo del Novecento*, 174.

10. Letter dated 6 April 1919 and cited in *Pirandello–Martoglio, carteggio inedito*, ed. Zappulla Muscarà, 182. My italics.

11. July 1924, interview in *Grandi Firme*, cited in Pietro Milone, 'Prefazione' to *Uno, nessuno e centomila* (Milan: Garzanti, 1993), pp. lvi–lxxix at p. lxii. Milone compares *Uno, nessuno e centomila* to Pirandello's own, famously ascetic last will and testament, speaking of the 'romanzo testamentario che Pirandello conclude non dissimilmente dalle sue disposizioni testamentarie che prevedevano la

dispersione al vento [...] delle sue ceneri' ('Prefazione', p. lxxii). For Pirandello's 'Mie ultime volontà da rispettare', see *Spsv* 1289.

12. 'Conversando con Pirandello', published in *Epoca*, 5 July 1922 and cited in Vicentini, *L'estetica di Pirandello*, 221. Pietro Milone insists that the quotation is '"quasi un riepilogo", non "un epilogo" (come erroneamente riportato da molti), tanto meno se visto come palinodia della natura critica dell'opera pirandelliana'; Milone, p. lxi.

13. Cited in Mario Forti, *Idea del romanzo italiano fra '800 e '900* (Milan: Garzanti, 1981), 93.

14. Stefano Pirandello, 'Prefazione' to *Uno, nessuno e centomila* , reprinted in *Tr* II, 1057–60 at 1060.

15. Stefano also calls the novel a 'breviario di fede' (*Tr* II, 1060): 'breviario' has, etymologically, both a liturgical and a summarizing meaning. As an example of the symbiotic relationship between critical and paratextual pronouncements, see the critic Antonio Di Pietro's description in 1951 of *Uno, nessuno* as a 'breviario, un libro ascetico', cited in Guglielminetti, *Il romanzo del Novecento*, 162.

16. Tilgher, 'Il teatro di Pirandello', in *Studi sul teatro contemporaneo*, 135–93.

17. Ibid. 190–1.

18. Ibid. 189.

19. Cited in Illiano, 'Momenti e problemi di critica pirandelliana', 143.

20. The most striking example of this acceptance of the terms in which Pirandello has posited the novel is probably Stefano Miliotto's 'Premessa' to the volume *Nuvole e vento*, the proceedings of the 1989 'Convegno di Studi Pirandelliani', devoted to *Uno, nessuno e centomila*. Milioto transcribes parts of Pirandello's declarations about *Uno, nessuno e centomila* without comment, lending the institutional weight of the Centro di Studi Pirandelliani to Pirandello's interpretation and positioning of his work; 'Premessa', to Stefano Milioto (ed.), *Nuvole e vento: introduzione alla lettura di Uno, nessuno e centomila* (Agrigento: Centro Nazionale di Studi Pirandelliani, 1989), 9–10. There are countless critical works on *Uno, nessuno* which adopt a similar perspective on the novel: see, amongst others, Paola Pestarino, 'Ipotesi sulle redazioni manoscritte di *Uno, nessuno e centomila*': she describes *Uno, nessuno* as a '*summa*' of Pirandello's narrative (p. 442); Gaspare Giudice calls it 'l'opera-definizione, l'aureo libretto o codice, del pirandellismo', *Luigi Pirandello*, 411; Arcangelo Leone de Castris refers to the 'carattere di bilancio preventivo e di premessa ideale, ma anche di bilancio consuntivo e di effettiva epigrafe, che il romanzo rivela'; *Storia di Pirandello*, 199; similarly, Georges Piroué writes that 'in *Uno, nessuno e centomila*, Pirandello dresse un bilan, il rédige un testament, il s'érige à lui-même un brillant tombeau'; *Luigi Pirandello: sicilien planétaire* (Paris: Denoël, 1988), 256. Giovanna Rigobello elaborates on this description by calling the novel 'il compendio dell'intera opera letteraria di Pirandello [...] ne costituisce la *summa* sul piano sia ideologico sia estetico' which 'compendia la *Weltanschauung* pirandelliana'; 'La parola e il silenzio in *Uno, nessuno e centomila*', in Enzo Lauretta (ed.), *Pirandello e la parola* (Agrigento: Centro Nazionale di Studi Pirandelliani, 2000), 197–210 at 197–9. The term '*summa*' also appears in Maria Antonietta Grignani's discussion of the novel, '*Uno, nessuno e centomila*: la scrittura', in Milioto (ed.), *Nuvole e vento*, 111–22 at 111.

21. See Guglielminetti, 'Le vicende', 186, for more details on 'Ricostruire'.

22. Vittore Branca, 'La filologia', in id. and J. Starobinski (eds.), *La filologia e la critica letteraria* (Rome: Rizzoli, 1977), 13–109 at 82. Bessi and Martelli, concurring that 'noi non possediamo, una volta perduto l'originale, l'opera quale essa uscì dalla penna dell'autore; ma solo quella che ci è trasmessa dalla tradizione intera', set up a key distinction between 'l'opera d'arte come "fatto" (una critica, cioè, legata alla staticità del testo, una critica del "testo fisso") e la considerazione dell'opera d'arte come "atto"', recuperating the centrality of the composition process; Rossella Bessi and Mario Martelli, *Guida alla filologia italiana* (Florence: Sansoni, 1984), 77. This view is obviously the antithesis of the Crocean one: Benedetto Croce in his essay 'Illusioni sulla genesi delle opere d'arte documentata dagli scartafacci degli scrittori', referring to the polemic over the recent publication of *Gli promessi sposi*, criticized the so-called 'critica degli scartafacci', saying 'mi sdegnavo della "genesi" che costoro, per darsi un tono, dicevano di voler determinare nel capolavoro manzoniano, perché io sapevo che l'opera d'arte ha una genesi affatto ideale, che si trae dalla sua presenza stessa'; 'Illusioni sulla genesi delle opere d'arte documentata dagli scartafacci degli scrittori', *Quaderni della Critica*, 3 (1947), 93–4 at 93.

23. Guglielminetti, *Il romanzo del Novecento*, 165.

24. Annamaria Andreoli notes how, in one of the 'foglietti', this quotation read 'esperimento della *scomposizione* d'un Moscarda', strengthening the parallel between the breakdown of text and character; 'Nel laboratorio di Pirandello', 164 (my italics).

25. This episode is also a pastiche of *Tristram Shandy*, vol. 6, ch. 1: 'We'll not stop two moments, my dear Sir, – only, as we have got thro' these five volumes, (do, Sir, sit down upon a set – they are better than nothing) let us just look back upon the country we have pass'd through. –' Laurence Sterne, *Tristram Shandy* (Oxford: Oxford University Press, 1990), 329. This has obvious parallels in Moscarda's 'State, state pure sdraiato comodamente su la vostra greppina. Io seggo qua. Dite di no?' (*Tr* II, 767).

26. Moscarda's addresses to the reader are indicative of his humoristic fear that his narrative cannot be properly understood by his reader, as in this example when he enters the notary's studio: 'Ma io ero, entrando nello studio, in uno stato d'animo, che voi non vi potete immaginare. Come potreste immaginarvelo, scusate, se vi pare ancora la cosa più naturale del mondo entrare nello studio d'un notaro per stendere un atto qualsiasi, e se dite che lo conoscete tutti questo notaro Stampa?' (*Tr* II, 815)

27. On the traditionally comic function of intertitles, see Giancarlo Mazzacurati, 'L'arte del titolo, da Sterne a Pirandello', in id. (ed.), *Effetto Sterne* (Pisa: Nistri-Lischi, 1990), 294–332. For a typology of the narrative functions of the title see Giovanni Cappello, 'Retorica del titolo', in AA.VV., *Il titolo e il testo* (Padua: Editoriale Programma, 1992), 11–26.

28. Genette, *Paratexts*, 302.

29. Dorrit Cohn points out the function of such 'perigraphic apparatus' as footnotes or endnotes, which constitute a 'textual zone intermediating between the narrative text itself and its extratextual documentary base'; *The Distinction of Fiction* (Baltimore: Johns Hopkins University Press, 1999), 115. Pirandello's footnote obviously places the text firmly in the tradition of *Tristram Shandy*'s myriad mock references; however, his use of lists such as the bullet-pointed

'RIFLESSIONI' and 'CONCLUSIONI' (*Tr* II, 759) is also imitative of Alberto Cantoni's use of similar typographic expedients in *Un re umorista* (1891).

30. Ann Caesar has pointed to the influence of mock autobiographies such as Ugo Foscolo's *Il sesto tomo dell'io* (1790) and Carlo Dossi's *Vita di Alberto Pisani* (1871) on *Uno, nessuno: Characters and Authors in Luigi Pirandello*, 134. In my opinion, Dossi's text is particularly significant for Pirandello's for its embedding within it of several other tales, all supposedly written by the hero.

31. For more details on the shifting functions of proper names in Pirandello see Luigi Sedita, *La maschera del nome: tre saggi di onomastica pirandelliana* (Rome: Istituto dell'Enciclopedia Italiana, 1988).

32. Paul de Man expresses the difference in referential importance of the proper name in autobiography and fiction thus: 'Autobiography seems to depend on actual and potentially verifiable events in a less ambiguous way than fiction does; it seems to belong to a simpler mode of referentiality, of representation and of diegesis [...] its deviations from reality remain rooted in a single subject, whose identity is defined by the uncontested readability of the proper name'; 'Autobiography as de-facement', *MLN* 94 (1979), 919–30 at 920. This definition ignores, however, the confusion caused by fictional autobiography on the referential plane, and, De Man points out, by the figurative nature of autobiography itself.

33. Philippe Lejeune, *On Autobiography*, trans. Katherine Leary (Minneapolis: University of Minnesota Press, 1989); see pp. 3–30 for the discussion of the autobiographical pact.

34. Foucault, 'What is an author?', 147.

35. Edward Said, *Beginnings* (London: Granta, 1985), 83.

36. The decentred narrative has Moscarda's narrative voice being expropriated by other characters in the form of free indirect style; however, there is also a concomitant expropriation by Gengè of Moscarda's words, suppressing Moscarda as originator of his own discourse; for example: '"Quando mai tu ti sei occupato di codeste cose?" Più che mai stupiti, quasi atterriti, rivolsero gli occhi a cercare in me chi aveva proferito le parole ch'essi avevano pensato e che stavano per dirmi. Ma come! Le avevo dette io?' (*Tr* II, 827).

37. Mario Costanzo, 'Note', 1093. Giovanni Macchia also identifies 'Stefano Giogli' as the source for *Uno, nessuno*, calling it 'la novella da cui nacque l'idea del romanzo'; *Pirandello o la stanza della tortura*, 63.

38. Giudice, *Luigi Pirandello*, 60–1.

39. Macchia, *Pirandello o la stanza della tortura*, 69. Mario Ricciardi, who has elsewhere paid close attention to the layering of Pirandellian narratives, agrees with Macchia about the ambiguity of the direction of the borrowings in *Uno, nessuno e centomila*: '*Uno, nessuno e centomila* può essere un "raccoglitore" di tante esperienze pirandelliane, segnalate con la citazione, la ripresa, la presenza significativa, ma può anche essere un'opera stratificata in cui convergono, in tempi successivi, modi di scrittura, intenzioni ideologiche e scelta di poetica che, solo agli inizi degli anni '20, assumono la forma precisa del romanzo pubblicato'; '*Uno, nessuno e centomila*: il romanzo della scomposizione della personalità', in Milioto (ed.), *Nuvole e vento*, 23–47 at 24.

40. Guglielminetti, *Il romanzo del Novecento*, 170.

41. Louis Hay writes of the functions of genetic criticism that it 'deals with the

relation between the text and its genesis, and with the mechanics of text production, the activity of the writing subject'; 'Does text exist?', *Studies in Bibliography*, 41 (1988), 64–76 at 68. Genette classifies the documents which constitute a pre-text as including 'hypotextual sources, anecdotes, preparatory documents, outlines, drafts, "clean" MSS and proofs'; *Paratexts*, 396.

42. Ibid. 402.

43. Rigobello, 'La parola e il silenzio in *Uno, nessuno e centomila*', 199.

44. Cappello also suggests the metaphors of the 'collage', the 'patchwork' and the 'montaggio'; 'La confessione della rovina', in Lauretta (ed.), *La 'persona' nell'opera di Luigi Pirandello*, 141–74 at 158–61.

45. Donati, *La solitudine allo specchio*, 10.

46. Mazzacurati, *Pirandello nel romanzo europeo*, 288. Mazzacurati also produces an economic metaphor for the manuscript of *Uno, nessuno*, calling it 'un deposito, quel manoscritto finale, che si è ingrossato, assottigliato, poi di nuovo rinfollito negli anni, secondo un criterio di approvvigionamento e di sperpero' (288–9); this description ties *Uno, nessuno* more closely to *Suo marito*, which I discussed in economic terms. Mario Forti calls the novel both a reservoir ('serbatoio') and jotter ('brogliaccio'); Forti, *Idea del romanzo italiano fra '800 e '900*, 93.

47. 'Non conclude' was published in *La preparazione* in 1909, and is reprinted in *Effetto Sterne*, 433–9.

48. Douglas Radcliff-Umstead refers to the 'final pantheistic serenity' of Moscarda's concluding words, *The Mirror of our Anguish* (London: Associated University Presses, 1978), 273; Alison Booth writes of the 'pantheism' of the ending; 'Mystics, madmen and mendicants: the visionary element in Pirandello', *Yearbook of the British Pirandello Society* 7 (1987), 11–31 at 21; similarly, Gian-Paolo Biasin in *Literary Diseases: Theme and Metaphor in the Italian Novel* (Austin: University of Texas Press, 1975), 124; De Castris famously referred to Moscarda's 'catarsi mistica', 'suo disporsi al godimento panico della natura'; *Storia di Pirandello*, 203. Pietro Milone, however, links the metaliterary finale, as I have done, to an act of 'scrittura sempre inconclusa', 'Prefazione', p. lxxxv.

49. This is a direct echo of the 1910 *novella*, 'Il dovere del medico' (see *Na* I, 427–8).

50. Barilli says that 'l'epifania della coperta precede di poco quella finale con cui Vitangelo, e con lui, Pirandello, prende congedo da noi: epifania ormai tanto allargata da confondersi con la presenza generale dell'Essere'; *La linea Svevo-Pirandello*, 226.

51. This conflict between writing and work is considered by Walter Ong in his discussion of the transition from orality to a typographical culture: 'print encourages a sense of closure: a sense that what is found in a text has been finalized, has reached a state of completeness'; *Orality and Literacy* (London: Methuen, 1982), 133. This kind of closure began with the rise of print culture in the eighteenth century and its consequent linking of originality with artistic commodification, which I discussed in relation to *Suo marito*. Using this argument, I would argue that Moscarda asserts his storytelling originality in the closing soliloquy, opposing it to a view of originality based on words or works as property.

52. Guglielminetti, 'Le vicende', 204.

53. Said, *Beginnings*, 22.

CONCLUSION

In this book I aimed to question the idea of a linear movement from 'L'umorismo' to the climactic text *Uno, nessuno e centomila*, and thus undermine ideas of a simple chronological progression in Pirandellian narrative: it may seem that I have merely reconstituted this diachronic movement, as my study ends with a reading of *Uno, nessuno e centomila*, interpreted in the light of narrative processes derived from 'L'umorismo'. However, my reading of the metanarrative nature of *umorismo* posits the tropes of metaphor and epiphany as narrative processes which are emblematic of Pirandello's fragmented and repetitive texts as a whole, and which, as tropes which contain and interrogate ideas of repetition and originality, enact a continual movement between past and present. 'L'umorismo' should therefore be read not as a 'source' text which 'explains' Pirandello's narrative, but rather as a site where the issues which criss-cross Pirandello's narrative intersect: itself a text that was rewritten, 'L'umorismo''s fictions of theory and theories of fiction show that the communication or 'intercambiabilità' between Pirandello texts ensures that progression is always undercut by regression.

Similarly, at times it is difficult to separate the categories of quotation, self-plagiarism and repetition, as they tend to elide. What is indisputable is that, as well as embodying ideas of textual authority, authorship and ownership, such processes of textual displacement, fragmentation and reconstitution force us to question our notions of text itself. Just as the 'scomposizione' of Moscarda as narrator and author-figure encourages the reader to interrogate any unitary or totalizing view of the text created by the 'real' author and readers, Pirandello's practice of self-quotation requires us to direct our attention to the multiplicity of texts which compose one single text and to think carefully and critically about ideas of chronology, origins and echoes. The tensions between past and present which Pirandello's texts demonstrate, both in their own modes of composition and in the devices which structure them, show that, inevitably, Pirandellian closure is circularity masquerading as a straight line.

BIBLIOGRAPHY

Works by Pirandello

Carteggi inediti con Ojetti–Albertini–Orvieto–Novaro–De Gubernatis–De Filippo, ed. Sarah Zappulla Muscarà (Rome: Bulzoni, 1980).

Epistolario familiare giovanile (1886–98), ed. Elio Providenti (Florence: Le Monnier, 1986).

Giustino Roncella, nato Boggiòlo, ed. Corrado Simioni and Maria Griffini (Milan: Mondadori, 1980).

Her Husband, translated and with an introduction by Martha King and Mary Ann Frese Witt (Durham, NC and London: Duke University Press, 2000).

Maschere nude, 2 vols. (Milan: Mondadori, 1958).

Maschere nude, ed. Alessandro D'Amico, 2 vols. (Milan: Mondadori, 1986).

Novelle per un anno, ed. Mario Costanzo, 3 vols. (Milan: Mondadori, 1985–90).

Pirandello–Martoglio, carteggio inedito, ed. Sarah Zappulla Muscarà (Milan: Pari, 1980).

Saggi, poesie, scritti varii, ed. Manlio Lo Vecchio-Musti (Milan: Mondadori, 1977).

Suo marito, ed. with an introduction by Rita Guerricchio (Florence: Giunti, 1994).

Taccuino di Harvard, ed. Ombretta Frau and Cristina Gragnani (Milan: Mondadori, 2002).

Tutti i romanzi, ed. Giovanni Macchia and Mario Costanzo, 2 vols. (Milan: Mondadori, 1973).

L'umorismo (Lanciano: Carabba, 1908).

L'umorismo, ed. Salvatore Guglielmino (Milan: Mondadori, 1987).

L'umorismo, ed. with an introduction by Pietro Milone (Milan: Garzanti, 1995).

Uno, nessuno e centomila, ed. with an introduction by M. Guglielminetti (Milan: Mondadori, 1997).

Uno, nessuno e centomila, ed. Pietro Milone (Milan: Garzanti, 1993).

I vecchi e i giovani, ed. Massimo Onofri, introduction by Nino Borsellino (Milan: Garzanti, 1993).

Secondary Literature

ABBA, GIUSEPPE CESARE, *Da Quarto al Volturno: noterelle d'uno dei Mille* (Bologna: Zanichelli, 1918).

ABRAMS, M. H., *The Mirror and the Lamp* (New York: Norton, 1958).

—— *Natural Supernaturalism: Tradition and Revolution in Romantic Literature* (London: Oxford University Press, 1971).

ALESSIO, ANTONIO, 'Colori e metafore nell'immagine pirandelliana', in Enzo Lauretta (ed.), *Pirandello e la lingua* (Milan: Mursia, 1994), 177–83.

ALFONZETTI, BEATRICE, 'La scrittura selvaggia: l'immagine di Grazia Deledda in *Suo marito*', in Ugo Collu (ed.), *Grazia Deledda nella cultura contemporanea*, 2 vols. (Nuoro: Satta, 1992), ii. 285–303.

ALONGE, ROBERTO, 'Madri, puttane, schiave sessuali e uomini soli', in Alonge et al. (eds.), *Studi pirandelliani: Dal testo al sottotesto* (Bologna: Pitagora, 1986), 91–110.

ANDERSSON, GÖSTA, *Arte e teoria: studi sulla poetica del giovane Luigi Pirandello* (Stockholm: Almqvist & Wiksell, 1966).

—— 'Pirandello saggista, lettore di Gabriel Séailles', in Paola Giovanelli (ed.), *Pirandello saggista* (Palermo: Palumbo, 1982), 303–19.

ANDREOLI, ANNAMARIA, 'Nel laboratorio di Pirandello', in *Taccuino segreto di Luigi Pirandello* (Milan: Mondadori, 1997), 127–215.

ANGELINI, FRANCA, 'Un nome e una donna', in A. Buttafuoco and M. Zancan (eds.), *Svelamento: Sibilla Aleramo: una biografia intellettuale* (Milan: Feltrinelli, 1988), 64–72.

—— 'Scenes and texts: perspectives in Pirandello criticism', in Biasin and Gieri (eds.), *Luigi Pirandello*, 23–34.

ARCHI, PAOLO, *Il tempo delle parole* (Palermo: Palumbo, 1992).

ARGENZIANO MAGGI, MARIA, *Il motivo del viaggio nella narrativa pirandelliana* (Naples: Liguori, 1977).

ARISTOTLE, *Poetics*, trans. Stephen Halliwell, Loeb Classical Library 23 (London: Heineman, 1973).

—— *'Art' of Rhetoric*, trans. J. H. Freese, Loeb Classical Library 22 (London: Heineman, 1975).

BÀCCOLO, LUIGI, *Luigi Pirandello* (Milan: Bocca, 1949).

BAKER, ALAN R. H., and BIGER, GIDEON (eds.), *Ideology and Landscape in Historical Perspective* (Cambridge: Cambridge University Press, 1992).

BALDASSARRI, RITA, 'Una fonte per *I vecchi e i giovani* di Luigi Pirandello: *Gli avvenimenti di Sicilia* di Napoleone Colaianni', *Ipotesi 80*, 18–19 (1986–7), 26–54.

—— '*I vecchi e i giovani* e le varianti: rieccheggiamenti della scrittura di Colaianni', *Ipotesi 80*, 21–2 (1987–8), 19–40.

BANDI, GIUSEPPE, *I mille*, in *Memorialisti dell'Ottocento*, ed. G. Trombatore, 3 vols. (Milan and Naples: Ricciardi, 1953).

BARBINA, ALFREDO, *Bibliografia della critica pirandelliana 1889–1961* (Florence: Le Monnier, 1967).

BARILLI, RENATO, *L'azione e l'estasi* (Milan: Feltrinelli, 1967).

—— *La barriera del naturalismo* (Milan: Mursia, 1980).

—— 'Il comico in Bergson, Freud e Pirandello', in A. Alessio (ed.), *L'enigma Pirandello* (Ottawa: Canadian Society for Italian Studies, 1988), 318–35.

—— *La linea Svevo-Pirandello* (Milan: Mursia, 1981).

—— *Pirandello, una rivoluzione culturale* (Milan: Mursia, 1986).

BARTHES, ROLAND, 'The death of the author', in *Image–Music–Text* (London: Flamingo, 1984), 142–8.

—— *The Rustle of Language*, trans. Richard Howard (Oxford: Blackwell, 1986).

BATTAGLIA, SALVATORE, *I facsimile della realtà* (Palermo: Sellerio, 1991).

—— 'Palazzeschi e l'arte dell'anacronismo', *Filologia e letteratura* 68 (1971), 501–13.

BEER, GILLIAN, *Darwin's Plots* (London: Routledge and Kegan Paul, 1983).

BEJA, MORRIS, *Epiphany in the Modern Novel* (London: Peter Owen, 1971).

BERGSON, HENRI, *Laughter*, in *Comedy*, ed. Wylie Sypher (Baltimore: Johns Hopkins University Press, 1980).

BESANT, ANNIE, and LEADBEATER, C. W., *Thought-Forms* (London: Theosophical Publishing Society, 1905).

BESSI, ROSSELLA, and MARTELLI, MARIO, *Guida alla filologia italiana* (Florence: Sansoni, 1984).

BIASIN, GIAN-PAOLO, *Italian Literary Icons* (Princeton: Princeton University Press, 1985).

—— *Literary Diseases: Theme and Metaphor in the Italian Novel* (Austin: University of Texas Press, 1975).

—— *Malattie letterarie* (Milan: Bompiani, 1976).

—— and GIERI, MANUELA, 'Pirandello at 360 degrees', in eid. (eds.), *Luigi Pirandello*, 3–22.

———— (eds.), *Luigi Pirandello: Contemporary Perspectives* (Toronto: University of Toronto Press, 1999).

BIDNEY, MARTIN, *Patterns of Epiphany* (Carbondale, Ill.: Southern Illinois University Press, 1997).

BINET, ALFRED, *Alterations of Personality*, trans. H. G. Baldwin (London: Chapman and Hall, 1896).

BINI, DANIELA, 'La creazione artistica come sconfitta della morte', in Lauretta (ed.), *Pirandello e l'oltre*, 233–43.

—— 'La storia come maschera', in Lauretta (ed.), *Pirandello e la politica*, 199–207.

—— 'Woman as creator: Pirandello's *L'innesto*', *Pirandello Studies* 17 (1997), 34–45.

BLACK, MAX, *Models and Metaphors* (Ithaca: Cornell University Press, 1962).

—— *Perplexities: Rational Choice, the Prisoner's Dilemma, Metaphor, Poetic Ambiguity and Other Puzzles* (Ithaca: Cornell University Press, 1990).

BLAZINA, SERGIO, 'Rassegna di studi pirandelliani: i romanzi (1961–1983)', *Lettere italiane*, 36 (1984), 69–131.

BONIFAZI, NEURO, *Teoria del fantastico: il racconto fantastico in Italia: Tarchetti–Pirandello–Buzzati* (Ravenna: Longo, 1982).

BOOTH, ALISON, 'Mystics, madmen and mendicants: the visionary element in Pirandello', *Yearbook of the British Pirandello Society* 7 (1987), 11–31.

BOOTH, WAYNE, *The Rhetoric of Fiction* (Chicago: University of Chicago Press, 1969).

BORLENGHI, ALDO (ed.), *Pirandello o dell'ambiguità* (Padua: R.A.D.A.R., 1968).

BORSELLINO, NINO, *Immagini di Pirandello* (Cosenza: Lerici, 1979).

—— *Ritratto di Pirandello* (Bari: Laterza, 1983).

BOWIE, MALCOLM, *Freud, Proust and Lacan: Theory as Fiction* (Cambridge: Cambridge University Press, 1987).

BRANCA, VITTORE, 'La filologia', in id. and Jean Starobinski (eds.), *La filologia e la critica letteraria* (Rome: Rizzoli, 1977), 13–309..

BREDIN, HUGH, 'Roman Jakobson on metaphor and metonymy', *Philosophy and Literature* 8/1 (1984), 89–103.

BRIDGEMAN, TERESA, 'On the likeness of similes and metaphors: Jarry's *Les jours et les nuits*', *Modern Language Review* 91 (1996), 65–77.

BRIOSI, SANDRO, *Il senso della metafora* (Naples: Liguori, 1985).

BROOK, CLODAGH J., *The Expression of the Inexpressible in Eugenio Montale's Poetry* (Oxford: Oxford University Press, 2002).

BROOKS, PETER, *The Melodramatic Imagination: Balzac, Henry James, Melodrama and the Mode of Excess* (New York: Columbia University Press, 1984).

—— *Reading for the Plot* (Cambridge, Mass.: Harvard University Press, 1992).

BURKE, EDMUND, 'The sublime' (1757), in Isaac Kramnick (ed.), *The Portable Enlightenment Reader* (London: Penguin, 1995), 329–33.

BURKE, KENNETH, *A Grammar of Motives* (New York: Prentice-Hall, 1945).

CAESAR, ANN, *Characters and Authors in Luigi Pirandello* (Oxford: Clarendon Press, 1998).

CALABRESE, STEFANO, 'Etica dell'azione e intreccio nel romanzo storico italiano', *Rivista di letterature moderne e comparate* 46/1 (1993), 47–67.

CAMILLERI, ANDREA, *Biografia del figlio cambiato* (Milan: Rizzoli, 2000).

CANTELMO, MARINELLA, 'Vedere, far vedere, essere visti: dalla *Weltanschauung* dell'autore alla visione narrativa', *Strumenti critici* 11 (1996), 111–35.

—— (ed.), *L'isola che ride: teoria, poetica e retoriche dell'umorismo pirandelliano* (Rome: Bulzoni, 1997).

CANTONI, ALBERTO, *Il demonio dello stile: tre novelle* (Milan: Lombardi, 1987).

—— *Un re umorista* (Rome: Lucarini, 1991).

CAPPELLO, GIOVANNI, 'La confessione della rovina', in Lauretta (ed.), *La 'persona' nell'opera di Luigi Pirandello*, 141–74.

—— *Quando Pirandello cambia titolo: occasionalità o strategia?* (Milan: Mursia, 1986).

——— 'Retorica del titolo', in AA.VV., *Il titolo e il testo* (Padua: Editoriale Programma, 1992), 11–26.

CAPUTO, RINO, 'La letteratura nel romanzo', in *Giornata di studi nel primo cinquantenario della morte di Luigi Pirandello* (Rome: La Nuova Copisteria, 1988), 75–90.

——— '*I vecchi e i giovani*: l'occasione "storica" di Pirandello', *Trimestre* 6 (1972), 443–66.

CARCHIA, GIOVANNI, *La retorica del sublime* (Bari: Laterza, 1990).

CARDUCCI, GIOSUÈ, *Prose* (Bologna: Zanichelli, 1909).

CARETTI, LANFRANCO, *Antichi e moderni* (Turin: Einaudi, 1976).

CASELLA, PAOLA, *L'umorismo di Pirandello: ragioni intra- e intertestuali* (Florence: Cadmo, 2002).

CAVE, TERENCE, *Recognitions: A Study in Poetics* (Oxford: Clarendon Press, 1990).

CAZALÉ BÉRARD, CLAUDE, 'Effetti di una storia interrotta: strategie dell'esito nelle *Novelle per un anno* di L. Pirandello', *Rivista di studi pirandelliani* 6/7 (1991), 51–71.

CECCHI, EMILIO, and SAPEGNO, NATALINO (eds.), *Storia della letteratura italiana*, 9 vols. (Milan: Garzanti, 1979).

CERINA, GIOVANNA, *Pirandello, o, la scienza della fantasia: mutazioni del procedimento nelle Novelle per un anno* (Pisa: ETS, 1983).

CHIUMMO, CARLA, '"Nel vuoto di un tempo senza vicende": natura e storia ne *I vecchi e i giovani*', *Studi e problemi di critica testuale* 62/1 (2001), 173–97.

COHN, DORRIT, *The Distinction of Fiction* (Baltimore: Johns Hopkins University Press, 1999).

——— 'Optics and power in the novel', *New Literary History* 26 (1995), 3–20.

COLAIANNI, NAPOLEONE, *In Sicilia, gli avvenimenti e le cause* (Rome: Perino, 1894).

COLUMMI CAMERINO, MARINELLA, 'Il narratore dimezzato: legittimazioni del racconto nel romanzo storico italiano', in AA.VV., *Storie su storie: indagine sui romanzi storici* (Vicenza: Neri Pozza, 1985), 95–119.

COMPAGNON, ANTOINE, *La seconde main ou le travail de la citation* (Paris: Seuil, 1979).

CONSOLO, VINCENZO, *Di qua dal faro* (Milan: Mondadori, 1999).

COOPER, DAVID, *Metaphor* (Oxford: Blackwell, 1986).

CORSINOVI, GRAZIELLA, 'Rassegna pirandelliana (1973–78)', *Otto/Novecento* 3 (1979), 357–67.

COSTANZO, MARIO, 'Per un'edizione critica di *Uno, nessuno e centomila*', *Quaderni dell'Istituto di Studi Pirandelliani* 1 (1973), 109–19.

CROCE, BENEDETTO, 'Illusioni sulla genesi delle opere d'arte documentata dagli scartafacci degli scrittori', *Quaderni della critica* 3 (1947), 93–4.

——— 'Luigi Pirandello', in *Letteratura della nuova Italia*, 6 vols. (Bari: Laterza, 1940), vi. 359–77.

——— 'Luigi Pirandello—"L'umorismo"', *La critica* 7 (1909), 219–23.

—— *Problemi di estetica* (Bari: Laterza, 1910).

CULLER, JONATHAN (ed.), 'The call of the phoneme', in id. (ed.), *On Puns: the Foundation of Letters* (Oxford: Blackwell, 1986), 1–16.

—— *On Deconstruction* (London: Routledge, 1983).

—— *The Pursuit of Signs* (London: Routledge, 1981).

CURI, FAUSTO, 'L'umorismo di Pirandello nel sistema della modernità letteraria', in Nicolosi and Moretti (eds.), *L'ultimo Pirandello: Pirandello e l'Abruzzo*, 19–61.

DANESI, MARCEL, *Vico, Metaphor and the Origin of Language* (Bloomington: Indiana University Press, 1993).

DASHWOOD, JULIE, 'I momenti eccezionali di Pirandello: *umorismo*, novelle e "paradiso terrestre"', in Lauretta (ed.), *Pirandello e l'oltre*, 169–78.

DE ANGELIS, PALMIRA, *L'immagine epifanica: Hopkins, D'Annunzio, Joyce. Momenti di una poetica* (Rome: Bulzoni, 1989).

DE CERTEAU, MICHEL, *The Writing of History* (New York: Columbia University Press, 1988).

DE DONATO, GIGLIOLA, 'Un "personaggio da romanzo": Grazia Deledda in *Suo marito* di Pirandello', *Rivista di studi pirandelliani* 6/7 (1991), 21–41.

DE MAN, PAUL, *Allegories of Reading* (Yale: Yale University Press, 1979).

—— 'Autobiography as de-facement', *MLN* 94 (1979), 919–30.

—— *The Rhetoric of Romanticism* (New York: Columbia University Press, 1984).

DE OBALDIA, CLAIRE, *The Essayistic Spirit* (Oxford: Clarendon, 1995).

DEBENEDETTI, GIACOMO, *Il romanzo del Novecento* (Milan: Garzanti, 1971).

DELLA COLETTA, CRISTINA, *Plotting the Past: Metamorphoses of Historical Narrative in Modern Italian Fiction* (West Lafayette, Ind.: Purdue University Press, 1996).

DERRIDA, JACQUES, *Dissemination*, trans. Barbara Johnson (London: Athlone, 1997).

—— *The Margins of Philosophy*, trans. Alan Bass (Brighton: Harvester, 1982).

DI BELLA, ELIO, *Risorgimento e anti-Risorgimento a Girgenti: mezzo secolo di lotte politiche nella realtà storica e nella narrativa pirandelliana* (Agrigento: Edizioni Centro Culturale Pirandello, 1988).

DI GIURO, V. (ed.), *Manuale enciclopedico della bibliofilia* (Milan: Bonnard, 1997).

D'INTINO, FRANCO, *L'antro della bestia: le Novelle per un anno di Luigi Pirandello* (Caltanissetta: Sciascia, 1992).

DONATI, CORRADO, *Bibliografia della critica pirandelliana 1962–1981* (Florence: La Ginestra, 1986).

—— *Luigi Pirandello: nella storia della critica* (Fossombrone: Metauro, 1998).

—— *La solitudine allo specchio* (Rome: Lucarini, 1980).

DOSSI, CARLO, *Vita di Alberto Pisani* (Turin: Einaudi, 1976).

ECO, UMBERTO, 'The frames of comic freedom', in Thomas A. Sebeok (ed.), *Carnival!* (New York and Berlin: Mouton, 1984), 1–9.

—— 'Semiosi naturale e parola nei *Promessi sposi*', in G. Manetti (ed.), *Leggere I promessi sposi: analisi semiotiche* (Milan: Bompiani, 1989), 1–16.

—— *Sugli specchi e altri saggi* (Milan: Bompiani, 1985).

FERRANTE, LUIGI, 'La poetica di Pirandello', in *Atti del Congresso Internazionale di Studi Pirandelliani* (Florence: Le Monnier, 1967), 371–8.

FERRONI, GIULIO, 'Pirandello', in Walter Binni (ed.), *I classici italiani nella storia della critica*, 3 vols. (Florence: La Nuova Italia, 1977), iii. 57–129.

FINOCCHIARO CHIMIRRI, GIOVANNA, 'La donna scrittrice fra Capuana e Verga', in AA.VV., *Les femmes écrivains en Italie aux 19^c et 20^c siècles* (Aix-en-Provence: Université de Provence, 1993), 25–37.

FOLEY, BARBARA, *Telling the Truth: The Theory and Practice of Documentary Fiction* (Ithaca: Cornell University Press, 1986).

FORTI, MARIO, *Idea del romanzo italiano fra '800 e '900* (Milan: Garzanti, 1981).

FOSCOLO, UGO, *Tutte le opere*, 2 vols. (Turin: Einaudi, 1995).

FOUCAULT, MICHEL, 'What is an author?', in J. V. Harari (ed.), *Textual Strategies: Perspectives in Post-Structuralist Criticism* (Ithaca: Cornell University Press, 1979), 141–60.

FRUMAN, NORMAN, 'Originality, plagiarism, forgery and romanticism', *Centrum* 4/1 (1976), 44–9.

GAZICH, NOVELLA, '"Con occhi nuovi": modalità narrative nelle *Novelle per un anno*', *Rivista di studi pirandelliani* 11 (1997), 29–34.

—— 'Per una tipologia della novella pirandelliana', *Otto/Novecento* 5 (1992), 43–56.

GEERTS, WALTER (ed.), '*I vecchi e i giovani*: la portata del romanzo storico', in M. Rossner and F.-R. Hausmann (eds.), *Pirandello und die europäische Erzahlliteratur des 19. und 20. Jahrhunderts* (Bonn: Romanistischer, 1990), 50–7.

GENETTE, GÉRARD, *Fiction and Diction*, trans. Catherine Porter (Ithaca: Cornell University Press, 1993).

—— *Narrative Discourse*, trans. Jane E. Lewin (Oxford: Blackwell, 1980).

—— *Palimpsests: Literature in the Second Degree*, trans. Channa Newman and Claude Doubinsky (Lincoln: University of Nebraska Press, 1997).

—— *Paratexts*, trans. Jane E. Lewin (Cambridge: Cambridge University Press, 1997).

GHIDETTI, ENRICO, *Malattia, coscienza e destino: per una mitografia del decadentismo* (Florence: La Nuova Italia, 1993).

GIOANOLA, ELIO, *Pirandello: la follia* (Genoa: Il Melangolo, 1983).

GIOVANELLI, PAOLA (ed.), *dicendo che hanno un corpo* (Modena: Mucchi, 1994).

GIUDICE, GASPARE, *Luigi Pirandello* (Turin: UTET, 1963).

GLYNN, RUTH, 'Presenting the past: the case of *Il nome della rosa*', *The Italianist* 17 (1997), 99–116.

GRANATELLA, LAURA, 'Proposta per una lettura del mito maternocentrico come metafora dell'atto creativo', in S. Milioto (ed.), *La donna in Pirandello* (Agrigento: Centro Nazionale di Studi Pirandelliani, 1988), 11–21.

GRIGNANI, MARIA ANTONIETTA, 'Incursioni al femminile nei romanzi di Pirandello', in Milioto (ed.), *La donna in Pirandello*, 23–35.

—— '*Uno, nessuno e centomila*: la scrittura', in Milioto (ed.), *Nuvole e vento*, 111–22.

GRIMALDI, EMMA, *Come un quadro sottosopra: aspetti e problematiche del femminile in alcune opere di Pirandello* (Cava de' Tirreni: Avagliano, 2001).

GROOM, NICK, *The Forger's Shadow* (London: Picador, 2002).

—— 'Forgery or plagiarism?', *Angelaki* 1–2 (1993–4), 41–51.

GUBAR, SUSAN, 'Birth of the artist as heroine', in C. Heilbrun and M. Hyonnet (eds.), *The Representation of Women in Fiction* (Baltimore: Johns Hopkins, 1983), 19–59.

GUERRA, LIA, 'Fragmentation in *Dubliners* and the reader's epiphany', in Rosa M. Bosinelli (ed.), *Myriadminded Man: Jottings on Joyce* (Bologna: CLUEB, 1986), 41–9.

GUGLIELMINO, SALVATORE, 'Retroterra e implicazioni del saggio sull'*umorismo*', in Milioto (ed.), *Pirandello e la cultura del suo tempo*, 143–55.

GUGLIELMINETTI, MARZIANO, *Il romanzo del Novecento italiano: strutture e sintassi* (Rome: Riuniti, 1986).

—— 'Le scrittrici, le avanguardie, la letteratura di massa', in Zappulla Muscarà (ed.), *Letteratura siciliana al femminile*, 11–25.

—— 'Le vicende e i significati di *Uno, nessuno e centomila*', in Lauretta (ed.), *Il 'romanzo' di Pirandello*, 183–207.

HAY, LOUIS, 'Does text exist?', *Studies in Bibliography* 41 (1988), 64–76.

HUTCHEON, LINDA, 'Literary borrowing... and stealing: plagiarism, sources, influences, and intertexts', *English Studies in Canada* 12/2 (1986), 229–39.

ILLIANO, ANTONIO, *Introduzione alla critica pirandelliana* (Verona: Fiorini, 1976).

—— *Metapsichica e letteratura in Pirandello* (Florence: Vallecchi, 1982).

—— 'Momenti e problemi di critica pirandelliana: "L'umorismo", Pirandello e Croce, Pirandello e Tilgher', *PMLA* 83/1 (1968), 135–43.

ILLICH, IVAN, *In the Vineyard of the Text: A Commentary to Hugh's Didascalion* (Chicago: University of Chicago Press, 1993).

ISER, WOLFGANG, *The Act of Reading: A Theory of Literary Response* (Baltimore: Johns Hopkins University Press, 1991).

JAKOBSON, ROMAN, *Language in Literature*, ed. Krystyna Pomorska and Stephen Rudy (Cambridge, Mass.: Harvard University Press, 1987).

—— 'Two aspects of language and two types of aphasic disturbance', in Krystyna Pomorska and Stephen Rudy (eds.), *Language in Literature* (Cambridge: Harvard University Press, 1987), 95–114.

JOYCE, JAMES, *Epifanie (1900–1904)*, ed. Giorgio Melchiori (Milan: Mondadori, 1982).

—— *Stephen Hero* (London: Panther, 1977).

KAWIN, BRUCE, *The Mind of the Novel: Reflexive Form and the Ineffable* (Princeton: Princeton University Press, 1982).

KERMODE, FRANK, *The Sense of an Ending* (Oxford: Oxford University Press, 1968).

KING, GEOFF, *Mapping Reality: An Exploration of Cultural Cartographies* (London: Macmillan, 1996).

KLEM, LONE, 'Certi momenti di silenzio interiore', in Lauretta (ed.), *Pirandello e l'oltre*, 313–24.

—— '*Umorismo* in atto: accenni ad una interpretazione integrale dei *Sei personaggi in cerca d'autore*', in Enzo Lauretta (ed.), *Il teatro nel teatro di Pirandello* (Agrigento: Centro Nazionale di Studi Pirandelliani, 1977), 39–52.

KRISTEVA, JULIA, *Desire in Language*, trans. Thomas Gora, Alice Jardine and Leon S. Roudiez (Oxford: Blackwell, 1993).

KROHA, LUCIENNE, 'Scrittori, scrittrici e industria culturale: *Suo marito* di Pirandello', *Otto/Novecento* 19/5 (1995), 167–82.

—— *The Woman Writer in Late Nineteenth-Century Italy* (Lampeter: Mellen, 1992).

LACROIX, M. JEAN, 'La *novella* pirandelliana come maieutica della personalità', in Enzo Lauretta (ed.), *La 'persona' nell'opera di Pirandello* (Milan: Mursia, 1990), 205–20.

LAKOFF, GEORGE, and JOHNSON, MARK, *Metaphors We Live By* (Chicago: University of Chicago Press, 1980).

LANARO, GIORGIO, 'La critica alle *Finzioni dell'anima* nella cultura italiana del primo Novecento', *Rivista critica di storia della filosofia* 37 (1982), 430–42.

LATTARULO, LEONARDO (ed.), *Il romanzo storico* (Rome: Riuniti, 1978).

LAURETTA, ENZO, *Luigi Pirandello: storia di un personaggio 'fuori di chiave'* (Milan: Mursia, 1980).

—— (ed.), *Pirandello e la politica* (Milan: Mursia, 1992).

—— (ed.), *Pirandello e l'oltre* (Milan: Mursia, 1991).

—— (ed.), *Il 'romanzo' di Pirandello* (Palermo: Palumbo, 1976).

LEADBEATER, C. W., *The Astral Plane* (Madras: Theosophical Publishing House, 1977).

LEJEUNE, PHILIPPE, *On Autobiography*, trans. Katherine Leary (Minneapolis: University of Minnesota Press, 1989).

LEONE DE CASTRIS, ARCANGELO, *La polemica sul romanzo storico* (Bari: Cressati, 1959).

—— *Storia di Pirandello* (Bari: Laterza, 1962).

LEPSCHY, ANNA LAURA, 'Gallina's *La famegia del santolo* and Pirandello's *Tutto per bene*', *Yearbook of the British Pirandello Society* 6 (1986), 19–35.

LO VECCHIO-MUSTI, MANLIO, *Bibliografia di Pirandello* (Milan: Mondadori, 1937).

LUGNANI, LUCIO, *L'infanzia felice e altri saggi su Pirandello* (Naples: Liguori, 1986).

LUKÀCS, GEORG, *The Historical Novel*, trans. Hannah and Stanley Mitchell (London: Merlin, 1962).

LUPERINI, ROMANO, *L'allegoria del moderno* (Rome: Riuniti, 1990).

MACCHIA, GIOVANNI, 'Luigi Pirandello', in Cecchi and Sapegno (eds.), *Storia della letteratura italiana*, ix. 441–92.

——— *Pirandello o la stanza della tortura* (Milan: Mondadori, 2000).

MCFARLAND, THOMAS, *Originality and Imagination* (Baltimore: Johns Hopkins University Press, 1985).

MALATO, ENRICO, 'Filologia e critica', in AA.VV., *La critica del testo* (Rome: Salerno, 1985), 3–23.

Manuale enciclopedico della bibliofilia, ed. Vittorio Di Giuro (Milan: Bonnard, 1997).

MANZONI, ALESSANDRO, *On the Historical Novel*, trans. and with an introduction by Sandra Bermann (Lincoln: University of Nebraska Press, 1984).

——— *Opere*, ed. Riccardo Bacchelli (Milan and Naples: Ricciardi, 1953).

——— *I promessi sposi* (Florence: La Nuova Italia, 1978).

MARCHESINI, GIOVANNI, *Le finzioni dell'anima* (Bari: Laterza, 1905).

MARTINELLI, LUCIANA, 'Silvia Roncella (una lettura di *Suo marito* di Luigi Pirandello)', in Zappulla Muscarà (ed.), *Letteratura siciliana al femminile*, 103–23.

——— *Lo specchio magico: immagini del femminile in Luigi Pirandello* (Bari: Dedalo, 1992).

MASIELLO, VITILIO, 'L'età del disincanto: morte delle ideologie e ontologia negativa dell'esistenza nei *Vecchi e i giovani*', in Lauretta (ed.), *Pirandello e la politica*, 67–87.

——— *I miti e la storia* (Naples: Liguori, 1984).

MAZZACURATI, GIANCARLO, 'L'arte del titolo, da Sterne a Pirandello', in id. (ed.), *Effetto Sterne: la narrazione umoristica in Italia da Foscolo a Pirandello* (Pisa: Nistri-Lischi, 1990), 294–332.

——— 'Il personaggio: l'imputato di turno', in Stefano Milioto (ed.), *Gli atti unici di Pirandello (tra narrativa e teatro)* (Agrigento: CNSP, 1978), 181–8.

——— *Pirandello nel romanzo europeo* (Bologna: Il Mulino, 1987).

MEIJER, PIETER DE, 'Una fonte dei *Vecchi e i giovani*', *La rassegna della letteratura italiana* 67 (1963), 481–92.

MELTZER, FRANÇOISE, *Hot Property: The Stakes and Claims of Literary Originality* (Chicago: University of Chicago Press, 1994).

MENSI, PINO, *La lezione di Pirandello* (Florence: Le Monnier, 1974).

MICOCCI, CLAUDIA, 'Silvia Roncella e/o Giustino Boggiòlo', in Lauretta (ed.), *Il 'romanzo' di Pirandello*, 125–41.

MILIOTO, STEFANO (ed.), *La donna in Pirandello* (Agrigento: Centro Nazionale di Studi Pirandelliani, 1988).

——— (ed.), *Le novelle di Pirandello* (Agrigento: Centro Nazionale di Studi Pirandelliani, 1980).

——— (ed.), *Nuvole e vento: introduzione alla lettura di Uno, nessuno e centomila* (Agrigento: Centro Nazionale di Studi Pirandelliani, 1989).

——— (ed.), *Pirandello e la cultura del suo tempo* (Milan: Mursia, 1984).

MOSES, GAVRIEL, *The Nickel was for the Movies* (Berkeley: University of California Press, 1995).

NARDELLI, FEDERICO, *L'uomo segreto: vita e croci di Luigi Pirandello* (Milan: Mondadori, 1932).

NASH, CRISTOPHER, *World-Games: The Tradition of Anti-Realist Revolt* (London: Methuen, 1987).

NICHOLS, ASTON, *The Poetics of Epiphany: The Nineteenth-Century Origins of a Modern Literary Moment* (Tuscaloosa: University of Alabama Press, 1987).

NICOLOSI, FRANCESCO, 'Su *I vecchi e i giovani* di Pirandello', *Le ragioni critiche* 19–20 (1976), 64–86.

——— and MORETTI, VITO (eds.), *L'ultimo Pirandello: Pirandello e l'Abruzzo* (Chieti: Vecchio Faggio, 1988).

NIEVO, IPPOLITO, *Le confessioni d'un italiano* (Milan: Mondadori, 1996).

OLNEY, JAMES, *Metaphors of the Self* (Princeton: Princeton University Press, 1972).

ONG, WALTER, *Orality and Literacy: The Technologizing of the Word* (London: Methuen, 1982).

O'RAWE, CATHERINE, 'Pirandello's "macchinetta infernale and lente diabolica": *Umorismo*'s devilish double visions', *Pirandello Studies* 20 (2000), 102–16.

ORR, MARY, *Intertextuality: Debates and Contexts* (Oxford: Polity, 2003).

PAGANO, TULLIO, 'Modernisms: from Bergson's laughter to Pirandello's humour', *The Italianist* 17 (1997), 44–59.

PALADINO, VINCENZO, 'L'"altrove" di Pirandello', *Otto/Novecento* 19 (1995), 53–69.

PARKE, NIGEL, 'Stifled cries and whispering shoes: rites of passage in the modern epiphany', in Tigges (ed.), *Moments of Moment*, 207–32.

PARKER, PATRICIA, 'The metaphorical plot', in David S. Miall (ed.) *Metaphor: Problems and Perspectives* (Brighton: Harvester, 1982), 133–57.

PARRINI, ELENA, *La narrazione della storia nei Promessi sposi* (Florence: Le Lettere, 1996).

PASINI, FERDINANDO, *Luigi Pirandello, come mi pare* (Trieste: La Vedetta Italiana, 1927).

PATRIZI, GIORGIO, *Pirandello e l'umorismo* (Rome: Lithos, 1997).

PAVEL, THOMAS, *Fictional Worlds* (Cambridge, Mass.: Harvard University Press, 1986).

PESTARINO, PAOLA, 'Ipotesi sulle redazioni manoscritte di *Uno, nessuno e centomila*', *Rassegna della letteratura italiana* 7 (1978), 442–65.

PIROUÉ, GEORGES, *Luigi Pirandello: sicilien planétaire* (Paris: Denoël, 1988).

PROVIDENTI, ELIO, *Archeologie pirandelliane* (Catania: Maimone, 1990).

——— 'Note di bibliografia sulle opere giovanili di Luigi Pirandello', *Belfagor* 23 (1968), 721–40.

PUGLISI, FILIPPO, *L'arte di Pirandello* (Messina: D'Anna, 1958).

QUINLAN, MAURICE J., 'Swift's use of literalisation as a rhetorical device', *PMLA* 82 (1967), 516–21.

RADCLIFF-UMSTEAD, DOUGLAS, *The Mirror of our Anguish* (London: Associated University Presses, 1978).

—— 'Pirandello and the psychoanalysis of history', *Canadian Journal of Italian Studies* 12 (1989), 76–98.

RAGUSA, OLGA, *Pirandello* (Edinburgh: Edinburgh University Press, 1980).

RICCIARDI, MARIO, *La rivincita della letteratura* (Turin: Stampatori, 1979).

—— '*Uno, nessuno e centomila*: il romanzo della scomposizione della personalità', in Milioto (ed.), *Nuvole e vento*, 23–47.

RICHARDS, I. A., *Philosophy of Rhetoric* (Oxford: Oxford University Press, 1965).

RICOEUR, PAUL, *Interpretation Theory: Discourse and the Surplus of Meaning* (Fort Worth: Texas Christian University Press, 1976).

—— *The Rule of Metaphor* (Toronto: University of Toronto Press, 1975).

—— *Time and Narrative*, 3 vols. (Chicago: University of Chicago Press, 1988).

RIGNEY, ANN, *The Rhetoric of Historical Representation* (Cambridge: Cambridge University Press, 1990).

RIGOBELLO, GIOVANNA, 'La parola e il silenzio in *Uno, nessuno e centomila*, in Enzo Lauretta (ed.), *Pirandello e la parola* (Agrigento: Centro Nazionale di Studi Pirandelliani, 2000), 197–210.

RORTY, RICHARD, *Philosophy and the Mirror of Nature* (Oxford: Blackwell, 1998).

ROSE, MARK, 'The author as proprietor', *Representations* 23 (1988), 51–85.

RUSSO, LUIGI, *Dal Manzoni al Gattopardo: ritratti e disegni storici* (Florence: Sansoni, 1981).

RUTHVEN, K. K., *Faking Literature* (Cambridge: Cambridge University Press, 2001).

SAID, EDWARD, *Beginnings* (London: Granta, 1985).

SALIBRA, LUCIANA, *Lessicologia d'autore: studi su Pirandello e Svevo* (Rome: Edizioni dell'Ateneo, 1990).

SALINARI, CARLO, *Boccaccio, Manzoni, Pirandello* (Rome: Riuniti, 1979).

—— *Miti e coscienza del decadentismo italiano: D'Annunzio, Pascoli, Fogazzaro e Pirandello* (Milan: Feltrinelli, 1960).

SALSANO, ROBERTO, *Pirandello novelliere e Leopardi* (Rome: Lucarini, 1980).

SANTOVETTI, OLIVIA, 'Digressive art as humorous art', *Pirandello Studies* 20 (2000), 117–34.

SCHOLES, ROBERT, and KAIN, RICHARD (eds.), *The Workshop of Daedalus: James Joyce and the Raw Materials for A Portrait of the Artist as a Young Man* (Evanston, Ill.: Northwestern University Press, 1965).

SCIASCIA, LEONARDO, *Opere*, 3 vols. ed. Claude Ambroise (Milan: Bompiani, 1987–97).

—— (ed.), *Omaggio a Pirandello* (Milan: Bompiani, 1987).

SCRIVANO, RICCARDO, *Finzioni teatrali* (Messina: D'Anna, 1982).

—— 'Società e religione nel "teatro dei miti"', in Nicolosi and Moretti (eds.), *Pirandello e l'Abruzzo*, 87–107.

—— '*I vecchi e i giovani* e la crisi dell'ideologia' in Lauretta (ed.), *Pirandello e la politica*, 41–66.

SÉAILLES, GABRIEL, *Essai sur le génie dans l'art* (Paris: Alcan, 1911).

SEARLE, J. R., 'Metaphor' in A. Ortony (ed.), *Metaphor and Thought* (Cambridge: Cambridge University Press, 1981), 92–123.

SEDITA, LUIGI, *La maschera del nome: tre saggi di onomastica pirandelliana* (Rome: Istituto dell'Enciclopedia Italiana, 1988).

SENNETT, RICHARD, *The Conscience of the Eye* (London: Faber, 1990).

SIPALA, PAOLO, *Capuana e Pirandello: storia e testi di una relazione letteraria* (Catania: Bonanno, 1974).

SPINAZZOLA, VITTORIO, *Il romanzo antistorico* (Rome: Riuniti, 1990).

—— '*I vecchi e i giovani*', in AA.VV., *Studi in memoria di Luigi Russo* (Pisa: Nistri-Lischi, 1974), 423–55.

SPRINGER, CAROLYN, *The Marble Wilderness: Ruins and Representation in Italian Romanticism 1775–1850* (Cambridge: Cambridge University Press, 1987).

STARKIE, WALTER, *Luigi Pirandello 1867–1936* (Berkeley: University of California Press, 1965).

STASSI, M., '"Quel ramo del lago di Como": la natura nei *Promessi sposi*: tra idillio e storia', in G. Barberi-Squarotti (ed.), *Prospettive sui Promessi sposi* (Turin: Tirennia, 1991), 15–42.

STELLA, VITTORIO, 'Pirandello e la filosofia italiana', in Milioto (ed.), *Pirandello e la cultura del suo tempo*, 5–30.

STERNE, LAURENCE, *Tristram Shandy* (Oxford: Oxford University Press, 1990).

STEWART, SUSAN, *Crimes of Writing: Problems in the Containment of Representation* (Oxford: Oxford University Press, 1991).

STILLINGER, JACK, *Multiple Authorship and the Myth of Solitary Genius* (Oxford: Oxford University Press, 1991).

SWEETSER, E. E., *From Etymology to Pragmatics* (Cambridge: Cambridge University Press, 1990).

TAYLOR, CHARLES, *Sources of the Self: The Making of the Modern Identity* (Cambridge: Cambridge University Press, 1989).

THOMASSON, ANNIE, *Fiction and Metaphysics* (Cambridge: Cambridge University Press, 1997).

TIGGES, WIM, 'The significance of trivial things: a typology of literary epiphanies', in id. (ed.), *Moments of Moment*.

—— (ed.), *Moments of Moment: Aspects of the Literary Epiphany* (Amsterdam and Atlanta, Ga.: Rodopi, 1999).

TILGHER, ADRIANO, *Studi sul teatro contemporaneo* (Rome: Libreria di scienze e lettere, 1923).

TODERO, FABIO, 'Pirandello e la fabbrica del successo: l'autore e il pubblico in *Suo marito*', in G. Petronio (ed.), *Scrittore e lettore nella società di massa* (Trieste: LINT, 1991), 531–53.

TODOROV, TVETZAN, *The Fantastic*, trans. R. Howard (Ithaca: Cornell University Press, 1975).

TOMASELLO, GIOVANNA, 'La donna ne *La nuova colonia*', in Milioto (ed.), *La donna in Pirandello*, 57–63.

VERGA, GIOVANNI, *I Malavoglia* (Milan, Mondadori, 1992).

—— *Mastro-don Gesualdo*, ed. Carla Ricciardi (Milan: Mondadori, 1993).

VICENTINI, CLAUDIO, *L'estetica di Pirandello* (Milan: Mursia, 1972) (repr. with additions, 1985).

—— 'I "furti" di Pirandello e l'illusione della forma artistica', in R. A. Syska-Lamparska (ed.), *Ars dramatica: studi sulla poetica di Luigi Pirandello* (New York: Lang, 1996), 43–54.

WEISKEL, THOMAS, *The Romantic Sublime: Studies in the Structure and Psychology of Transcendence* (Baltimore: Johns Hopkins University Press, 1976).

WHITE, HAYDEN, *Metahistory: The Historical Imagination in Nineteenth-Century Europe* (Baltimore: Johns Hopkins University Press, 1985).

—— 'The Narrativization of Real Events', *Critical Inquiry* 7 (1981), 793–8.

—— *Tropics of Discourse* (Baltimore: Johns Hopkins University Press, 1978).

WIMSATT, J., 'The mirror as a metaphor for literature', in P. Hernadi (ed.), *What is Literature?* (Bloomington: Indiana University Press, 1978), 127–40.

WOODMANSEE, MARTHA, 'The genius and the copyright: economic and legal conditions of the emergence of the author', *Eighteenth-Century Studies* 17 (1984), 425–48.

WOOLF, VIRGINIA, *To the Lighthouse* (London: Penguin, 1992).

ZANGRILLI, FRANCO, *Lo specchio per la maschera: il paesaggio in Pirandello* (Naples: Cassitto, 1994).

—— '"L'umorismo"—poetica morale', *Rivista di studi pirandelliani* 6 (1980), 26–41.

ZAPPULLA MUSCARÀ, SARAH (ed.), *Letteratura siciliana al femminile* (Caltanissetta: Sciascia, 1984).

INDEX